Town in the Ruhr

Town in the Ruhr

A Social History of Bochum, 1860-1914

David F. Crew

Columbia University Press • New York • 1979

The Andrew W. Mellon Foundation, through a special grant,
has assisted the Press in publishing this volume.

Library of Congress Cataloging in Publication Data
Crew, David F 1946-
    Town in the Ruhr.

    Bibliography: p.
    Includes index.
    1.   Bochum—Social conditions.   2.   Labor and
laboring classes—Germany, West—Bochum—History.
3.   Social mobility—Germany, West—Bochum—History.
I.   Title.
HN458.B57C73   309.1'43'55   78-31526
ISBN 0-231-04300-7

Columbia University Press
New York   Guildford, Surrey

For My Parents: George and Olivia Crew

Contents

Tables

Figures

Preface

IN WRITING THIS book, I have incurred a number of debts that I am glad I can at last publicly acknowledge. Without the financial assistance provided by Cornell University, the German Academic Exchange Service (DAAD), and the Columbia University Summer Research Fellowship program, the archival work in Germany on which this study is based could not have been undertaken. My appreciation must also be extended to the personnel of a number of archives and libraries. In Bochum, Dr. Helmuth Croon and the staff of the Stadtarchiv Bochum were extremely helpful at an early stage in my research when encouragement was sorely needed. Without the benefit of Dr. Croon's encyclopedic knowledge of so many aspects of the history of the Ruhr region, there is much that I would have missed. My thanks also to the staff of the Ruhr University Library in Bochum, in which I spent many pleasant evening hours. I must also express my gratitude to the municipal administration of the city of Bochum for allowing me access to family registers in the Rathaus as well as to Friedrich Krupp Hüttenwerke AG for permitting me to consult the company archives of the *Bochumer Verein.*

In Münster, I was given a great deal of help and guidance by the staff of the Staatsarchiv. And special thanks to Dr. Richard Tilly for making it possible for me to obtain photocopies of some necessary documents in the Staatsarchiv after I had left Germany. Outside of Germany, I have also been helped by librarians at the Cornell University Graduate Library, Columbia's Butler Library, the New York Public Library, and the British Library, London.

My intellectual debts cannot be as straightforwardly apportioned. My teacher, Mack Walker, deserves even more credit than he is probably aware of; right up to the present day, his work as an historian continues to be an important inspiration to me. I owe a similar debt of gratitude to another accomplished historian, Phyllis Mack. I hope this book meets at least some of their expectations.

Like most books which began as dissertations, this work has undergone a lot of revision before appearing in final form. Over the last few years several individuals have helped me greatly in the process of recasting and refining a rough original. James J. Sheehan at Northwestern University very kindly read the entire manuscript at an early stage and offered both encouragement and constructive criticisms. A colleague at Columbia University, Hugh Neuburger, provided timely aid at short notice with chapter 1. And Geoff Eley, Emmanuel College, Cambridge, took time out from his own busy schedule to read the entire, revised version of the manuscript. Finally, I benefited from the comments provided by a number of scholars who read parts of this book which appeared earlier as journal articles: Theodore Hershberg and George Alter at the Philadelphia Social History Project, Michael Katz, Peter Stearns, Daniel Walkowitz, Stephan Thernstrom, Charles Tilly, Jürgen Kocka, and Herbert Kisch.

Without the support and criticism of a number of other colleagues and friends, my understanding of what this book involved would not have been able to develop as much as it did and it would have contained far more errors, infelicities, and oversights than it now does. In England, where much of the book was rewritten, I have special debts to Susan Pennybacker, Geoff Eley, Jane Caplan, and all the members of the King's College Social History Seminar at Cambridge; to Stephen Hickey in London, who graciously allowed me to read the manuscript of his Oxford University doctoral dissertation on the Ruhr miners in the comfort of his home; to Pat Thane and the members of the Seminar in Modern Social History, University of London. In Germany, I must extend my thanks to Hans-Ulrich Wehler, Jürgen Kocka and the editors of *Geschichte und Gesellschaft*, to Hartmut Kaelble, Freie Universität, Berlin, and to Professor Werner Conze at the University of Heidelberg, for their support and encouragement, direct and indirect. And then, finally, in the United States, my colleagues in the history department at Columbia, Professor Allan Silver in the Columbia sociology department, and all my undergraduate and graduate students who have, in the last four years, repeatedly forced me to rethink most of my ideas about history.

I have appreciated the remarkable efficiency with which the editors at Columbia University Press have moved the manuscript from typescript to print. My gratitude must also be expressed to the editors of the *Journal of Social History* and of *Geschichte und Gesellschaft* for allowing me to include material in this book which was originally published in part in those journals.

Naturally, the faults this volume contains are my responsibility alone.

David F. Crew
New York City, 1979

Introduction

IN LESS THAN two decades, German historiography has been reshaped; a new, critical history has developed since the mid-1960s, written by the younger generation of West German historians who have, in many ways, rejected or reassessed the historical concerns and approach to the German past shared by their elders in the profession. For the older German historians, schooled in the tradition of Ranke and Meinecke, the central problem of German historiography was the *Primat der Aussenpolitik*, that is to say, the dominating role played in modern German history by that country's position in world affairs. Much of their work concentrated on high politics and diplomacy and often tended to be uncritically nationalistic, designed to give Germans a sense of pride in their past. However, the publication of Fritz Fischer's *Griff nach der Weltmacht* in 1961 did much to challenge the continuing validity of that historical enterprise. Fischer's book charged that the leaders of Wilhelmine Germany had developed plans for the domination of Europe before 1914 and that they bore the responsibility for the outbreak of World War I. Fischer's charges concerning German war guilt had an explosive impact on diplomatic historians, but it was their broader implications that impressed many of the younger members of the historical profession. Fischer's work had in fact helped open the way to a critical reassessment not only of Wilhelmine foreign policy, but of the domestic politics of the Kaiserreich. For, if it were true, as Fischer's arguments seemed to suggest, that there

were closer parallels between German foreign policy in the
two world wars than had previously been assumed, then it
seemed to some younger historians at least, that there might
also be similarities, indeed even considerable "continuities,"
between the political structures of the Kaiserreich and the
Third Reich.[1] While the older generation of German historians
had argued that Hitler and the rise to power of the Nazis were
basically aberrations in German history, the younger generation now began to question whether the real origins of the
Third Reich and of Germany's "persistent failure to give a
home to democracy in its liberal sense," as Ralf Dahrendorf
put it in 1965, were not perhaps to be traced back to the
Wilhelmine period.[2]

Certainly Dahrendorf thought so. As a sociologist, his
immediate brief was to demonstrate to his readers that, despite
the defeat of Nazism, the creation of a formally democratic
republic, and the fact that Germany was one of the most
advanced industrial nations in the West, it remained even in
the 1960s a fundamentally "illiberal society."[3] This, Dahrendorf argued, could be demonstrated by observing almost any
area of contemporary German life, ranging from the social
structure and patterns of social and geographic mobility, to
education, to the treatment of children, the mentally ill, the
aged and the dying, and even to internal family relationships.[4]
Dahrendorf traced the source of this persistent "illiberalism"
and "unmodernity" to Germany's period of industrialization
in the late nineteenth century. During these years, Germany
industrialized "quickly and thoroughly" but, strikingly for
Dahrendorf, without the social and political consequences
that were associated with this process in the "first industrial
nation," England. Germany rapidly became an advanced
industrial power, but not a liberal democratic state. Indeed,
Dahrendorf argued, "instead of developing it, industrialization in Germany swallowed the liberal principle."[5] The
answer to this paradox Dahrendorf discovered in Germany's
unique pattern of industrialization, which afforded the traditional, preindustrial, and premodern elites the ability, through
the state which they controlled and which in turn protected

them, to retain power against what was in any case a weak, hapless, and submissive bourgeoisie:

It is the mixture of feudal and national elements that makes for the peculiar and consequential pattern of industrialization in Germany. . . . Because Germany was a latecomer on the stage of the industrial nations of Europe—or so one might argue—she could not afford the luxury of a gradual capitalist development. Because she industrialized late, she had to industrialize quickly and thoroughly. This could be accomplished only if the state took a strong hand in the process, that is, by tighter organization and control than the capitalist principle would permit. Thus came about a combination of modern economic patterns and an authoritarian political order . . . Imperial Germany absorbed industrialization quickly and thoroughly. But she assimilated this process to the social and political structures by which she was traditionally determined. There was no place in these structures for a sizable, politically self-confident bourgeoisie . . . The state held a prominent place in the traditional structures; for that reason it took part, as promoter and owner, in the process of economic development. The state . . . thus managed to use the new power of industry to strengthen the old power of tradition.[6]

Indeed, Dahrendorf concludes that, since Imperial Germany did not experience the "lively diversity of the market . . . that which is polemically capitalist anarchy," it cannot be characterized as "in the full sense of the term . . . capitalist . . . Imperial Germany developed into an industrial, but not into a capitalist society . . . while the economic superstructure (as one might say in an ironic reversal of Marx's terms) is assimilated, the social and cultural context remains unchanged."[7]

None of the new generation of German historians would necessarily consider themselves to be Dahrendorfian disciples; nevertheless, many of them have shared his desire to demonstrate to the German public the disjunction in contemporary Germany between democratic political forms and the "real" democratization of society.[8] Moreover, they have adopted much the same basic approach to Germany's past. Accepting the notion of Germany's social and political "misdevelopment" since industrialization (an idea which implicitly assumes a "correct" and "normal" historical path against which German errors can be measured),[9] they have sought to explain Germany's "backwardness" by emphasizing the importance of the "failed bourgeois revolution" and the survival and continued domination of preindustrial, premodern, and precapitalist power elites and ideological traditions during the Wilhelmine era.[10]

But the contribution of this "new orthodoxy" certainly does not rest on the fact that it has given detailed historical dimension to Dahrendorf's rather sketchily outlined argument. Indeed, the new generation of critical German historians has done much to revive and promote the study of German social history, a field that, despite the great tradition of German sociology established in the late nineteenth century (Weber, Simmel, Tönnies) and some promising beginnings in the period up to 1933, had been virtually obliterated by the Nazi takeover or else shunted into the backwaters of *Volkskunde*.[11] For "it was in social history," as Richard Evans has recently pointed out, that the younger generation of German historians came to believe "that the key to the internal structure and development of Imperial Germany was to be found."[12]

Still, German social history, as it began to develop under their auspices, has taken on a form and substance quite different from its British, American, and French counterparts. Whereas older traditions of Marxism in England, the *Annales* school in France, and sociology and the New Left in America have both legitimized and stirred interest in the historical explanation of areas neglected by traditional historians—ranging from labor history through crime, riots, popular culture, women, family history and social mobility, what collectively and very loosely came to be designated as history "from the bottom up"[13]—the new generation of German historians began to produce a social history written very much "from the top down."[14] This was certainly no accident; indeed it reflected the interpretation of German social and political history that they were in the process of formulating and which received its most succinct articulation in Hans-Ulrich Wehler's *Das Deutsche Kaiserreich, 1871–1918*. According to Wehler, one of the central historical issues of the Wilhelmine period

was "the defence of inherited ruling positions by pre-industrial elites against the assault of new forces."[15] Germany's
failure to achieve the social and political modernization that
would have been commensurate with the economic transformation it was experiencing during this period was primarily
the result of the variegated methods of social and political
control exercised by the preindustrial elite to maintain its
social and political power.[16] In Wehler's analysis, then, Imperial Germany appears as a society whose essential features
were very much determined *from above*.

The weakness of the Wehlerian approach is not simply
that, by giving little weight to the experience and activities of
the great mass of the German people it fails to provide us with
a rounded social history of Germany during a critical period of
transition, but rather that social history "from the top down"
contributes little to our theoretical understanding of the relationship of industrialization to social change.[17] The failure of
German society and politics to develop in directions considered appropriate and necessary to what is thought to be the
"normal" logic of industrial capitalism has been explained
primarily by reference to the obstructionist influences of
preindustrial elites and ideological traditions.[18] Consequently,
it has not been necessary to devote much thought to the
question of whether such a universal logic exists in the first
place, a question which detailed investigation of the specific
nature of the development of industrial capitalist production
and social relations in their German context (as opposed to the
study of the supposedly preindustrial, precapitalist forces presumed to be preventing their full emergence) might have
provided an answer. In the end, then, German social history
"from the top down" makes it too easy to forget, as one young
English historian has recently pointed out, that "Wilhelmine
society contained the most dynamic capitalism in Europe, and
it is this rather than "feudal" continuities which needs our
primary attention."[19] It is hoped that this study will go some
way to answering that need.

One local history of a German industrial town will hardly
lay bare all the social changes that Germans experienced
during the course of industrialization; but the necessity of

undertaking this kind of work is more obvious in German history than perhaps anywhere else. In the United States, spurred on by the work of Stephan Thernstrom, a whole generation of young historians has already produced a formidable number of local history monographs, which, while too often rigidly restricted to analyzing patterns of social and geographical mobility abstracted from the broader social and political context, have nevertheless contributed a good deal to our understanding of social structure and social change in nineteenth-century American communities.[20] Local history is also a well-established tradition in France, and recently some American and English students of French history have been exploring aspects of the social histories of French cities as varied as Marseilles, Carmaux, Rouen, Lyons, Armentières, and Paris.[21] And, of course, as Richard Evans points out, "one of the great strengths of British historiography lies in its traditions of local history."[22] Yet, despite the fact that one of the earliest West German works of social history, Wolfgang Köllmann's book on nineteenth-century Barmen, was a local study of Germany's Manchester, and even though this same author has argued that local history is an essential building block of social history, local studies (with the exception of some recent and promising work) have not generally engaged the interest of German historians.[23]

Yet, as necessary as local studies may well be, if German social history is eventually to become as densely developed as its British and to some extent its French counterparts, they must be approached warily, for they can be full of pitfalls. Not the least of these, as John Foster has recently pointed out, is that the local community is necessarily incomplete as a social structure. This is particularly true of the later nineteenth century in continental Europe, when local communities and their inhabitants became progressively more integrated into and consequently had their experience shaped by not only regional but national and even international economic, social, and political structures and processes of change. No single local study, nor even a mosaic of local studies, could therefore hope to produce a "total social history," for even the sum of all these parts would not add up to a complete whole.[24]

That does not and must not mean that local historians can only define their task as simply trying to provide a case study of this or that particular type of town, village, or region, or even demonstrating the considerable diversity that exists within a social landscape. Local historians can be (as their subjects were historically) integrated into the broad structures and processes of change. It is a question really of asking how and in what ways the experience of the local community fits into the national experience and how, in what ways, and to what extent local areas participated in, contributed to, were affected by, and reacted to the large-scale social, economic, and political transformations that changed much of Europe during this period.

But this is a difficult task. It requires the ability to cultivate a feeling for the diversity and uniqueness of local experience while at the same time not getting lost in it; a tolerance for closework, yet the ability not to get bogged down in it. Perhaps the best way to start nurturing these rather contradictory talents (which I make no particular claim to have achieved) is at the very beginning, in the choice of topic. While many researchers will be tempted to search out the "typical" or "representative" community in which to invest their efforts, it may be argued that no community is strictly "typical" of more than a rather limited number of cases. Communities can however be exemplary in the sense that they both contained and reflected some essential characteristics, often in an extreme and accentuated form, of an emerging social system. The extreme case can often be extremely revealing and it is precisely for that reason that I have focused this analysis on one of the fastest growing, industrial towns in Germany's most dynamic industrial region during the critical period of that country's transformation into an industrial society.[25]

The subject of this study is the city of Bochum in the Ruhr valley, Germany's industrial heartland. At the beginning of the nineteenth century the Ruhr was an area of few towns, backward agriculture, and poor people, geographically close to the main routes of medieval and modern commerce but "always remote from them in spirit."[26] In 1825 the whole Ruhr area contained only about 250,000 inhabitants. The wooded, hilly region of the Sauerland and the Siegerland to the south of the river Ruhr, where the soil was very poor, developed into a major iron-working center before the nineteenth century; Remscheid and Solingen were already metallurgical centers by 1800. But "the plain north of the river . . . held little attraction and offered small prospects of gain" for industrial development at this time.[27]

The main center of this area was the Hellweg, a region of early human settlement of walled cities and compact nucleated settlement. It had formed since early times the most used routeway of the region, and along it there developed quite early in the Middle Ages a sequence of regularly spaced towns of commercial importance; Essen, Bochum, Dortmund, Unna, Werl, Soest . . . They had changed little by 1800. They remained medieval in aspect and even in function. Even as late as 1823 the city of Essen had not expanded to the limits set by its medieval walls. Soest was in 1800 the largest of the Hellweg towns, but it had only 5,000 inhabitants. Dortmund and Essen had but little more than 4,000 each, and Bochum only 2,000. . . . The burgesses of the smaller towns lived chiefly by their agriculture. Within the town of Bochum there had been only a few years earlier 300 head of cattle, and Roden committed himself to the opinion that Wattenscheid, now a coal-mining center, could never have any but an agricultural future.[28]

Yet in 1848, when the Englishman Banfield traveled through the Ruhr valley, he found that "castles, ruins and factories rapidly succeeded each other."[29] The depletion of ores and the inability of charcoal-smelted iron to compete with iron smelted with coke had put the Siegerland and Sauerland industry into a decline. But now the rich resources of the Ruhr coalfield were beginning to be seriously exploited; the old open workings and tunnels driven into hillsides were replaced by new deep mines in the Hellweg. They found ready markets in the Ruhr's expanding iron and steel works, and "an intimate and functional relationship between blast furnace, steel works, coal mine and cokery" began to emerge. Steel was produced from iron by a variety of methods; but most important for the Ruhr was the success of Jacob Mayer and Friedrich

Krupp in producing high-quality cast steel suitable for the moving parts of machines in the 1830s and 1840s; "Its manufacture lay at the root of the modern supremacy of the German machine tool industry." In turn the manufacture of cast steel encouraged industrial concentration in the coalfields because it required large quantities of coal. Mayer set the pattern for later expansion when, after careful consideration of a location, he moved his works from Lendersdorf near Aachen to Bochum in 1842.[30]

With this concentration of industry came a dramatic increase in the population and in the size of the Ruhr's urban centers; after 1871 the province of Westphalia experienced the largest population increase and the fastest growth of urban population of any province in Germany. By the end of the century four major urban-industrial centers had emerged along the Hellweg: Duisburg, Essen, Bochum, Dortmund. Of these four, Bochum seemed best suited for the purposes of my study, not just because it was representative of the process of rapid industrialization and urbanization in the Ruhr during the late nineteenth century, but because—in certain aspects— it was an extreme example. Essen, Duisburg, and Dortmund all had industrialized and urbanized earlier and at a somewhat slower pace, and by the end of the nineteenth century they had become more settled, attracting proportionately fewer new arrivals seeking work in their mines and foundries.[31] Bochum is thus an excellent example of a community confronting all the social developments that are associated with rapid industrialization and urban growth; its citizens lived in one of the farthest outposts of the industrial frontier.

The sources on which this study is based are primarily materials preserved in the municipal archive of the city of Bochum. Of great importance were the official administrative reports of the city government published annually by the executive body to provide the city council members with a detailed commentary on a wide variety of topics. These reports provide a wealth of information on the economic, social, and demographic history of the town, and they are also indispensable as sources for the attitudes and responses of the community leaders. Supplementing them and providing extremely useful information on the economy and on social policy are the yearly reports of the Bochum Chamber of Commerce. The administrative reports cover the period 1860–1914; the Chamber of Commerce reports run from the early 1870s to 1914.

Bochum was also fortunate enough to have an assiduous local historian who collected a huge amount of material relating to the economic, social, and political development of the community. This was never published, but the manuscript notes for the history, along with numerous copies of contemporary documents, are preserved in the city archive. For the analysis of social and occupational mobility in chapter 3, I employed several sources of social data that may not be familiar to most German historians. Chief among these were the *Adressbücher* or city directories for the period 1880–1901, which provide information on occupation, residence, and homeownership for all adult working inhabitants of the city. In addition to the city directories, I also employed manuscript lists of school attendance at the city's secondary schools *(Akten der Schulverwaltung der Stadt Bochum, Städtische Hauptkasse, Schulgeldhebelisten)*, a manuscript marriage register for the year 1900 *(Rathaus Bochum, Standesamt Bochum(Mitte), Familienbuch, 1900)* and a manuscript list of apprentices at the Bochumer Verein *(Werksarchiv Friedrich Krupp Hüttenwerke AG, Gusstahlwerk Bochumer Verein, 25000, Nrs. 1–5)*. The company archives of the Bochumer Verein also provided extensive materials on company housing and welfare policies. Other major sources included the files of the local newspaper, the *Märkischer Sprecher*, documents of the Landrat's office *(Stadtarchiv Bochum. Acta des Königlichen Landrathsamtes des Landkreises Bochum, 475–483 and 1000)*, and strike reports, contained in the *Staatsarchiv Münster* (P.A. Reg. Arnsberg, I,I,I,1463; I.24–I.34).

one

Society and Economy

The Industrial Revolution in Bochum

WHEN THE LUTHERAN *Rektor* Friedrich August Volkhart wrote his chronicle of Bochum in 1842, he described a backwater country town of 4,200 inhabitants, many of whom still worked land in the *Feldmark* and kept a cow or a goat which they pastured in the common meadow. A hundred merchants, eighteen innkeepers, and seventy-six master artisans supplied the needs of the community and the surrounding small agricultural villages. Only the unfortunate few who could find no other livelihood worked in the town's marginal industry.[1] Following a pattern characteristic of many poor European agricultural regions, weaving had been carried on in the area since the eighteenth century; in 1788 there were some twenty-six linen weaving masters in Bochum, and early in the nineteenth century a local merchant built a small textile factory.[2] There were also a few manufacturing specialities. Coffee mills were produced in small shops; in 1791 there were ten of them employing fifty men altogether. Tin ornaments for coffins were made by hand, and there was a small factory for spinning tobacco.[3]

But by mid-century almost all these "industries" were in decline; domestic and factory textile production succumbed to the more efficient competition of the Rheinland textile centers early in the century, the manufacture of coffee mills moved to Hagen in the 1850s, and by 1860 the coffin ornaments were being made in Iserlohn. An inquiry conducted in 1842, the same year Volkhart wrote his chronicle, showed that of the forty-five local businesses earning more than 200 thlr. per year not one was an industrial enterprise (Table 1.1).[4]

Yet, ironically, 1842 also witnessed the establishment of the town's first significant modern industry, a foundry built by a Swabian craftsman and a Magdeburg banker. They had been attracted to the area by the growing availability of coal that was just beginning to be extracted from the first deep mines, one of which had been sunk only the previous year near the neighboring village of Hamme.[5]

At first industrial growth in the city was slow, sometimes hesitant. Although a townsman looking around him in 1858, when the first occupational census was taken, would realize that Bochum was no longer just a country market town (Table 1.2), he could not imagine that by the end of the century his city would be one of Germany's "industrial metropolises." Manufacture and mining had expanded considerably, but they still coexisted with other, more traditional forms of employment.

Artisan production, primarily for the local market, and day labor, much of it in agriculture, still employed more than 35 percent of the working population in 1858; work in the city's new factories and in the local mines employed another 30 percent. But within the next fifteen years this balance decidedly shifted in favor of industry. Industry did not replace older forms of employment; it simply outstripped their rather modest growth rates at a dizzying pace. While the absolute

Table 1.1 Businesses Earning More than 200 Thalers in 1842

Business	Number	Business	Number
Tailors	8	Confectioner	1
Turners	2	Bookbinders	3
Merchants	2	Upholsterer	1
Surgeon	1	Saddlemaker	1
Cabinetmakers	3	Capmaker	1
Watchmakers	3	Coppersmith	1
Blacksmiths	3	Retail dealer	1
Baker	1	Grocer	1
Tinsmith	1	Barber	1
Horse dealer	1	Iron dealer	1
Shoemakers	2	Goldworker	1
		Auctioneer	1

Table 1.2 Occupational Distribution in 1858

Economic Sector	N	%
Civil servants	176	4.7
Renters and pensioners	23	0.6
Commercial and industrial proprietors	208	5.5
Innkeepers	44	1.2
Master artisans	362	9.6
Journeymen and apprentices	437	11.6
Street musicians	14	0.4
Carters, freighters	14	0.4
Factory workers	806	21.3
Miners	359	9.5
Day laborers, male	471	12.5
Day laborers, female	57	1.5
Servants, male	370	9.8
Servants, female	437	11.6
Total	3,778[a]	100.2[b]

SOURCE: StAB, VB, 1860–61, p. 12.
[a]Total population: 8,797.
[b]Total percent is more than 100 due to rounding.

numbers of artisan masters (although not journeymen and apprentices) as well as innkeepers, civil servants, and members of the free professions had increased only a few percentage points by 1871, the number of inhabitants now working in factories and mines had risen by over 300 percent. Whereas the industrial sector employed only about 30 percent of the population in 1858, in 1871 it gave jobs to over 54 percent (Table 1.3).

For the next half century, industry absolutely dominated the city's economy. By 1882 the industrial sector employed almost 80 percent of the working population. In subsequent decades other sectors (particularly trade and transport) began to offer more people jobs, but industry still provided work for over 70 percent of the adult population (Table 1.4).

During the 1870s and 1880s this industrial growth was onesided; it was primarily an expansion of heavy industry. In 1882 the city's mines and foundries employed almost two-thirds of the industrial labor force. Metalworking and machine building, attracted to the city by the growth of the mines and foundries but still in their infancy, offered work to fewer than 8 percent of those employed in industry. Provision of consumer services and goods was still primitive; only the food, clothing, and building trades had sizable labor forces. But within the next thirteen years the grip of heavy industry on the industrial sector noticeably loosened; metalworking, machine building and construction had all made sizable gains by 1895, in fact doubling their percentage of the industrial labor force, while the proportions employed in the mines and foundries had dropped some 18 percent. By 1907 metalworking and machine building together employed almost 20 percent of industrial workers, while building provided jobs for almost 14 percent. This was a significant shift in the direction of economic expansion, since it considerably widened the range of employment opportunities in industry.

Moreover, the expansion of the metalworking, machine building, and construction trades noticeably increased the opportunities not only for manual but for white collar jobs,

Table 1.3 Occupational Distribution in 1871

	Male		Female		Total	
Economic Sector	N	%	N	%	N	%
Agriculture	28	0.3	17	0.3	45	0.3
Mines and foundries	1,092	12.3	561	10.5	1,653	11.6
Large and small industry, including building	4,184	47.1	1,853	34.8	6,037	42.5
Master craftsmen[a]	389	4.4			389	2.7
Journeymen and apprentices[b]	360[c]	4.1			360[c]	2.5
Trade	471	5.3	339	6.4	810	5.7
Transport	161	1.8	96	1.8	257	1.8
Lodging and refreshments	86	1.0	81	1.5	167	1.2
Personal service	1,567	17.6	1,782	33.4	3,349	23.6
Civil service, free professions	218	2.5	190	3.6	408	2.9
Without occupation	39	0.4	7	0.1	46	0.3
Poor/inmate of hospital/ prison	185	2.1	211	4.0	396	2.8
No occupation given	108	1.2	195	3.7	303	2.1
Total	8,888	100.1[d]	5,332	100.1[d]	14,220	100.0

SOURCE: StAB, VB, 1871, pp. 9–11.

[a]Figure derived from report on the *Gewerbesteuer*, VB, 1871.

[b]Figure estimated on the basis of ratio of journeymen and apprentices to masters in 1860. VB, 1860–61.

[c]Approximate.

[d]Total percents do not equal 100 due to rounding.

Table 1.4 Employment in Economic Sectors, 1882, 1895, 1907

	1882		1895		1907	
Economic Sector	N	%	N	%	N	%
Agriculture	94	0.7	111	0.6	538	1.2
Industry and crafts	10,286	79.6	12,904	70.4	34,273	74.5
Trade and transport	1,681	13.0	3,194	17.4	7,320	15.9
Domestic service and day labor	293	2.3	979	5.3	1,306	2.8
Civil service and free professions	560	4.3	1,130	6.2	2,556	5.6
Total	12,914	99.9[a]	18,318	99.9[a]	45,993	100.0

SOURCE: *Statistik des Deutschen Reiches*, N.F. Bd. 2/2; N.F. Bd. 117; Bd. 210/2.
[a]Total percents do not equal 100 due to rounding.

since in these trades the ratio of white collar to manual
employees was comparatively high. The mining industry
employed only one white collar worker for every twenty-
seven manual laborers in 1886 and one for every twenty-six in
1907. But in metalworking this ratio was one to eight in 1907,
in machine building one to three, and in construction one to
eleven.[6]

The consumer trades were not so fortunate, but they did at
least manage to keep pace with the general rate of economic
growth. Undoubtedly the social characteristics of Bochum's
consumer market imposed definite limitations on expansion.
Since at least 75 percent of all potential customers were working class men and women who could usually afford only the
most necessary items of food and clothing, there was little
opportunity or incentive for producers and suppliers to
branch into specialty or luxury areas of production.[7] Thus
almost all the men employed in the food trade in 1895 were
ordinary bakers, butchers, and brewers, while the clothing
trade gave work to several hundred seamstresses and tailors,
but only eleven clothes washers, forty-eight milliners, two
hatters, four cap-makers, eight furriers, and, significantly, no
producers of that symbol of middle-class status, gloves (Table
1.5).[8]

By the late nineteenth century, then, the city's economy
was far more diversified and complex than it had been during
the early stages of industrialization. Alongside the handful of

large industrial enterprises that employed over two hundred workers each, there were now some two thousand small manufacturers and merchants, each giving work to fewer than fifty. (Table 1.6).[9]

Nevertheless, this growing structural diversity should not blind us to the fact that Bochum's economy continued to be heavily dependent on the two major industries—coal mining and iron and steel production. In 1861 the city government observed that "Bochum's wellbeing falls and rises with mining . . . as a consequence of the intimate connections between mining and trade and commerce whenever mining is in trouble, so too, all the other businesses suffer, down to the very smallest."[10] The situation had not really changed very much some thirty-nine years later, when the Chamber of Commerce remarked that

As a consequence of the dominant position which these two branches of industry [coal mining and iron and steel production] occupy in our district—both together employ some 90 percent of the approximately 120,000 industrial workers—the condition of the other branches of industry as well as of trade are essentially dependent, in this year as in every other, on the intensity of business [in these two main industries].[11]

Table 1.5 Industrial Employment, 1882, 1895, 1907

	1882		1895		1907	
Economic Sector	N	%	N	%	N	%
Mines and foundries	6,256	62.8	5,709	44.6	15,709	45.8
Stone and earthwork	59	0.6	124	1.0	884	2.6
Metalworking	578	5.8	1,426	11.1	5,071	14.8
Machine building	153	1.5	311	2.4	1,712	5.0
Chemicals	37	0.4	42	0.3	287	0.8
Luminous materials	48	0.5	46	0.4	116	0.3
Textiles	18	0.2	34	0.3	85	0.2
Paper, leather	116	1.2	178	1.4	302	0.9
Woodworking	289	2.9	587	4.6	861	2.5
Food	494	5.0	753	5.9	1,641	4.8
Clothing, cleaning	1,034	10.4	1,326	10.4	2,632	7.7
Building	811	8.1	2,081	16.3	4,623	13.5
Printing	65	0.7	159	1.2	332	1.0
Artistic trades	5	0.1	26	0.2	16	0.04
Total	9,963	100.2[a]	12,802	100.1[a]	34,271	99.94[a]

SOURCE: *Statistik des Deutschen Reiches, Bd. 2/2; Bd. 117; Bd. 210/2.*
[a]Total percents do not equal 100 due to rounding.

Table 1.6 Size of Enterprises in 1907

Economic Sector	Percent of Enterprises Employing:							
	1	2–3	4–5	6–10	11–50	51–200	201–1,000	Over 1,000
Mines and foundries	–	–	–	–	18.8	37.5	25.0	18.8
Stone and earthworks	14.3	5.7	–	5.7	71.4	2.9	–	–
Metalworking	18.9	26.1	19.8	21.6	7.2	5.4	0.9	–
Machines	27.2	29.3	8.1	8.1	16.2	10.1	1.0	–
Chemicals	8.3	16.7	58.3	–	–	16.7	–	–
Wood byproducts	–	–	–	16.7	50.0	33.3	–	–
Textiles	60.0	30.0	10.0	–	–	–	–	–
Paper	8.7	52.2	13.0	13.0	13.0	–	–	–
Leather	45.3	39.6	11.3	3.8	–	–	–	–
Woodworking	30.3	34.2	16.8	7.8	10.3	0.6	–	–
Food	15.3	49.3	17.9	11.6	4.5	1.1	0.3	–
Clothing	60.9	26.8	5.8	4.4	1.9	0.2	–	–
Cleaning	47.5	42.4	3.2	4.4	2.5	–	–	–
Building	25.2	23.9	11.1	13.4	19.6	5.6	1.3	–
Printing	25.6	25.6	9.3	16.3	18.6	4.7	–	–
Artistic trades	66.7	33.3	–	–	–	–	–	–

SOURCE: *Statistik des Deutschen Reiches, Bd. 217/I, p. 159.*

The Ownership of the Means of Production and Distribution

In 1858, when Bochum's industrial revolution had just begun, about 10 percent of the city's working population owned businesses (Table 1.7). There were as yet no large industrial enterprises, and only 1.6 percent of the work force were proprietors of large mercantile establishments or small factories. The great majority of business owners, then, were small merchants and traders, artisans with their own shops, and innkeepers. But the growth of heavy industry rapidly altered this pattern. By 1871 the business owning class had shrunk to approximately 5 percent of the working population, and within their ranks there emerged a tiny stratum of large industrial enterprises for which a special tax bracket had to be expressly created. By 1875 there were five of them in the city: the Bochumer Verein, the Bochumer Eisenhütte, the Gesellschaft für Stahlindustrie, and the Scharpenseel and Schlegel breweries.[12]

From 1871 to 1907 there were few additions to the ranks of the city's super-capitalists (see Table 1.6). However, the process of economic diversification that began in the late

1880s obviously created new opportunities for people to acquire small businesses. Thus by 1882 the proportion of small merchants had already doubled, although thereafter it dropped again. The shop-owning artisans, who had almost disappeared from the assessment lists in 1882, also began to increase, so that by 1907 they accounted for some 2 percent of the working population. Moreover, the 1907 figures also show the existence of a large stratum of marginal one-man businesses, amounting to almost 1 percent of the labor force. Certainly these men were not wage earners, yet it is doubtful that the economic situation of many of them was much better than that of skilled factory workers (see p. 141). Although being "independent" may have been a source of social prestige, the people who acquired it in this fashion probably paid a high price in terms of long hours, hard work, and constant insecurity.[13]

Table 1.7 Assessed Business Owners as Percentage of the Working Population

	1858		1871		1882		1895		1907	
	N	%	N	%	N	%	N	%	N	%
Large industrialists	–	–	1	0.01	6	0.05	8	0.04	76	0.2
Large merchants	61	1.6	84	0.6	213	1.6	298	1.6	241	0.5
Small merchants	148	3.9	336	2.4	605	4.7	735	4.0	1,194	2.6
Innkeepers	44	1.2	107	0.8	191	1.5	199	1.1	300	0.7
Artisans	120	3.2	138	1.0	54	0.4	150	0.8	950	2.1
Millers	2	0.1	4	0.03	–	–	–	–	–	–
Teamsters	11	0.3	12	0.1	1	0.01	26	0.1	–	–
Peddlers	–	–	51	0.4	–	–	–	–	–	–
Total	386	10.3	733	5.34	1,070	8.26	1,416	7.64	2,761	6.1
One-man shops (not assessed)									1,748	3.8

SOURCE: The figures for 1858, 1871, 1882, and 1895 were derived from the reports on the *Gewerbesteuer* in StAB, VB for these years. Large industrialists were considered to be those assessed in Class AI, large merchants in Class AII, small merchants in Class B, artisans in Class H. The figures for 1895 are actually derived from the 1892 report, the last year the city council gave details on the *Gewerbesteuer* assessments. The 1907 figures are an approximation based on the 1907 *Betriebszählung* using the categories devised by W. Köllmann, *Sozialgeschichte der Stadt Barmen im 19. Jahrhundert* (Tübingen: J. C. B. Mohr/Paul Siebeck, 1960), p. 292, and therefore differ somewhat from the official standards used to tax businesses.

Table 1.8 Social Structure in Bochum and Barmen (in Percent)

	Bochum		Barmen	
	1858	1907	1861	1907
"Capitalists"	1.6	0.3	1.4	1.4
Merchants and manufacturers	5.4	3.1	2.2	5.7
White collar and civil servants	4.7	9.2	2.5	11.0
Artisan masters	3.2	4.1	4.3	6.6
TOTAL "Mittelstand"[a]	13.3	16.4	9.0	23.3
"Proletaroide"[a]	6.5	4.6	11.1	4.3
Proletariat	78.5	78.7	78.5	71.0

SOURCE: Figures for Bochum calculated according to the guidelines set out in Köllmann, *Sozialgeschichte der Stadt Barmen im 19. Jahrhundert*, pp. 289–90. Figures for Barmen from Köllmann, p. 104.
[a]Following Köllmann's categorization.

In any case even if these one-man businesses are included among the ranks of the proprietary class, this still does not make the whole group a very large one, especially in comparison to a town like Barmen, where industrial and commercial ownership was considerably less concentrated. Consequently social structure in Bochum was much more visibly polarized. Employing Köllman's categories for the sake of comparison, we find that in 1907 the working class in Barmen comprised 71 percent of the population; in Bochum, however, it accounted for 78 percent. Twenty-three percent of Barmen's inhabitants were *Mittelstand* (including white collar workers and civil servants) and 1.6 percent were "capitalists," compared to 16 and 0.3 percent in Bochum (Table 1.8).

The Distribution of Income

Like the distribution of industrial and commercial property, the distribution of income in Bochum became intensely polarized during the early phase of industrialization. Although some of the more glaring inequalities of income distribution began to be somewhat smoothed out by the early twentieth century, massive imbalance still remained the main characteristic of the local income structure. To measure the magnitude of income inequality I have employed a simple device, the Lorenz curve, which allows us to compare the proportion of people earning income with the proportion of total income they received (Fig. 1.1). A completely equal distribution could only occur if, say, 25 percent of the population earned 25 percent of all income, 50 percent earned 50 percent, and so on. It is represented here by the diagonal line running from bottom left to upper right of the figure; the degree to which the curve representing actual income distribution slopes away from this diagonal indicates the magnitude of income inequality.[14]

In 1895 the people earning less than 3,000 marks represented 93 percent of all taxpayers in the city, yet they received only about 65 percent of total income. That meant the remaining 7 percent were earning almost 35 percent of total income, of which 15 percent was received by the top 1 percent alone. By 1907 the sharpness of this imbalance was no longer quite as pronounced; now 94 percent of the taxpayers earned less than 3,000 marks per year, but received about 80 percent of all

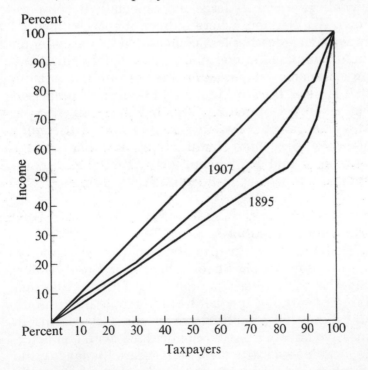

1.1 Distribution of Income, 1895 and 1907

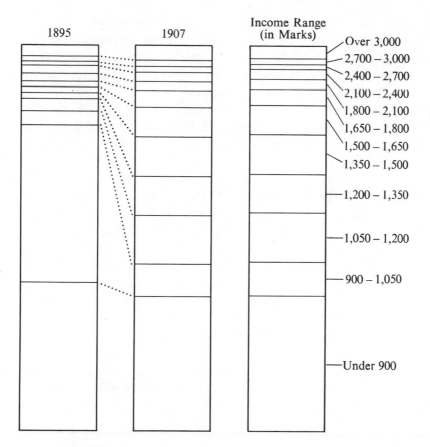

1.2 Income Ranges, 1895 and 1907

income. The percentage of total income flowing into the hands
of the remaining 6 percent who earned above 3,000 marks was
correspondingly reduced to slightly less than 20 percent. As
the steepness of the dotted lines in Figure 1.2 indicate, the
income range 1,050–1,650 marks underwent a dramatic
increase during this period. Cross-tabulation of income and
occupation from the 1901 tax registers indicates that this
income range was heavily populated by the higher paid
unskilled workers, skilled workers (especially skilled metalworkers), and lower level white collar employees including
office messengers and helpers, secretaries, and even some
foremen and factory officials. (For complete figures on income
distribution among taxpayers see Table 1.9.) Assuming that

roughly the same relationship between income and occupation existed in 1907 as in 1901, then the more privileged strata
of the working class plus lower level white collar workers
were growing faster than any other groups in the later stages
of industrialization. This development undeniably worked to
smooth out some of the most glaring inequalities of income
distribution that had characterized Bochum during the early
phases of industrialization. However, against this two other
facts must be balanced. First, in 1895, 38.8 percent of the
working population earned less than 900 marks; by 1907 this
had dropped only to 35.8 percent (Table 1.10). Second, the top
1 percent of taxpayers were no less privileged in 1907 than
they had been in 1895; once again they received about 15
percent of all income earned in the city.

The Industrial Revolution in Bochum created a relatively
complex, highly stratified community offering considerably
more opportunities for employment and mobility than either
the preindustrial town from which it had grown or the rural
villages and small towns from which many of its new inhabitants were coming. Yet the range of possibilities and the scope
of opportunities were severely restricted by the economic
processes that had created them; industrialization intensified

Table 1.9 Income Distribution among Taxpayers

	1895		1907	
Income Range (in Marks)	Cumulative % of Taxpayers	Cumulative % of Income	Cumulative % of Taxpayers	Cumulative % of Income
900–1,050	67.9	40.2	12.9	7.6
1,050–1,200	73.3	43.9	31.8	20.5
1,200–1,350	78.0	47.5	47.8	32.9
1,350–1,500	80.9	50.0	64.9	47.7
1,500–1,650	83.1	52.1	76.8	59.1
1,650–1,800	85.2	54.3	83.6	66.2
1,800–2,100	87.4	56.8	88.1	71.4
2,100–2,400	89.9	60.3	90.9	75.2
2,400–2,700	91.7	63.0	92.7	77.9
2,700–3,000	93.0	65.3	94.0	80.1
Over 3,000	100.0	100.0	100.1[a]	100.0

SOURCE: StAB, VB, 1895 and 1907.
Note: Since only the amount of tax paid and not income received was reported,
income had to be calculated indirectly.
[a]Total percent is more than 100 due to rounding.

Table 1.10 Income Distribution among the Working Population

Income Range (in Marks)	1875		1882		1895		1907	
	N	%	N	%	N	%	N	%
Under 420	7,644	44.8	3.079	22.8				
420–660	1,163	6.8	1,851	13.7				
660–900	4,146	24.3	6,277	46.5	7,577	38.8	18,159	35.8
900–1,050	807	4.7	381	2.8	8,131	41.6	4,216	8.3
1,050–1,200	1,683	9.9	507	3.8	648	3.3	6,150	12.1
1,200–1,350	519	3.0	237	1.8	561	2.9	5,203	10.2
1,350–1,500	275	1.6	255	1.9	346	1.8	5,583	11.0
1,500–1,650	168	1.0	126	0.9	263	1.3	3,880	7.6
1,650–1,800	122	0.7	157	1.2	246	1.3	2,220	4.4
1,800–2,100	72	0.4	87	0.6	266	1.4	1,479	2.9
2,100–2,400	102	0.6	124	0.9	305	1.6	915	1.8
2,400–2,700	71	0.4	55	0.4	210	1.1	574	1.1
2,700–3,000	69	0.4	112	0.8	157	0.8	414	0.8
Over 3,000	240	1.4	258	1.9	838	4.3	1,980	3.9
Total	17,001	100.0	19,500	100.0	19,548	100.2[a]	50,773	99.9[a]

SOURCE: StAB, VB, 1875, 1882, 1895, and 1907. See also Joseph Frings, *Die Einkommens- und Vermögensverhältnisse im Regierungsbezirk Arnsberg.*

[a]Total percents do not equal 100 due to rounding.

the extremes of wealth and poverty, power and impotence, and increased the social distance between strata.[15] This basic fact of local social structure must inevitably have imprinted itself deeply on the minds and the behavior of the people who lived in Bochum. But just as important as these structural factors were the dynamics created by the new industrial economy. As early as the 1860s, Bochum's inhabitants discovered that their material well-being was now dependent on the business cycle in heavy industry and that the town had become vulnerable to developments in the German and in the world economy of which most of Bochum's inhabitants must often have had only the slightest knowledge or understanding.

The Economics of Coal

Bochum properly entered the industrial age during the international boom of the 1850s—"a period," observed Mayor Greve in 1860,

which, not without some justification, has been termed the Californian Age, called forth by an often over-extensive speculation which was supported and encouraged by the stream of money flowing here from all parts of Germany. . . . with the result that a quite exceptional exertion of all productive forces has taken place.[16]

Much of the new capital attracted to the Ruhr went into the development of coal mines. In 1800 there had been 158 mines in Oberbergamtsbezirk Dortmund; in 1850 there were still only 198, but by 1860 there were no less than 281, a 42 percent increase in one decade. "We cannot restrain ourselves from a feeling of astonishment," Greve observed, "when we look back over the development of mining during the last decades . . . The capital which is invested in mining, runs into the millions."[17]

But the expectations attached to these investments were rapidly frustrated in the late 1850s when the industrial boom turned into a crisis:

The evil consequences of the general financial and commercial crisis, which, like a devastating torrent, broke over Europe at the end of 1857, have, after reaching this district, spread over it with increasing intensity . . . the money which many believed to have in their hands has been turned to dust overnight.[18]

Mining was badly hit. Coal production, which had increased almost threefold in a decade, quickly began to exceed the dwindling demand and coal prices fell heavily— Greve estimated a decline of as much as 50 percent in the three years before 1860.[19] Under these competitive conditions, declining prices meant declining profits for the coal industrialists, unless production costs could in turn be cut, markets expanded, and/or production in the industry as a whole restricted to bring supply more in line with demand.[20] In the late 1850s, Ruhr coal industrialists were not yet prepared to accept collective restriction of their output, so they could turn only to the first two responses. Since nineteenth century German coal mining was heavily labor intensive, with wages accounting for as much as 60 percent of total production costs, any serious attempt to reduce production costs inevitably centered on wage cutting.[21] Local mineowners tried that in the late 1850s, but they were running a losing race against the precipitous price drop; Greve noted that even though wages had been reduced at several local mines, coal prices were so low that production costs could scarcely be covered.[22] Mineowners also contemplated the possibility of compensating for price declines by selling greater quantities in new markets; however, the Ruhr coal industry was not particularly well situated to accomplish this in the 1850s. Its inland position made it dependent on rail transport, and, as Greve observed, at the freight rates charged by the Berg-Mark railway, "the market-area for local coal still remains extremely limited."[23]

The local coal industry struggled on until the early 1860s but then revived when a new upturn in the iron industry increased demand and raised prices; for the next fifteen years, coal experienced comparative prosperity. Indeed, for a time it seemed that coal might not succumb to the general economic decline that started in the Bochum area in 1874—although the Chamber of Commerce characterized the condition of the iron industry that year as "very sad," it noted that coal was still resisting the economic downturn. Nevertheless, by 1876 coal too was in serious trouble; that year prices dropped so dramatically that they were not to reach the 1875 level again until 1889.[24]

Coal industrialists responded, as they had done in the late 1850s, by paring production costs and increasing output. But since the depression that started in the mid-1870s was to prove deeper and more enduring than the industrial crisis of the late 1850s, this pattern of response had considerably more serious consequences. Wages were drastically reduced within the space of four years; in 1874 the average shift wage for miners was 4.05 marks. By 1878/79 it had dropped to 2.40 marks. Indeed, by that year the Chamber of Commerce had to admit that "the workers can only supply themselves with the absolutely necessary means of existence . . . a further reduction of the costs of production seems impossible, since wages and the cost of materials have been pressed down to the lowest level." Moreover, workers found that for these lower wages they were being required to work harder than ever before: "The mine administrations . . . are trying to increase the labor effect as much as possible. Productivity has been screwed up to the top."[25]

At the local Ritterburg mine, production per man/year rose by some 42.5 percent between 1875/76 and 1878/79, and at the Präsident mine a remarkable 63.9 percent production increase was recorded for the period 1874/75 to 1877/78 (Table 1.11). Even if miners at these two pits were working more shifts per year during this period than they had previously, these figures still indicate a considerable intensification of daily labor within a relatively short period of time.[26] One can imagine what this meant for even the basic physical condition of mineworkers. Table 1.11 also illustrates another irony of the situation confronting mineworkers during this period; although more coal was being mined there was actually less work to be had; at both mines, employment dropped off noticeably after 1875, although it revived somewhat earlier at the Präsident. In the district as a whole, men were being laid off or put on short time from 1876 onwards: the Chamber of Commerce noted that "in December, 1876 and the beginning of 1877 . . . the work force [of our mines] . . . was reduced by 10 percent on the average . . . at many mines, each week, several shifts have not been worked." Short time and layoffs in local mines were again reported in 1878 and 1879 and remained recurrent features of local minework throughout the 1880s and even into the 1890s.[27]

Faced with considerable unemployment, drastically reduced income, and at the same time heavier work loads, miners must have found the coal owners' response to crisis in the industry more than a little difficult to comprehend. But to the industrialists themselves, the logic of their actions was

Table 1.11 Productivity at Two Local Mines

	Ritterburg			Präsident	
Year	Men	Tons/Men/ Year	Year	Men	Tons/Men/ Year
1870	285	478.5	1874/75	2401	1057.8
1875/76	194	1357.8	1875/76	1085	2747.2
1876/77	141	1512.3	1876/77	1198	2976.2
1877/78	129	2359.4	1877/78	1189	2927.2
1878/79	161	2808.9	1878/79	1043	2798.1
1879/80	159	2470.1	1879/80	1103	2384.3

SOURCE: StAB, VB, for specific years.

both perfectly clear and inescapable: "with ever declining prices—these now amount to scarcely a quarter of the 1873 prices for lower quality coals—the efforts [of the mines] to hold their heads above water by increasing their market until the return of a better business juncture has caused them to engage in even further increases of production."[28]

But, in the end, increasing production as a response to crisis was, as the Chamber of Commerce later observed, simply "suicidal." In 1879 the Chamber dourly reported that with "the most recent price figure of 25 marks [per ton] . . . the not inconsiderable . . . expansion of the market area means nothing more than that the valuable substance of our coal stores must be flung away, in part without profit, often even without covering the basic costs of production . . . But the loss of a part of the costs of production is the lesser evil compared . . . to the reduction of production or complete closing down of the operation." Moreover, the Chamber of Commerce judged that a further reduction of production costs seemed impossible as wages and cost of materials had already been pushed to the lowest level. Consequently, "there can be no doubt that by now coal production is at the point at which the question 'to be or not to be' directly confronts it."[29]

However, the coal industry was rescued from the apocalypse by the slow revival of the iron trades in late 1879 and early 1880. Yet the problems of the industry had not been solved: although prices began to rise at the end of 1879 they had only reached the levels of 1861–62 and 1864–69 and did not reach the 1875 level again until 1889.[30] Throughout the 1880s the same complaints were repeatedly voiced by the Chamber of Commerce: despite the fact that the coal market had revived and production increased, prices stubbornly refused to rise significantly and sometimes even declined. It became increasingly apparent to many coal industrialists that unbridled free competition was not to their best advantage, that at times it could be ruinous, and that the rules of the game would therefore have to be amended.[31] The first step in this direction was taken on October 29, 1879, when an agreement to reduce production was signed in Dortmund. The agreement had a rather limited effect; in 1882 the Chamber of Commerce admitted that overproduction had not been eliminated but simply kept within bounds. Moreover, a significant minority of coal companies, particularly the larger and stronger ones, continued to believe that competition worked to their advantage. But eventually stronger initiatives were taken: at the end of September 1890 the Dortmund Kohlenverkaufsverein was formed, followed in December by the A-G Bochumer Kohlenverkaufsverein. Finally, in February 1893, the most comprehensive and strongest organization in the industry, the Rheinisch-Westfälisches Kohlensyndikat, was formed. Looking back on the first two years of its activity, the Chamber was glad to report that the coal syndicate had finally been able to ensure that "production was adapted to demand and the price held steady." In later years, the Chamber's enthusiasm for the Kohlensyndikat grew even stronger; by 1909 it was prepared to argue that failure to renew the syndicate would "shake the whole industrial district and all the branches of industry that are active in it . . . in a way that the district has not experienced since the sad times after 1873."[32]

But although cartels may indeed have improved the coal industry's position in the domestic market, Ruhr coal producers could not be content just to sell coal on better terms at home. At an early point, exporting became an important element of the industrialists' response to crisis in the domestic market. In the wake of the 1857–58 downturn, Mayor Greve pointed to the successes of the Hibernia mine, which sent coal to Russia, Portugal, and North and South America, and suggested that with lower freight rates, German coal might well be able to compete with the English.[33] In later years the Ruhr coal industry developed a considerable export trade, and local industrialists repeatedly discussed the possibilities for further expanding their export markets, but they were most intensely preoccupied with the export question during periods of crisis in the domestic market. Selling more coal abroad became a regular response to a depressed domestic market and one which the formation of cartels served only to encourage. During the downturn that began in 1876, the Chamber of Commerce observed that many coal companies were pushing into exports just to stay alive.[34] In 1885, when prices were again under heavy pressure and the immediate prospects in the domestic market looked discouraging, the Chamber argued that exports could play a particularly important role. Similarly, in the summer of 1890, when domestic prices dropped sharply, "significant amounts of coal and coke [were] being delivered to foreign countries."[35] In 1908, however, the attempt to escape into foreign markets ran into trouble when Ruhr coal producers discovered that the downturn which had depressed the German market had also touched the other industrial countries: "only to a very restricted degree was German industry able to create for itself a substitute for the failing domestic market by intensifying its foreign business.[36]

Yet, as important as the export trade was, it was certainly not regarded by Ruhr coal producers as being particularly profitable. Indeed, in order to compete with the British, French, and Belgians in the western European markets that had become the Ruhr's main export areas, Ruhr coal producers regularly had to sell at, and sometimes below, cost. Although 1910 was perhaps an extreme year, it nevertheless revealed a pattern common to much of the period. That year, the Chamber of Commerce reported, exports had risen considerably, but "a large portion of this additional export was nothing more than the disposing of goods for which no place could be found in the domestic market and to be sure at prices which, as a result of the strong foreign competition, come precariously close to or are indeed lower than the costs of production."[37] Nevertheless, the Chamber went on to argue that

The possibility of this expanded foreign market is very valuable for us, because it eases the burden on the domestic market, it guarantees continued . . . employment for industry and workers, it ensures the position of Germany's commerce and industry on the world market. But, in general, this additional export does not represent a good, profit bringing business and can scarcely be seen as an indication of a rising business cycle.[38]

Naturally, Ruhr coal industrialists did hope that their export trade could eventually be made not only more extensive but also more lucrative.[39] However, even if the export trade was not particularly profitable, it was still vital to the industry. Cartels combined with tariffs could mitigate the problem of overproduction in the domestic market, but cartels posed their own problems, for although they could maintain prices in the domestic market, they could not regulate demand. In a domestic downswing, then, the total revenues of coal producers would decline—a serious proposition for an industry in which fixed costs were relatively high and could not readily be reduced.[40] As the Chamber of Commerce pointed out in 1911, "the expenditures for administration, drainage and ventilation, etc. always remain the same regardless of whether a lot or a little is produced."[41] Added to this was the cost of servicing a sizeable debt. In this situation, exports provided a progressively more important means of relief; exported coal could not be sold at domestic prices because of intense foreign competition, but it could be gotten rid of at prices which would at least help to defray a portion of the fixed costs of the enterprise. Indeed, it can be argued that the formation of cartels actually allowed, even encouraged, coal producers to sell coal on the world market at "low and even dumping prices," since they kept domestic prices relatively high.[42] Cartels and exports, then, were complementary elements of the coal producers' response to crisis in the coal industry.

However, Ruhr coal producers could not simply rely on cartels to keep prices high enough in the domestic market so that they could undersell competitors in foreign markets. The Ruhr coal industry still had to contend with the fact that "in the years immediately preceding 1914, British coal was delivered at the pithead more cheaply than in any other part of Europe.[43] Consequently Ruhr coal industrialists had to be as economical as possible with production costs, and that meant primarily labor, since, as we have seen, mining was heavily labor intensive.[44] Since manual labor was not extensively replaced by mining machines before the war, that meant first of all that Ruhr producers had to ensure that wages did not rise above levels that would allow them to continue to compete effectively with the British, and in this regard they were relatively successful.[45] As late as 1913, average earnings per shift in the Ruhr, although higher than in any other major continental coal producing region, were still lower than in Great Britain.[46]

Second, since the British lead "owed nothing to an economy of low wages" but rather was based on "a marked superiority in labour productivity,"[47] German producers had to ensure that they could at least match and if possible overtake British rates of output per man, and in this too they were relatively successful. In the quarter century after 1890, labor productivity declined in all the major western European coal-producing nations as mines got older and deeper and the seams got harder to work. But whereas the British experienced a decline of no less than 20 percent in output per man between 1884–88 and 1909–13, the Germans had to tolerate only a 6 percent decline during the same period, with the result that "by 1914 the German miner was producing as much coal as his British counterpart."[48]

Undoubtedly, this growing German challenge to British hegemony stemmed in good part from basic differences in the age and geological conditions of mines in the two countries: "since development had come late in . . . Germany, maturity and decline in productive efficiency which followed it could be expected to be delayed . . . particularly in the case of Germany whose reserves of workable coal were greater than those of either Britain or France."[49] Nevertheless, at least some part of the difference must also be attributed to the fact that, especially after the turn of the century, Ruhr coal industrialists engaged in a prolonged and relatively successful effort to maintain (and sometimes to increase) output per man by extending the actual working day[50] and by speeding up the pace of work underground. As a 1905 agitational pamphet put it,

Dig coal, dig coal; that is the pressing order of the day.[51]

The Economics of Iron and Steel
Like coal, the iron and steel industry had attracted considerable investment in the fifties and sixties. By 1864 the Chamber of Commerce could report that the Bochumer Verein "has

expanded its installations in the most splendid way year by
year and now numbers over 1,000 workers" and by 1869 it was
reporting that "the works enjoy not only full employment, but
are partially not in a position to meet all requirements. Naturally this increased industrial and commercial traffic has been
of the most salutary influence on our city."[52] But, as with coal,
the boom in iron and steel turned into a crisis in the mid
1870s. In 1874 the situation of the iron industry was described
as

extremely sad and at the moment still without any prospect of
improvement. The numerous deficits that the previous year brought,
the . . . capital reductions which followed as a consequence, the
blast furnaces that have been blown out, the works which have been
shut down show clearly the heavy pressures which burden this
branch of business.[53]

Quite naturally, a good deal of this pressure fell on the
workers employed in the iron and steel industry. Unemployment rapidly became severe; whereas the Bochumer Verein
gave work to 5,900 men in 1873 (including miners), by 1874 it
had reduced its workforce to 3,500. By the time the Iron
Enquiry Commission took the testimony of the director of the
Bochumer Verein, Louis Baare, in November 1878, unemployment was widespread in Bochum County. People were so
desperate that they "offer themselves to work for 15 Sgr. daily,
but for that we cannot use them, they cannot live from that.
Even at our present wages, the workers cannot subsist."[54]

Shift wages at the company had been reduced from an
average of 4.28 marks in 1873 to 2.95 marks in 1879, and
average annual earnings had declined from 1,152 to 912 marks
in the same period. In response to the question whether wages
could be reduced even further, Baare flatly stated that "we
have already undercut the minimum that we must give the
workers in order that they can sufficiently nourish themselves
and still work [damit sie überhaupt aushalten]. . . . I think it is
impossible to reduce wages still further."[55]

Moreover, those workers who could find jobs had not only
to accept less money but to work much harder:

The men have definitely had their strength reduced. For example, a
boilerman who now earns 2.3 Marks must now look after four boiler

fires and work three hours more, and whereas he used to stoke 50–60 *Scheffels* of coal, now he must stoke 140. The performance of the men is overexerted. They can also neither find nor take work in the mines since they are not suited to it and cannot earn enough on piece rates (*im Gedinge*).[56]

Trying to explain the origins of the crisis to his board members in 1875, Baare focused on the problem of overproduction. Unlike the coal industry, iron and steel had undergone considerable technological change, which remarkably increased its productive capacity.[57] In particular, Baare pointed to the discovery of the Bessemer converter (1856) and the Siemens-Martin open hearth furnace (1864), which made possible the manufacture of cheap steel:

Whereas previously cast steel could only be made in small crucibles with a 60 pound capacity by means of a four hour smelting process, Bessemer applied large iron vessels [so-called converters] in which he could, by means of only a half-hour smelting process and with much less fuel, produce a hundred times, later even two and three hundred times the amount of steel.[58]

Unfortunately, this increased productive capacity was progressively unable to find a domestic market. By the mid-1870s the problem had reached crisis proportions: "In deplorable contrast to overproduction now stands the reduction of consumption as a consequence of the downturn of so many other branches of business and the resultant restriction of demand on the part of the railways."[59]

Baare felt that the problem could only be solved when many foundries closed down; that did in fact happen and not just in Germany.[60] But Baare's suggestion was certainly not conceived as a long-term answer; when the economy revived, expansion would and did obviously begin again in the iron and steel industry,[61] and it was clear to Bochum's industrialists that overcapacity would continue to be a permanent fact of the industry's existence since the technology involved seemed to have taken on a life of its own.[62] Overproduction, the Chamber of Commerce rather philosophically observed in 1885, "is a necessary consequence of the discoveries which have been pushing to mass production in the last decades in the area of the iron and steel industry."[63]

Necessities, although accepted, can still be dealt with. The crisis of the 1870s in the iron and steel industry and the slump that continued on through the 1880s were seen by Bochum's industrialists not just as the consequence of their own overproduction but of the "overproduction among industrial countries that has been going on for five years" and pointed specifically to the "colossal overproduction of the English iron industry." The first order of business, then, was to establish a safe domestic market in which foreign producers could no longer dump their own surplus production.[64] The answer to that problem was the protective tariff of 1879, for which local industrialists pushed hard, and whose salutary effects they were pleased to observe in 1882.[65] Previously, during the periods of crisis, England had saturated the German market with cheaply priced goods; this time, however, Bismarck's tariff policy had protected German producers. But as Levy pointed out in his study of German cartels,

The duties on iron and steel would have been ineffective if competition among the producing companies within the Reich had brought prices down below the level of "world market prices" plus duty and freight. The only way to avoid this was to fix prices through the medium of cartels, syndicates and conventions.[66]

Consequently, between 1879 and 1882, no fewer than eighteen cartels were formed in the iron industry covering products ranging from pig-iron to semi-manufactures, sheets, and pipes. In 1896 the Pig Iron Syndicate was formed, with headquarters in Düsseldorf, and in 1904 twenty-seven large German steelworks accounting for 83.5 percent of German steel production joined together to found the German Steel Works Association,[67] an organization whose renewal, three years later, the Bochum Chamber of Commerce assessed as "the most important event of the year 1907 for the whole iron [and steel] industry."[68]

However, cartelization made rather more uneven progress in iron and steel than in the coal industry because of the much greater heterogeneity of output.[69] As Feldman points out,

Horizontal organization was most suitable for the cruder products; pig iron and the so-called A-products [semis, rails, and structural steel]. These items were uniform and demonstrated little variation in quality. They were easily marketed through a single sales organization, and this explains why the most effective and advanced of prewar cartels in this industry were the Pig Iron Syndicate . . . and the Steel Works Association . . . At no time, however, did it prove possible to syndicalize the so-called B-Products [bars, bands, plate, and rolled wire] . . . the maximum accomplishment in this area had been the creation of quota arrangements . . . for the B-Products in 1904, but this arrangement deteriorated and finally collapsed in 1912.[70]

Indeed, the B-Products sector remained highly unstable throughout this period, as the example of the Walzwerkverband indicates. In 1892 the Chamber of Commerce reported that the Walzeisenverband was coming under heavy pressure in the domestic market from noncartel works. The following year it was forced to lower its prices in order to continue competing, and in 1893/94 the Verband actually fell apart, whereupon an even more intense price competition ensued. Similar consequences were feared when the Bar Iron Syndicate was dissolved in 1911.[71]

The volatility of the B-Products sector can be interpreted simply as failure on the part of the iron and steel industry to exert the same degree of control over domestic production and prices that the coal industry had earlier achieved. Yet the failure to organize the B-Products sector might more accurately be seen as the direct result of the successful cartelization in A-Products. Indeed, Feldman argues that since they were

unable to make more than modest profits on the successfully syndicalized A-Products, the large mixed works dominating the Steel Works Association made increasing use of their self-consumption rights . . . to produce B-Products. . . . There was every reason to believe that the unquestionable stabilization of prices in the A-Products had led to a dramatic expansion—probably an overexpansion—of production of B-Products, which served as a "safety-valve" . . . for the mixed works. The latter . . . needed to cover their fixed costs through maximum production and were at the height of their expansionist propensities.[72]

This tactic was obviously a gamble; a successful one in years in which the domestic market for B-Products was good, but then there would also be years like 1895/96, when "the prices for products not protected by the syndicates have dropped so far down that only some individual plants with very good equipment are able to achieve [even] moderate profits, but most companies work without profit."[73]

As with coal, then, cartelization in iron and steel had not solved the problem of overproduction that had led the industry into crisis in the 1870s, but simply shifted it onto a different plane. Protective tariffs plus the combination of regulated sales of A-Products and possibilities for expansion (and higher profits) in the B-sector might well have been seen by iron and steel industrialists as the components of a successful domestic market policy. But at the same time, they also realized that the new technological developments in iron and steel had raised the efficient scale of production to such a high level that the industry could not be content to rely solely, or even primarily, on the domestic market. They were therefore forced to admit that "the prosperity and the pain of our heavy iron industry ... is contingent on smooth sales to foreign countries."[74]

Exports were particularly important to Bochum's iron and steel producers, when the domestic market was in trouble. From the late 1870s on into the early 1880s, the exceptionally bad condition of the domestic market put Ruhr producers under special pressure to find those "sales paths to far away countries" that Baare had discussed in his 1875 report. Although by no means profitable—the Chamber of Commerce report of 1878/79 argued that "such an export trade as has taken place in the year 1878 borders close on suicide"—these exports nevertheless "by defraying general costs allow [the industry] to carry on the hard battle which it has been fighting since 1874." Or as Baare put it in his 1875 report, "although we renounce ... direct profits, we satisfy ourselves with the advantage that ... the employment of our works and our workers is being paid for by foreigners." Indeed, "without strong exports" the Chamber of Commerce argued in 1881, "the relatively small quantity of domestic demand for railway material would require significantly higher production costs, and there would not be, as there is now, many millions flow-

ing in from foreign countries . . . for workers' wages, railway
tariffs and agricultural products."[75]

Indeed, throughout the period, whenever the domestic
market turned down there was a rush to export. In 1887/88, a
year labeled by the Chamber of Commerce as not particularly
"glittering," the Bochumer Verein sent no less than 51.2 percent of its total production out of the country. Another downturn in 1890/91 prompted local industrialists to get foreign
contracts even at unprofitable prices in order, as they said, to
avoid cutbacks and layoffs. In 1893/94, described as "one of
the worst years in recent history," the Chamber of Commerce
observed that the "increase in exporting which has set in
during this reporting year indicates only the sad situation of
the industry which must make great sacrifices in order to
retain its core of stable workers [Arbeiterstamm]."

Similarly in 1894/95, it was reported that "works which
lack sufficient jobs are seeking by means of price reductions to
get new contracts in foreign markets." And again in 1900, the
Chamber noted that although exports made scarcely any
money they at least kept business going.[76]

However, export markets were not simply a useful safety
valve for surplus production during periods of domestic crisis: they were a permanent necessity of the industry. Even in
years in which the domestic market was good, exports
accounted for a sizable percentage of local iron and steel
production. In 1890, a relatively good year, the Bochumer
Verein still exported 29.9 percent of its production. And even
in 1899, a rather exceptional year in which "although exports
have by no means diminished, they have lost [in relative]
importance insofar as the great mass of new production in the
iron industry is being absorbed by the domestic market," the
Chamber of Commerce warned that "as happy . . . as this . . .
capacity of the domestic market to consume is, we must still
point to the importance of caring for foreign business. If we
once begin to slack off here, there will be bitter retribution in
the next period of downturn."[77]

But making headway or even holding ground in the
export trade was no easy task for Ruhr iron and steel producers. The protective tariff (and progressively the cartels) helped

to make the domestic market relatively secure and thereby give Ruhr producers the ability to be competitive in world markets, yet that competition was at best intense and at worst murderous.[78] Great Britain was obviously the main rival. Almost as soon as the protective tariff was erected, the battle between English and German products which had earlier been waged within German markets now shifted to the European export market:

This time the English industry has had to confine itself to running competition with us ... in German export markets in southern Europe. Our export prices must in consequence take on a declining tendency which naturally our foundry works cannot afford to resist, even when this means renouncing direct profits so that they can hold onto the field which has been won with so much effort and such great sacrifice.[79]

Similarly, the Chamber of Commerce reported in 1882 that the Bochumer Verein was having great difficulty with British competition as demand in the British colonies and other overseas markets had recently declined, so that British producers were turning to European countries where German manufacturers had their best customers.[80]

In these initial confrontations in the late 1870s and early 1880s, German producers were distinctly disadvantaged by three main factors. First, British labor was at this point more productive, meaning that British labor costs were lower. Second, England enjoyed the advantage of cheap sea transport, which alone equaled some 10 percent of the worth of steel rails. And, finally, German costs were higher because German producers had to make Bessemer steel with foreign low phosphor ore, whereas the British had large domestic stores of low phosphor ironstone. These differences were sufficient in the late 1870s and early 1880s to ensure that the British could almost always underbid Ruhr producers in contract submissions to major foreign markets.[81]

However, the British were not the only people that Ruhr industralists had to worry about. Although a less serious contender in the long run, Belgium also put up stiff competition in some export markets. In 1887, for example, the Chamber of Commerce observed that "in Belgium much lower wages are paid than in German works and . . . therefore the German companies can only compete with the Belgians at a loss." In 1892 the Chamber of Commerce complained that local plants producing railway equipment were suffering from both heavy English and Belgian competition. Both countries were selling railway equipment at such low prices that German works could scarcely make a profit.[82] Moreover, toward the end of the century a new threat was added; in 1899 the Chamber of Commerce reported that "American competition, which in 1897 had menacingly appeared in continental and German markets, has made further progress this year."[83]

To meet the challenge of foreign competition, Bochum's iron and steel producers had to try to reduce the costs of their products in world markets. To achieve that goal a variety of initiatives were taken. Since transport costs figured so heavily and so disadvantageously in the price of German iron and steel exports, the state was repeatedly petitioned for reductions in rail freight charges.[84] As with coal, cartels helped to keep prices in the domestic market high enough to allow price cutting and dumping abroad.[85] Moreover, most of the Ruhr iron and steel companies began both to ensure their raw materials supplies and to escape coal cartel prices by engaging in vertical integration—the gradual acquisition of coal mines, iron mines, coke factories, etc.[86] The Bochumer Verein acquired its first coal mine in 1868, an iron ore pit in 1872/73; additional coal mines in 1882, 1889, 1890, 1894, and 1900; and a cokeworks in 1890. And the blast furnaces and steelworks were integrated with rolling mills and further production processes so that the industry gained not only economies of scale but of serial production.[87]

But perhaps the major thrust in cost cutting centered on labor saving technological innovation.[88] In his 1878 testimony before the Iron Inquiry Commission, Baare had made a comparison between the Bochumer Verein and the Clarence Iron Works that revealed that the German blast furnace required some 75.5 workers at a cost per shift of 221.005 marks, whereas a comparable English furnace needed only 24.37 workers at a cost of 90.046 marks. "The difference in price" between British and German iron, Baare concluded, "is therefore to be ascribed to the higher working capacity of the English. . . . It indicates clearly the superiority of the English worker and the lower working costs of the same."[89]

However, German producers very quickly began to improve the labor cost differential between themselves and the British by adopting extensive mechanization of production processes.[90] Indeed, German producers were in the forefront of European industrialists in this regard and were quick to adopt American iron and steel technology, at that time the most advanced in the world.[91] The Bochumer Verein, for example, had begun an extensive process of electrification of all its production processes (rolling mills, cranes, etc.) by the 1890s. In 1899 it modernized its rolling mills and after 1901 began to completely mechanize operations at its blast furnace.[92] When the members of the British Gainsborough Commission came through Bochum in 1906 they were quick to note the results.

Three years ago there was some comment because the Indian Railway Department ordered wheels and rails from these works . . . In general it is quite clear that everything is up to date as regards machinery . . . Their shops are very fine and we do not hesitate to say that we have seen nothing better in this regard since we left England. Two magnificent coupled engines, 1,200 and 800 nominal H.P. respectively, were particularly striking.[93]

Similarly, the investigations of the German Metalworkers' Union in 1910 revealed that

The pure unmeasurable achievements of modern technology are at their most successful . . . in modern foundry work. The operation of the foundries requires an extensive application of mechanical aids, since man alone is not in the position to subdue the powerful natural forces . . . which are ranged against him in the making of iron . . . a complete representation of the technical equipment in foundry works is for this reason . . . impossible, since almost every day brings further progress and improvements and one piece of equipment surpasses the other.[94]

The main thrust of these technological advances was to save on labor costs. As David Landes points out, "The effect of mechanical loading alone was to reduce a work force of 46 skilled and unskilled labourers per hearth to 16 and cut labour costs (allowing for the amortization of the additional capital) by 58 percent." In its survey, the German Metalworkers' Union noted that "in modern steel and rolling mills the crane dominates," then went on to illustrate the point by describing a new inclined hoist for loading Martin furnaces with scrap metal that needed only a crane operator at the scrap metal pile and a few laborers to shunt wagons (even this task could be performed by magnetic crane).[95] The same report also described the transformation of rolling mill technique:

In the rolling mills, hoisting instrument technology . . . has been transformed. Previously, to service the *Triostrassen*, the workers used "wands" which were operated by hand with steam or water under pressure. The work [with this equipment] required numerous workers on heavy [rolling] streets . . . But today reversing rollers are used.[96]

The returns of the new technology in the form of increased productivity per worker were considerable. The German Metalworkers' Union estimated, for example, that between 1890 and 1909 alone the total work force had expanded by some 79 percent but the production of pig iron had risen some 171.4 percent (i.e., a 60 percent tonnage increase per worker). The same report also pointed out that by no means all this increased productivity could be credited to the substitution of machinery for human effort; some of it, indeed if the union report was correct, a good deal of it, was also coming from an increased intensity of labor effort. On the one hand, the new technical improvements themselves quickened the pace of work: "the worker is required to service the machines, ovens and equipment quicker . . . he must adapt his working capacity to the fast tempo."[97]

But at the same time, it was clear that various piece rate wage systems were being utilized to step up labor intensity and thereby to increase productivity. "Piece work," Baare remarked in his 1875 report "is our Alpha and Omega." But "piece work in the foundries," the German Metalworkers' Union concluded in 1910, "is very often no real work any more but rather a hunting and driving that no longer has anything natural about it." Aside from piece work, employers provided a "stimulus to more intensive activity . . . through promising premiums or through wage reductions, or even through the systematic playing off of one shift against the other."[98]

Indeed, in the short run at least, employers could actually reduce labor costs by such methods without adopting new technology; at the Westfälische Stahlwerk (Weitmar) in the Bochum area it was reported that whereas there had been forty-two men working in the Feineisenwalzwerk in 1909 producing 90–100 tons per day, the same quantity was being made in 1910 with only thirty-two workers and this without noteworthy technological improvement.

Moreover, up until the war, Ruhr iron and steel producers enjoyed the benefit of this increased workers' productivity without having to make any significant concessions with regard to hours worked. In its 1910 report, the German Metalworkers' Union concluded that a reduction of working hours was necessary to relieve exhaustion among workers in the industry, and that such a reduction had been made possible by the increased productivity of the new machinery. Moreover, it suggested that a reduction of hours would also be in the interest of the iron and steel companies themselves, since they would be better able to compete with foreign producers in world markets if they had "a healthy, strong work force [rather] then . . . one that was overtired and damaged by long, heavy work."[99] Naturally, employers did not quite see it that way, since any significant reduction of working hours probably would require that three rather than the current two shifts be run in each twenty-four-hour period, thus adding to labor costs and endangering Germany's ability to compete with Great Britain. Right up until the war, working hours at the Bochumer Verein remained between ten and eleven per shift, and the rare local employer, like Heinrich Flottmann, owner of a machine building factory, who did reduce hours was severely censured by other industrialists and even threatened with boycott. And obviously, Ruhr iron and steel industrialists, like their counterparts in coal, would strenuously resist any working class efforts that would deny them their competitive advantage by raising wages or lowering productivity.[100]

The Metalworking and Machine Building Industries

Although Bochum's industrial economy was dominated by the mining of coal and the production of iron and steel, it did, as we have seen earlier, develop greater diversity toward the end of the century. One of the major areas of new growth was in metalworking and machine building—industries that located in Bochum to be close to the suppliers of their raw materials, iron and steel.[101] By 1907 metalworking and machine building together employed almost 20 percent of the working population. But, unlike coal, iron, and steel, this branch of local industry was not heavily capitalized and remained comparatively small in scale; by 1907 there were no fewer than 210 metalworking and machine building shops in the city, and the great majority of them employed fewer than ten men (93.7 percent in metalworking and 88.9 percent in machine building).[102]

Unlike coal, iron, and steel and, indeed, the metalworking and machine building industries elsewhere in Germany, the local industry did not develop a sizable export market before the war.[103] As late as 1911, the Chamber of Commerce observed that "in the main the market area is, as before, almost only the industrial district itself [i.e., Rhineland-Westphalia] and the potash district. Exports to foreign countries are not very important for most companies.[104]

Since the metalworking and machine building industries produced primarily machines and equipment used in mining and in the blast furnaces, they were extremely dependent on the business cycle as it affected local heavy industry. To give just two examples: During the late-1870s depression, Wilhelm Seippel, owner of a local factory that made miners' safety lamps, complained to the Chamber of Commerce that his business was bad since, under present economic conditions, the mines "restricted themselves primarily to having used and defective lamps repaired, but hold back from placing orders for new lamps as far as possible." On the other hand, a boom in heavy industry, especially mining, usually led to the situation described in 1911: "Increased production of coal has led to a growing demand for mining machinery, shaking chutes are especially in demand."[105]

The highly differentiated production of metalworking and machine building meant that it was far more difficult to achieve cartelization in this sector than it had been in either coal or iron and steel.[106] Consequently, sharp, often cutthroat, competition, reminiscent of the experience of coal, iron, and steel in the 1870s, continued in metalworking and machine building right up to the war. Naturally, this competition was particularly extreme during periods of economic downturn: in 1908, for example, the Chamber of Commerce reported that "sharp competition has broken out over contracts, which have become fewer and smaller . . . the works underbid each other in such a way that prices have reached such a low level that often the costs of production cannot be covered . . . most of the works have to show a reduction in profit."[107]

However, local metalworking and machine building industrialists do not seem to have been very happy about their profits regardless of whether their market was good or bad, since they constantly had to contend with being squeezed between the cartel prices charged by their suppliers, the iron and steel industry, and the much more rapidly fluctuating market prices they in turn received for their products. As the Chamber put it in 1907,

during boom periods the improvement of their selling prices cannot, as a rule, keep step with the rise of prices for primary and half-finished products. On the other hand, an economic downturn makes itself felt in immediate price reductions [in the finishing industries] so that a favorable business juncture is almost always of shorter duration than it is for primary and half-finished products. Because there is a lack of organization among the finishing industries, the extraordinarily sharp competition which sets in with business downturns drives prices down with such a swift tempo that any reduction of the cartel-supported raw material prices is thereby more than outweighed.[108]

Finally, the metalworking and machine building industries were, like coal, labor intensive. Although some local enterprises had already begun to install labor saving machinery in the 1870s,[109] the industry as a whole remained heavily dependent on relatively highly paid, skilled workers.

If less weight is laid on the total amount of wages here [in metalworking and machine building] than in the production of primary materials, then that is naturally clarified by the fact that the [absolute] number of workers in the production [of finished metal products] is, compared, for example, to mining, lower and therefore wage increases do not seem to fall so strongly into the balance. But people should not forget that . . . in finished production [there are] a larger number of different occupational types, molders, smelters, turners, fitters . . . etc. . . . all highly paid, skilled working men. . . . If, therefore, the net profits of the employers, as has been attested from all sides, have . . . not risen in proportion to sales, then this impairment of employers' profits in the metalworking industry surely has redounded to the benefit of the worker, for the most part.[110]

The fact that profit margins were often considered to be unsatisfactory, coupled with the more extreme price fluctuations experienced in the metalworking and machine building trades, had the effect of making local industrialists engaged in these sectors even more sensitive to labor costs than their counterparts in the coal, iron, and steel industries.[111] Yet, because they lacked the power that came from industrial concentration, metalworking and machine building enterprises did not have the same ability as heavy industry to contain their labor costs within the parameters that would ensure their economic viability.[112] In a variety of ways, then, metalworking and machine building stood out as instructive counterexamples to the general developmental trends in heavy industry. They showed quite clearly what happened when an industrial sector was incapable of organizing itself as heavy industry had done.

But to local industrialists, the ability to "organize" and "control" the economy, thus rendering it more predictable, benefited not only themselves; it also created a new security for the whole of German society. Because German industry had succeeded in organizing significant sectors of German economic life, the very nature of that economy had been transformed:

There will always be upswings and downturns in economic life, but, in the last few decades, at least in Germany, these have taken on an essentially milder form. Although in the years 1897–1900 and 1905–1907, we experienced periods of glittering boom ... these booms [still] reached an end; yet this did not mean that the whole economic building began to totter. In the same way, the downturn in the year 1900, while it brought some severe shakes, was in no way a crisis that could be compared to 1873 or 1857. The explanation for the possibility of a peaceful resolution of such periods of extreme economic tension can only be the regulation of economic life which has been made possible by the development of cartels which began in the major industries in the 1890s.[113]

More specifically, so local industrialists argued, the German working class had gained a great deal from this regulation of economic life:

The German working class has achieved a much better condition during the last twenty years ... this is to be ascribed to the fact that they have been completely spared periods of large income reductions, extensive unemployment or even impoverishment. ... Without the influence of the large cartels which, to a greater or lesser degree, control the market, business cycles would affect the working class much more sharply and create disorder in their livelihood as happened in earlier decades.[114]

Organization of the German economy had thus, according to local industrialists, diminished the material basis for class conflict. Indeed it could now be argued that both workers and industrialists shared a common interest in the perpetuation of "organized capitalism."[115] But just how much had the material condition of Bochum's industrial workers actually changed since the 1870s?

The Insecurity of Working Class Life

In 1875 Louis Baare, director of the Bochumer Verein, offered an estimate of household costs for a working class family of four to the Imperial Iron Enquiry Commission (Table 1.12).

Table 1.12 Estimate of Household Costs, 1875

Item		Cost/Day
Meat (Sunday only)		10 pfg.
Bread		60
Coffee and chicory (per week)		15
Potatoes		24
Butter, grease, lard		15
Vegetables		15
Fat		24
Spice, seasonings		2
Soap, including laundry		10
Coal and wood		10
Rent for 2 rooms with stall		27
Taxes		
Communalsteuer 9 mk.		
Klassensteuer 6 mk.		
School and church 9 mk.	Total taxes:	6
Sick Fund		2
Total	2 mk.	20 pfg.
Total per Year (not including clothing)	803 mk.	

SOURCE: StAB, Küppers Nachlass, NI 23a.

This year, 1875, marked the beginning of a severe depression, and the working population in the city was already beginning to be squeezed hard by it. Only about a quarter of male workers would not have had real problems feeding, housing, and clothing their families (Table 1.10). Another 25 percent who earned between 660 and 900 marks were still able to survive, but only with considerable difficulty. The bottom 50 percent who earned less than 660 marks were in real trouble unless they had working wives, daughters, or sons who helped keep family income above subsistence level. Only a few inhabitants had so far been forced onto the poor rolls—in 1875 the city authorities supported less than twenty-one in every thousand inhabitants—but their numbers were rapidly increasing. By 1878 the figure had risen to 44.7 and by 1879 it was up to 58.5 (Table 1.13).

On the other hand, 1882 signaled a period of recovery; more jobs became available, the demand for coal rose, and the numbers receiving support from the city dropped down to sixty-five per thousand.[116] And that year too, although the proportion of the work force earning more than 900 marks actually shrank, to about 16 percent, there were signs of

Table 1.13 Recipients of Permanent and Temporary Support (Per 1,000 Total Population)

Year	Permanent Support	Temporary Support
1866	29.6	
1867	31.3	
1868		
1869	29.3	
1870	33.3	
1871	33.1	
1872	34.1	
1873	29.6	
1874	29.3	
1875	16.5	4.4
1876	19.4	
1877		16.7
1878	25.6	19.1
1879	34.4	24.1
1880	35.0	20.9
1881	33.2	9.6
1882	33.4	15.7
1883	26.6	15.8
1884	25.1	19.5
1885	30.2	21.2
1886	30.2	23.0
1887	24.4	30.0
1888	20.3	28.3
1889	18.2	25.3
1890	17.1	
1891	19.5	19.6
1892	22.8	22.1
1893	25.2	26.6
1894	27.9	15.4
1895	28.2	11.8
1896	27.3	14.5
1897	25.8	19.8
1898	23.4	14.7
1899	21.0	9.4
1900	22.1	8.7
1901	23.6	11.7
1902	22.1	19.5
1903	21.8	24.9
1904		
1905		
1906	15.4	21.4

SOURCE: StAB, VB, 1866–1906.

improvement in the distribution of income at the lower levels. Whereas fewer than 25 percent had earned between 660 and 900 marks and 50 percent less than that figure in 1875, now, in 1882, almost 50 percent of the working population had edged into the 660–900 marks range, the threshhold of relative economic security for the working class.

Thirteen years later, in 1895, the Bochumer Verein hired on an additional 492 men, and average earnings increased slightly. The local Hasenwinkel and Engelsburg mines employed fewer workers than the year before, but wages were up.[117] This was, then, a year of moderate expansion in some sectors of the local economy, contraction in others, and slowly rising wages. But the improvement over 1875 was unmistakable; now only 40 percent of the working population earned under 900 marks, although twenty-eight in every thousand inhabitants received permanent and twelve temporary support from the city (Tables 1.10 and 1.13).

Finally, 1907, the highpoint of an economic revival that had started in the fall of 1905: "Production continues to expand and the demand simply cannot be satisfied . . . the labor market is very favorable to the worker and has created further wage increases for him." The Bochumer Verein took on 819 men that year, and average wages there rose from 1,328 to 1,415 marks. In local mines the shift wage for face workers was up from 5.29 to 5.98 marks. Only at the very end of the year was this prosperous picture marred by signs of an impending downturn: "The labor market has gotten somewhat worse, but up until now there have been no really disturbing consequences."[118]

The immediate result of this increasing unemployment in late 1906 was to force more people onto the poor rolls; fewer than twenty inhabitants in every thousand received permanent support that year, but already more than twenty had asked for temporary aid (Table 1.13). However, income had not been seriously affected; indeed, that year only about 36 percent of the working population earned less than 900 marks (Table 1.10).

Between 1870 and the early twentieth century, then, the income of the poorest groups in the community underwent a definite and permanent improvement. In the 1870s and 1880s, regardless of the condition of the labor market or the average level of wages, three-quarters of the working population could expect to earn less than 900 marks each year and therefore, according to Baare's estimate, lived at or near subsistence level. But by the 1890s, between a third and a half of the working population regularly earned more than 900 marks per year. Since inflation had not drastically affected real income in the meantime, this put them permanently above the survival line (Table 1.10).

Yet, as real and important as this long-term improvement was, insecurity and unpredictability still remained central features of working class life in Bochum. By the early twentieth century, fewer workers had directly to contend with plunging into outright destitution; yet the proportions of the working population who continued to confront economic insecurity remained high and fluctuated widely with the cycles of prosperity, recession, and depression. Table 1.14 helps to illustrate these patterns.

While it was true that business cycles became somewhat less extreme after the 1890s, as the Chamber of Commerce had maintained, layoffs, short-time, and wage cuts remained

Table 1.14 A Model of Income Fluctuation (in Percent)

Situation	Earning Less than 900 Mks.	Earning Less than 660 Mks	Supported poor
Case 1. Labor demand high, wages rising			
(a) in the 1870s–80s	75–80	25	6
(b) in the 1890s–1900s	35	10	2–3
Case 2. Unemployment, but wages holding			
(a) in the 1870s–80s	75–80	30	6–8
(b) in the 1890s–1900s	35	10–20	5
Case 3. Unemployment increasing, wages dropping			
(a) in the 1870s–80s	75–80	50	8
(b) in the 1890s–1900s	40–50	20–30	6

[a]Approximate.

recurrent features of working-class life in Bochum (Table 1.15). During the twenty-year period from 1870 to 1889, miners faced layoffs in no less than ten separate years and worked short-time and/or were subjected to wage cuts in five. Similarly, workers in the iron and steel industry were laid off in nine separate years, worked short-time in three, and experienced wage cuts in no less than eight.

After 1890, local workers had a somewhat better chance of holding onto their jobs; iron and steel workers faced layoffs in six of the twenty years between 1890 and 1909, miners in only four. Wage cuts were also less frequent; miners experienced wage reductions in four of these years, iron and steel workers in only two. However, working short-time, which often significantly reduced total income, actually became more common; miners were put on short-time in no less than nine of these years, iron and steel workers in no less than four.

Moreover, heavy industry did not give working class families the same opportunity to mitigate this economic insecurity as did other industrial contexts: textile towns, for example, or the more economically variegated metropolitan centers where there was greater demand for both female and child labor.[119] Throughout the course of its existence, the working class family in Bochum was probably more dependent on the income of the father than families in either of these other two types of cities. Consequently its position was that much more vulnerable and insecure.

Bochum provided relatively few sources of employment for women. In the textile town of Barmen, women made up no less than 26.5 percent of the workers in industrial and artisanal occupations in 1907, but in Bochum they were only 4.0 percent.[120] As Florence Bell observed in her description of an English counterpart to the Ruhr heavy industry city, "The position of the women of the working classes is different from that which they occupy in other big manufacturing towns, for the reason that . . . the iron trade, offers absolutely no field for women in any part of it.[121] In Bochum that obviously applied to the mining industry as well: In 1907 only two women in the entire city were reported to be working in mines or foundries.[122]

Table 1.15 Layoffs, Short-Time, and Wage Cuts in the Coal, Iron, and Steel Industries, 1870–1913

Year	Coal Layoffs	Coal Short-Time	Coal Wage Cuts	Iron and Steel Layoffs	Iron and Steel Short-Time	Iron and Steel Wage Cuts
1870						X
1871						
1872						
1873				X		
1874				X		X
1875				X		X
1876	X	X	X	X		X
1877	X	X	X	X		X
1878	X	X	X			X
1879	X					
1880						
1881						
1882	X					
1883	X	X		X	X	X
1884	X			X		X
1885			X	X	X	
1886	X	X	X			
1887	X					
1888	X					
1889				X	X	
1890		X		X		
1891	X	X		X		X
1892	X	X	X	X	X	X
1893			X			X
1894	X	X		X		
1895					X	
1896						
1897						
1898						
1899						
1900					X	
1901	X	X	X	X	X	
1902						
1903						
1904		X				
1905						
1906						
1907						
1908		X	X		X	
1909	X	X		X		
1910		X				
1911		X				
1912						
1913						

SOURCES: StAB, VB, annual Chamber of Commerce reports, and Küppers Nachlass, NI, 23a.

The women who worked in the nineteenth century were overwhelmingly young and single. In France in 1896, 52 percent of all single women worked, compared to 38 percent of those who were married (including agriculture). In Britain in 1911, 69 percent of all single girls but only 9.6 percent of married women were employed. In Bochum too, although only 4.6 percent of married women had full time employment in 1907, some 44.4 percent of all single girls were working.[123]

Joan Scott and Louise Tilly have suggested that for a good part of the nineteenth century the work of young, single women reflected the continuation and adaptation of "traditional peasant" and "lower class strategies" for family survival; daughters were put to work so that they would bring much needed income into the family. Obviously, we have no accurate way of measuring (without detailed family budget surveys) just how much income young girls could and did contribute to the working class family economy in Bochum, but some significant observations can be made simply on the basis of the published census data.[124] To begin with, even if all working daughters contributed to the family income, a considerable proportion of Bochum families could not have improved their economic position by drawing on daughters' wages, since only 44.4 percent of all single women in the city were working in 1907. Moreover, a considerable number of the young girls who did work would have been contributing income, not to families in Bochum but to their parents in the small towns and villages of Westphalia and West Prussia from which they had originally migrated. In 1907 the largest employer of single women was domestic service (N = 2,691 or 35.6 percent of all single women), but the great majority of domestic servants came from outside Bochum: 64.0 percent from Westphalia and 15.1 percent from West Prussia with only 18.3 percent having been born in the city.[125] Only a relatively small number of Bochum families could therefore have been deriving any measure of financial support from daughters who worked in domestic service.

Apart from domestic service, the job opportunities for young girls in Bochum were rather slim. Employment as a shopgirl in retail trade was one possibility. By 1907, 12.1

percent of all single women in the city found work here.[126] But it was clear that this form of employment was becoming an alternative rather than an addition to domestic service. In the same year, the Chamber of Commerce observed that "working as a sales girl lacks social status so that daughters from the better circles naturally try to find office work and the salesgirls are now recruited more from those classes which earlier regarded experience as a domestic servant as the most suitable preparation for their later careers as housewives." Some young girls might also find jobs in the small local clothing industry (N = 764 or 10.1 percent of all single women) and the food trades (N = 117 or 1.5 percent).[127] But, taken as a whole, the opportunities for daughters to gain income that might help the family were relatively limited.

Moreover, the nature of local industry, combined with the restrictions imposed by Prussian law, meant that young men found it difficult to get work before they were sixteen. A survey undertaken at the Bochumer Verein in 1887 indicated that the company employed only 86 workers under the age of sixteen (out of a total of 3,235). And in 1911, the Chamber of Commerce observed that "children under 14 years of age . . . are not employed in the Dortmund Mining District, while young workers between the ages of fourteen and sixteen find work only at the surface" where the wages were lower than underground.[128] After the age of sixteen, however, boys entered the labor market very rapidly. Indeed, it could be argued that the relative scarcity of work for young women put a special pressure on young men to find full-time employment so that they could contribute to the family income, as Table 1.16 suggests.

Until such time as sons and, to a lesser degree, daughters could go out to work, some families may have tried to ease their economic burdens by sharing their rent, a major item of working class expenditure, with boarders and lodgers.[129] Certainly, the available figures on household composition in 1910 do indicate that the heavy industry cities in the Ruhr, like Bochum, Dortmund, Duisburg, and Düsseldorf, all had relatively high proportions of households containing lodgers.[130]

Table 1.16 Age of Entry into the Labor Force (percentages employed in 1907)

Age	Male	Female
14–16	80.6	14.3
16–18	92.5	59.9
18–20	97.2	64.7

SOURCE: Calculated from *Statistik des Deutschen Reiches*, Bd. 210/2. See also chapter 4 of Stephen Hickey's forthcoming Oxford University dissertation on miners in the eastern Ruhr. I wish to thank Mr. Hickey for allowing me to read the completed chapters of this work.

However, this expedient still involved a minority of households at any given time (although it may have been resorted to temporarily by many more to weather some particular crisis), and it was not likely to be regarded as a particularly attractive solution to the family's income problems, since taking in lodgers exacerbated living conditions which were already overcrowded. As Niethammer and Brüggemeier have recently suggested, "Lodgers were taken in as long as it was necessary. When the oldest children were earning, their income could help to support their younger brothers and sisters and the lodgers became unnecessary."[131]

The economic position of the working class family in Bochum was therefore extremely insecure for a relatively long period of its life cycle. For the first fourteen to sixteen years, working class families had, in most instances, to rely solely on the earnings of the father and hence were "almost entirely dependent upon the health and physical condition of the breadwinner, any illness or accident affecting him at once plunges them into difficulties." In Bochum, economic difficulties resulting from the temporary or permanent incapacity of the father must have been quite common, since work in heavy industry was exceptionally dangerous and debilitating. Between 1905 and 1913, the mining and iron and steel industries had more accidents per thousand employed workers than any other branch of German industry for which statistics were recorded, and a relatively high proportion of these accidents caused the deaths of the workers involved. Moreover, as the city council observed in 1875, "every year a percentage of the working class . . . is rendered incapable of earning a living as a result of the heavy and fatiguing work in local factories, even disregarding the frequent incidence of accidents."[132]

When children finally did go out to work, the family's economic situation became somewhat less vulnerable, but this stage was relatively short, for sons and daughters would begin to leave home in their late teens and early twenties. Although children may well have continued to aid parents during emergencies and some may even have sent portions of their income home after they moved out, in most instances the main burden of support was thrust back onto the father, but now under conditions that made this final phase of the working class life cycle in Bochum even more difficult than the early years of marriage.[133] By the time their children had left home, most fathers would have been in their middle and late forties—just the point in their lives when their income was first seriously beginning to decline.[134] As Table 1.17 indicates, working class earning power started off slowly, built to a peak in the late thirties, then began to drop somewhat as the worker entered his forties, finally suffering very considerable erosion in the early fifties (although the income of skilled workers held up somewhat longer than that of the unskilled). Whereas some 90.9 percent of the workers in an income sample who were younger than 20 earned less than 1,050 marks in 1901, 66.5 percent of those aged 20–29 earned more than this figure as did 72.4 percent of those aged 30–39. Among the 40–49-year-old group, some 63.7 percent still earned more than 1,050 marks, but significantly, the percentage of workers in this age group earning less than 1,050 marks was larger than any younger age group, except for those under 20. Then, finally, by the time the worker reached 50 the chances were more than even that he would earn less than 1,050 marks per year, as declining physical strength and agility forced him to produce less or to seek a less demanding and lower paid job.

In short, then, "organized capitalism" did not radically transform the life situations of most of Bochum's working class. While working class income certainly had improved by the early twentieth century and while business cycles had moderated by comparison to the disastrous record of the

Table 1.17 Workers' Income over the Life Cycle

Age Group	Under 900 Mks.		900–1,050 Mks.		1,050– 1,200 Mks.		1,200– 1,350 Mks.		1,350– 1,500 Mks.	
	N	%	N	%	N	%	N	%	N	%
Under 20 (N = 66)	4	6.1	56	84.8	5	7.6	1	1.5	0	0.0
20–29 (N = 691)	9	1.3	223	32.3	368	53.3	64	9.3	27	3.9
30–39 (N = 390)	7	1.8	101	25.9	225	57.7	40	10.3	17	4.4
40–49 (N = 245)	18	7.3	71	29.0	108	44.1	37	15.1	11	4.5
50–59 (N = 114)	11	9.6	50	43.9	34	29.8	13	11.4	6	5.3
60–69 (N = 20)	10	50.0	6	30.0	3	15.0	1	5.0	0	
70 and over (N = 3)	3	100.0								
No age given (N = 8)	1		2		3		1		1	

SOURCE: This sample has been drawn from the manuscript tax schedule for 1901 (StAB, Staatssteuerrolle, 1901). It includes all individuals paying income tax who lived in the city's twelfth ward, an area of high concentration of incomes under 3,000 marks per year.

1870s, insecurity and unpredictability remained basic ingredients of working class life.[135] It would be unreasonable to suggest that this basic fact of their material existence did not significantly influence the way industrial workers regarded the world in which they lived. But the ways in which that influence could exert itself were by no means simple, uniform, or easily predictable. Workers might be moved to seek greater control over their lives by individual or collective action (or both combined). They might try to achieve upward mobility, if not for themselves then for their children, into more secure realms of the social structure. They might also come to the conclusion that it was necessary to gain greater control over their individual existences by engaging in collective action— strikes, trade unions, political activity. However, the insecurity and unpredictability of working class life could obviously work in quite different directions; workers might feel, for example, that committing family resources to achieving upward mobility was too risky an undertaking when these resources were already limited and insecure. Similarly, the vulnerability of the working class family economy and its heavy dependence on male breadwinners (all of whom might well be working in the same industrial sector) could make it difficult for workers to commit themselves to a strike for any length of time and might even discourage them from joining a union or engaging in political activity for which they might well be blacklisted by employers.[136] Moreover, the specific trajectory of the working class life cycle in heavy industry, which confronted the male breadwinner with the inescapable prospect that income would steadily decline from his early forties onward, may well have encouraged a cautious outlook and an unwillingness to take risks even at a younger age when his income was still good.[137] In the chapters that follow, one of our main tasks will be to suggest why different groups or types of workers would have found some of these responses more compelling than others.

two

Geographic Mobility

Anyone who came to know the city of Bochum twenty, thirty, forty or even fifty years ago and who came to visit it today after a long absence . . . would scarcely recognize it anymore . . . ! Next to the old part of the city a new one has grown up with magnificent regular streets and great open squares on which stately new buildings . . . are situated, all of which produces the impression of a metropolis.

In the city there is a flourishing manufacture of large iron products . . . and the immediate area has such large mines, that the work force of individual pits numbers not just in the hundreds, but in the thousands. It goes without saying that, as a result of these kinds of enterprises, a significant number of workers have had to move to the city.

Mayor Lange, 1886[1]

UNTIL THE 1840s, Bochum remained a small county seat and local market center whose population barely exceeded 4,000. But by 1907 it was an *Industriegrossstadt* with a population of over 120,000 and a labor force in excess of 50,000. Like other industrial cities in the Ruhr, Bochum grew by massive immigration during this period; by 1871 some two-thirds of the local inhabitants were migrants, most of them from the villages and small towns of neighboring Westphalia and the Rhineland (Table 2.1).[2]

By the mid 1880s, improved transportation and expanding employment opportunities were attracting people from regions of Germany much farther away, particularly from the impoverished rural districts of the east.[3] Local migrants from Westphalia and the Rhineland still supplied the bulk of new arrivals, but now there was a perceptible increase in the number of northeastern Germans (Table 2.2).[4]

By 1907, then, only 23 percent of the work force had been born in the city.[5] Yet, impressive as they are, these statistics scarcely hint at the actual volume of the migratory flow. Between 1880 and 1900 the population of Bochum rose from 32,798 to 64,702—an increase of 31,904. Net natural increase accounted for some 21,097 people, so we can assume that at least 10,807 migrants must have entered the city during these twenty years. In fact, local police records reveal that the actual volume of in-migration was much greater, totaling 232,092 persons. The huge discrepancy between these two figures is explained by the fact that, during the same period, at least 194,836 persons also left the city.[6] This was a remarkably volatile urban population; the net volume of population turnover during the two decades 1880–1900 amounted to thirteen times the total population in 1880 and almost fourteen times

Table 2.1 Regions of Origin in 1871

Born In	Percent
Bochum	33.1
Westphalia	39.5
Rhineland	12.5
Near migrant total	52.0
Hessen/Waldeck	8.4
Northeastern Germany[a]	0.6
Rest of Prussia	2.9
Rest of Germany	2.2
Foreign countries	0.9
Far migrant total	14.8

SOURCE: StAB, VB, 1871, p. 12.
[a]East and west Prussia and Posen.

Table 2.2 Regions of Origin in 1885 and 1907 (in Percent)

Born In	1885	1907
Bochum	41.5	36.5
Westphalia	30.2	34.4
Rhineland	9.9	5.4
Near migrant total	40.1	39.8
Hessen/Waldeck	6.5	2.6
Northeastern Germany[a]	3.7	11.9
Rest of Prussia	4.3	5.0
Rest of Germany	3.3	2.7
Foreign countries	0.5	1.5
Far migrant total	18.3	23.7

SOURCE: *Preussische Statistik. Die Endgültigen Ergebnisse der Volkszählung im preussischen Staate vom 1. Dez. 1885*, Ed. 90 (Berlin, 1888), p. 46; *Statistik des Deutschen Reichs*, Bd. 210, 2.

[a]East and West Prussia and Posen.

the net population increase by 1900 (Table 2.3). During every single year from 1880 to 1900 no less than 14, and sometimes as much as 20 percent of all the city's residents had just arrived in Bochum in the preceding twelve months.[7] It is unlikely that the majority of these newcomers stayed there beyond the next 365 days; for from 9 to 25 percent of the population also left the city each year and there is good reason to suspect that most of these out-migrants had also been among that year's recent arrivals.[8] Table 2.3 reveals this pattern of annual in- and out-migration.

Table 2.3 Rates of Population Turnover, 1880–1900 (per 1,000 of the average annual population)

Year	Arrivals	Departures	Year	Arrivals	Departures
1880	247	126	1890	229	197
1881	249	135	1891	261	205
1882	250	166	1892	190	186
1883	226	187	1893	211	173
1884	197	167	1894	210	185
1885	170	165	1895	210	189
1886	166	154	1896	256	203
1887	176	159	1897	265	231
1888	204	170	1898	286	235
1889	226	182	1899	288	257
			1900	288	254

SOURCE: Calculated from the reports of the Standesamt; StAB, VB, 1880–1900.

Although the fluidity of Bochum's population was remarkable, it was by no means exceptional. Official statistics for the period 1898–1902 reveal that average annual population turnover was similarly high in eighteen other large German towns, ranging from a low of 190 per 1,000 in Krefeld to a high of 600 per 1,000 in Charlottenburg. And in the Austrian city of Graz, William Hubbard has recently discovered that from 1880 to 1890 total mobility "amounted to twice the size of the city's population in 1890."[9]

Moreover, data on the percentage of inhabitants remaining in Bochum for a given period of time seem to fit the patterns of high population mobility uncovered by recent research on several American cities. Thus the persistence rate in Bochum after ten years was 44 percent, in Northampton, Massachusetts, 53 percent; in Rochester, New York, 20 percent; in Poughkeepsie, New York, 30 percent; in Atlanta, Georgia, 43 percent for white residents; and in Boston, Massachusetts, among household heads it ranged from 39 to 49 percent for three separate decades. The available evidence therefore seems to confirm the opinion of Bochum's city government that "continuous turnover of the population is typical of every large industrial city."[10]

Why did so many people leave Bochum during this period and so few remain? One way of answering that question is to examine the demographic, social, and economic traits that distinguished the out-migrants from the persisters. For out-migration was a highly selective, not a random process: age, marital status, occupation, individual social mobility, and fluctuations in the local business cycle all played a significant role in determining whether Bochum would be the migrant's final destination or simply a way station on the road to somewhere else.[11]

Age and Marital Status

The most commonly shared trait of both in- and out-migrants was their bachelorhood and their youth. Young male workers without spouses or children to care for were extremely mobile, whereas married couples tended to be much more stable. The

Chamber of Commerce's complaint in 1899 that there was "a good deal of job changing among young workers which inevitably disrupts production" was frequently repeated by local industrialists and is amply supported by available statistics. In 1885, for example, the ratio of single to married adults in the city as a whole was about 7:10, but among transient migrants it was roughly 9:1. And between 1880 and 1900, unmarried migrants, meaning for the most part men under the age of twenty-five, accounted for no less than 87 and sometimes as much as 93 percent of the transient population.[12]

Predictably, older, settled middle class contemporaries tended to regard this mobility as a moral problem, reflecting the restlessness and irresponsibility of youth. Young, single workers, so the argument ran, frivolously changed jobs whenever the spirit moved them. The behavior of these "immature and unworthy persons who waste their money in beer houses and low music halls as a result of the high wages they earn and the fact that they lack any family supervision" contrasted forcibly with "the families of the old settled workers and the neighboring rural families."[13]

Yet the dissimilar behavior patterns of single and married male workers owed more to the working class life cycle than to any real or imagined moral differences between them. From the time he left school at about age fourteen until he married, the manual worker felt little compulsion to settle down and had good reasons for moving frequently. On the negative side, the fact that he had only himself to support made it relatively easy for the single worker to leave jobs he did not like. Even in the middle of a severe depression in the local iron and steel industry when married workers at the Bochumer Verein were accepting wage cuts and longer hours just so they could keep their jobs, single men "try to do better for themselves by moving on." But single men did not always change jobs just to escape low wages or poor working conditions. Often there were positive attractions elsewhere, particularly the promise of high wages. In 1899, for example, the Chamber of Commerce noted that many young workers were even giving up their apprenticeships, and thus their prospects of eventually becoming skilled metalworkers, because "in the mines [they can] earn more than they would if they remained in the factories as apprentices." Far more than the married men, single workers were "at home wherever the best earning opportunities are offered."[14]

As young bachelors passing through Bochum, many manual workers may have "had the feeling that they did not have to remain permanently in their occupation, that they could perhaps still change their fate."[15] But that hope dimmed with marriage and parenthood. During the early, economically most difficult years, when children were still too young to contribute to family income, job changing may have seemed too risky to be worthwhile.[16] Steady work and a continuous income, even at the cost of considerable dissatisfaction with working conditions and wages, became more important to the married worker than the unsure prospect of improvement elsewhere. Local employers were well aware of this, and attempted to capitalize on it by trading a measure of security for the loyalty of their married men; thus they invested considerable amounts of money in company housing and other welfare schemes,[17] fired single workers first during depressions and, in at least one instance, even allowed married men to return to the job after a strike although the single workers had all been replaced by strikebreakers.[18]

Business Cycles and the Supply and Demand of Labor

The working class life cycle ensured that the great majority of men who left Bochum during these years would be young and single. But both the composition and the volume of the out-migrant flow also depended on fluctuations in the local business cycle and variations in the supply and demand of skilled and unskilled workers.

Workers were most easily uprooted from the city during periods of economic recession when jobs were scarce and wages low, especially if they were unskilled. In 1878, during a severe slump in the iron and steel industry, the president of the Bochumer Verein reported that "we are forever hiring on new hands, but they cannot earn enough to live, therefore they change jobs in an attempt to improve their situation and eventually end up going back to their homes."[19]

Many of these workers had only just arrived. They had come to Bochum because their "livelihood had gone on the rocks in their hometown"; now they discovered survival was no easier in the city. Barely "on the fringe of being able to earn a living" at the best of times, these new arrivals were plunged into total misery when a slump set in and demand for their physical strength and meager skills dried up. During these periods of poor wages and widespread unemployment, many found their way into the floating population, where "drunkenness, marital unhappiness, crimes and misery" must have made later return to a more settled existence extremely difficult.[20]

The return of prosperity made jobs in Bochum much easier to find; yet out-migration was actually higher when employment was full than it had been during the lean years. It would be reasonable to assume, as many contemporaries did, that this movement out of the city was a response to economic opportunities elsewhere and not the result of failure to find work in the city. In 1907, for instance, employers in the local metalworking and machine-building trades charged that large scale turnover resulted from the workers' efforts to "exploit the recent rise in prosperity . . . turnover during the whole year has reached almost four times the total average number of workers employed [but] when prosperity starts to taper off, the workers once again look for permanent employment."[21]

Yet these men were skilled and their experience certainly cannot be generalized to all migrants, most of whom were unskilled. For skilled workers enjoyed the special advantage of quite often being in short supply.

Now, as before, we have a deficiency of responsible and productive workers, especially tinsmiths, furnace smiths and tin finishers . . . even though the economy has started to enter another slump, the supply of trained workers is still much too small.[22]

These men undoubtedly moved because they could get better jobs elsewhere.[23] But unskilled workers were not in such an enviable position, for their chances of finding work were affected not only by economic fluctuations but by the migratory response itself. The potential reservoir of skilled labor outside the city was finite; but there were infinite numbers of unskilled men who could be drawn to Bochum as demand for their labor increased. If too many of these people descended on the city at one time, there would simply not be enough jobs to go around. Did the number of new arrivals who turned up in the city looking for work always correspond even roughly to the number of new positions? Or did the volume of in-migration exceed the capacity of the town's economy even though it was expanding? The answers to these questions determined the unskilled worker's fate in the local job market.

Figure 2.1 compares the ratios of unemployed migrant workers receiving aid from the voluntary organization, Verein

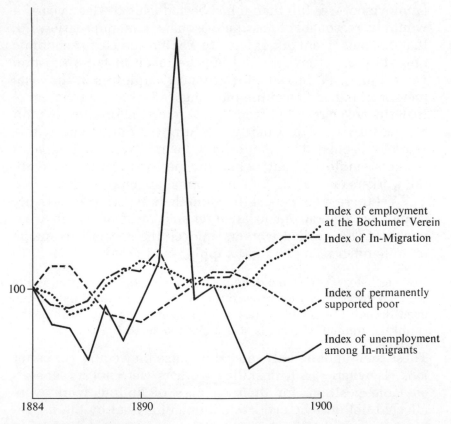

Index of employment at the Bochumer Verein

Index of In-Migration

Index of permanently supported poor

Index of unemployment among In-migrants

100

1884   1890   1900

2.1 In-Migration, Unemployment, and Business Cycles

gegen Strassen-und Hausbettelei, with the flow of new arrivals. It shows that as in-migration increased in response to growing prosperity, the percentage of unemployed new arrivals frequently rose rather than declined.[24] Despite expanding employment opportunities, destitution among in-migrants often became more, not less common. Though new jobs were being created, word of these opportunities was obviously generating a migratory response out of all proportion to the actual expansion of employment. This created a crisis of employment that must have seemed all the more bitter to those caught up in it, since it occurred within the midst of general prosperity.

Clearly, then, unskilled labor provided little opportunity or incentive for workers to stay in Bochum. Indeed, the city council explicitly recognized the connection between unskilled work and geographic instability when, shortly before the war, it observed that "the figures for migration are especially great in Bochum because the productive processes of mining require only a few skilled workers and can provide employment for large numbers of unskilled men."[25]

The out-migrant flow was therefore always disproportionately composed of unskilled and semiskilled workers, while skilled men were overrepresented among those who remained in the city. From Table 2.4 we can see that 44.5 percent of the sample persisting until 1890 was unskilled or semiskilled compared to 53.2 percent of the out-migrants. On the other hand, skilled workers and artisans made up 32.5 percent of the persisters but only 28.5 percent of the out-migrants.[26]

Moreover, the manual workers who left Bochum between 1880 and 1890 were disproportionately drawn from the ranks of the city's downwardly mobile. Men who found themselves slipping down from skilled to unskilled work seem to have lost the capacity and the incentive to create a stable foothold in the city for themselves and their families. But for men who held onto regular, well-paid, skilled jobs and sometimes even achieved a degree of upward mobility, Bochum seems to have been a considerably more attractive community (Table 2.5).[27]

Being able to live in one community for more than a few years was thus a considerable achievement in industrial Germany, since it meant that the worker had found and kept a regular, relatively attractive job with some prospects for advancement. Yet migrants, especially those from the distant provinces, found that the kinds of jobs that would make it possible for them to settle in Bochum were not readily accessible. Indeed, they were usually forced to accept the most unskilled, unhealthy, irregular, and hence most unsettled forms of work that the industrial community had to offer.

Mining and foundry work were, as Helmuth Croon observes, "from the seventies or eighties onward the occupation of the unskilled which every strong man could perform," as were chemical manufacture, stone- and earthwork, and some building jobs. It was widely recognized that minework,

Table 2.4 Occupational Status before 1890 of Persisting and Out-Migrating Sample Members

1880 Occupation	Persisting		Out-Migrating		Total Sample	
Unskilled/						
Semiskilled	N	%	N	%	N	%
Miners	49	10.0	78	12.4	127	11.4
Factory workers	102	20.9	141	22.5	243	21.8
Railway workers	7	1.4	7	1.1	14	1.3
Day laborers	42	8.6	87	13.9	129	11.5
Servants and service	10	2.0	16	2.5	26	2.3
Transport workers	5	1.0	3	0.5	8	0.7
Coke workers	3	0.6	2	0.3	5	0.4
	218	44.5	334	53.2	552	49.4
Skilled/Artisanal						
Metalworkers	21	4.3	37	5.9	58	5.2
Builders	33	6.7	28	4.4	61	5.5
Food, drink, clothing	39	8.0	18	2.9	57	5.1
Wood, furniture	31	6.3	15	2.4	46	4.1
Railway	1	0.2	1	0.2	2	0.2
Service and entertainment	5	1.0	3	0.5	8	0.7
Undifferentiated	29	6.0	77	12.2	106	9.5
	159	32.5	179	28.5	338	30.3
Non-manual Occupations	107	21.9	102	16.2	209	18.7
No gainful work	2	0.4	1	0.2	3	0.3
Invalided	3	0.6	12	1.9	15	1.3
Total	489	99.9	628	100.0	1,117	100.0

Table 2.5 Occupational Mobility Patterns of Skilled Out-Migrants and Persisters, 1880–1890 (in percent)

	Same Occupation	Unskilled/ Semiskilled	Other Skilled/ Artisanal	Nonmanual
Skilled metal-workers				
out-migrants	56.3	31.3	0.0	12.5
persisters	71.4	9.5	0.0	14.3[a]
Skilled builders				
out-migrants	57.1	23.8	14.3	4.8
persisters	72.7	12.2	3.9	12.0
All skilled/ artisanal workers				
out-migrants	60.5	18.4	15.8	5.2
persisters	64.7	10.4	15.0	9.8

[a]Total does not equal 100.00% since some members of the sample who were retired or invalided by 1890 were not included here.

the foundries, and the chemical industry took a heavy toll of the workers' energies and health. Throughout the second half of the nineteenth century, miners frequently complained about the early invalidism that resulted from their work. Foundry work too was hot, strenuous, and dangerous, and the men who worked at the blast furnaces suffered through long work days; as late as 1901 the German Metalworkers' Union complained that in local plants workers were still forced to put in eleven-hour days. Moreover, workers in all these unskilled positions had minimal job security.[28]

As Table 2.6 indicates, far migrants were most heavily concentrated in these unskilled and unhealthy trades, whereas the natives and local migrants tended more often to find jobs in skilled or artisan trades such as metalworking, machine building, instrument making, and woodworking. And although the published census figures do not allow us to distinguish the exact relationship between geographic origin and specific skill levels within these individual industrial sectors, analysis of the 1900 marriage register does confirm the patterns already indicated (Table 2.7).

More than 50 percent of skilled metalworkers marrying that year had been born in Bochum and the five surrounding counties. But among unskilled factory workers and miners, these figures were 25 percent and less than 33 percent respec-

Table 2.6 Occupation and Regional Origin in 1907

Occupational Group	All Migrants	Far Migrants	Natives	West-falen	Rhine-land	Hessen-Waldeck	N.E. Ger-many	Else-where
Stone and earthwork	96.2	81.8	3.8	10.2	4.2	1.7	31.0	49.1
Chemicals	89.9	59.6	10.1	18.8	11.5	1.4	36.9	21.3
Mines and foundries	83.8	46.8	16.2	43.1	3.9	3.1	24.0	9.7
Building	82.3	47.0	17.7	30.2	5.1	8.0	15.3	23.7
Wood by-products	79.6	38.3	20.4	31.0	10.3	0.0	27.6	10.7
Artistic trades	75.0	12.4	25.0	43.8	18.8	0.0	0.0	12.4
Cleaning	73.7	23.7	26.3	41.6	8.4	1.6	10.5	10.6
Food	73.0	22.7	27.0	41.6	8.7	2.1	5.2	15.4
Textiles	72.9	28.2	27.1	25.9	18.8	2.4	4.7	21.1
Machines and instruments	72.2	35.9	27.8	26.6	9.7	3.9	15.1	16.9
Printing	69.9	36.2	30.1	21.7	12.0	2.4	9.6	24.2
Woodworking	69.6	34.9	30.4	28.2	6.5	7.3	11.5	16.1
Metalworking	68.7	39.7	31.3	20.0	9.0	5.9	12.5	21.3
Leather	68.4	25.6	31.6	30.2	12.6	1.9	9.8	13.9
Paper	66.7	15.0	33.3	33.3	18.4	2.3	4.6	8.1
Clothing	62.7	26.9	37.3	29.1	6.7	4.7	11.3	10.9
All industry	77.4	38.2	21.6	34.3	5.9	4.3	18.5	15.4

SOURCE: *Statistik des Deutschen Reichs*, Bd. 210/2.

tively. Thus far migrants were disproportionately concentrated among the ranks of the city's working class "plebeians" (Table 2.8), where, like their American counterparts in Newburyport, Massachusetts, they soon discovered that it was a way of life to be constantly "buffeted about from city to city."[29]

Moreover, far migrants had much greater difficulty than either natives or near migrants in securing positions of power and authority in the industrial sector. Whereas natives and near migrants were most often the owners, managers, and

Table 2.7 Nativity of Men Marrying in 1900

Occupation	Born in Bochum and Five Surrounding Counties	
	N	%
Skilled metalworkers	40	51.3
Unskilled factory workers	39	25.3
Miners	38	32.7

SOURCE: Rathaus Bochum, *Familienbuch*, 1900.

Table 2.8 Regional Origin and Occupational Status Levels in Industry in 1907 (per 100 of each regional origin group employed)

	Owners and Managers	White Collar Workers	Manual Workers
Natives	8.1	8.4	83.5
All migrants	6.0	6.7	87.3
Near migrants	7.8	8.2	84.0
Far migrants	4.2	5.1	90.7
Hessen/Waldeck	6.3	5.9	87.8
Northeastern Germany	2.2	2.1	95.7
Rest of Germany	6.8	9.7	83.5
Foreign countries	2.5	4.2	93.3
Total work force	6.4	7.1	86.5

SOURCE: *Statistik des Deutschen Reiches*, Bd. 210/2.

white collar workers in industrial enterprises, far migrants found that they were more frequently consigned to the proletarian role in local industry; the northeastern Germans in particular had little hope of being anything more than manual workers. Men from the distant regions of Germany did somewhat better in trade and commerce, although northeastern Germans, who accounted for more than half of this group, still usually ended up as manual workers. And, in any case, whatever success far migrants might achieve in the commercial sector it was not enough to significantly improve their position in the economy as a whole, since so few of them worked in commercial trades; for every migrant employed in trade and commerce there were more than nine in industry.

Conclusion

In preindustrial Germany, being a settled member of a local community meant economic security, moral respectability, and personal honor. Only the poor and the dishonorable moved. As Wolfram Fischer argues,

Pauper- und Pöbelstand collect together all those who, for some social or legal reason have no *Heimat* . . . They are *heimat- und bindungslos*. Since they can nowhere find a sufficient permanent livelihood, it must be so.[30]

Beggars, vagabonds, soldiers, and journeymen traveled the countryside from town to town. Young men and women whose fathers' farms no longer had work for them set out for southwest Germany as "Schwabengänger" or to the Netherlands as "Hollandgänger."[31] But respectable members of the community stayed where they were.

The massive population movements that accompanied capitalist industrial development clearly disrupted these patterns; movement became the norm. Yet, although the scope and dimensions of geographic mobility had radically altered, the basic types of people who moved had not. It was true that in most industrial communities many of the respectable and wealthy citizens had originally been migrants. But if a person stayed on the move, then he was probably an economic failure and a social outsider. As we have seen, people usually left Bochum because they could not find or keep a job there, or because they could not earn enough to live.

On the other hand, those who had skilled jobs or nonmanual employment and therefore possessed a more secure livelihood, tended to remain in the city. Attitudes that condemned movement and valued stability were thus given fresh relevance by the conditions of the industrial-urban environment itself. Indeed, the settled and respectable inhabitants of the new industrial towns used the modern term "proletariat" to convey a very traditional image of the uprooted and homeless outsider:

It is at the very worst in this connection [economic, social, cultural, moral] with the families who have separated themselves from their *Heimatgemeinde*, without choosing a permanent residence elsewhere, but instead move around from one factory town to another, seeking their fortune everywhere, without finding it anywhere . . . [they] form a *Proletariat* that is totally destitute of all means of help every time there is a wage stoppage.[32]

Native, settled worker families were not considered to be part of this "proletariat"; the fact of being settled both bestowed and revealed moral qualities among them that were lacking in the floating population. "In general," wrote the Chamber of Commerce in neighboring Essen in 1876,

the local settled miners and factory workers are naturally diligent, thrifty, devoted and caring for their families . . . Another part of our

working population consists of migrants from all regions. If they
have set up permanent residence here for any length of time then
they strive to get up with the best of them ... But unfortunately
during periods of labor shortage, our locality becomes the refuge for
many elements that have experienced shipwreck in the course of
their lives and these people occasion many ... police investigations.
It is also to be expected that in such a variously composed working
population there is, here and there, [fertile] soil for Social Democratic agitation.[33]

But workers obviously had different reasons to be dis-
trustful of movement. By the end of the nineteenth century,
one observer has remarked, "Americans knew full well that
attachment to the community must be subordinated to the
advantages of mobility."[34] Yet American historians have
recently demonstrated that this myth certainly could not have
applied to the great majority of American workers, and the
evidence presented in this chapter suggests that much the
same would have to be said of the German workers who
moved into the industrial cities of the Ruhr.[35] Indeed, it is hard
to believe that job changing and movement from one city to
another was for most German workers anything more than a
threatening experience imposed on them by forces they could
not control. For some, particularly the young, not being tied to
one community could have represented a sort of freedom, but
it was a very hollow liberty, which allowed the discontented
to thumb their noses at authority for a time and to take a short
rest from difficult and unpleasant work, but which made no
real promise of improvement in their lives. And as they grew
older and took on the responsibilities of wives and children,
most male workers were undoubtedly prepared to relinquish
even this small measure of freedom if only they could find
steady work. It is doubtful that many would willingly have
sacrificed whatever degree of material security they had been
able to achieve in Bochum for the highly uncertain prospect of
advancement elsewhere.[36]

three

Social Mobility

For the individual proletarian, every prospect of working himself up out of the morass into which modern methods of production have thrust him by himself, through his own strength, have disappeared. He can only achieve his elevation through the elevation of the whole class to which he belongs.
  Karl Kautsky, "Comments on the Erfurt Program, 1912

They want to succeed in life, as it is called; the one to own a house, the other fine lodgings, the third expensive clothes, the fourth a life of pleasure in food, drink and dancing. In the education of their children some go much beyond what is possible for them. . . . When their means are not sufficient then discontent is immediately there. And envy, hatred . . . against all those who are better situated.
  Reports of the Kreissynode of Bochum (Hofstede, June 12, 1899)

TWO PICTURES OF the same subject: the first a statement of ideology the second rather a reproach to the lower classes than an accurate description of their condition, hopes, and prospects. But both are drawn on the same canvas and both portray a society in which there was little room to move, little chance for material progress, and a great gulf between opportunities and expectations that would inevitably lead to social conflict.

Since then, little has been added to our knowledge of the dimensions and processes of social mobility in industrial Germany.[1] Instead, we are forced to make assumptions based on the theories and clichés of other fields and disciplines, among which there is, unfortunately, no consensus. Students of social mobility disagree about the relative "openness" of industrial societies because they have not reached a common assessment of the effects of industrialization on social structure. On one side stand the partisans of American uniqueness. Their view, rooted in American folklore and supported by many scholars, is that rapid and widespread social mobility has been uniquely American while European industrial society has remained comparatively closed.[2] Opposition to that interpretation derives from what we might term the folklore of sociology and has been best articulated by Seymour Lipset and Reinhard Bendix.[3] Starting from the assumption that industrialization has basically similar consequences wherever it occurs, Lipset and Bendix have followed a trail of impressive but often ambiguous and incomplete statistics to reach the conclusion that social mobility is and has been widespread in all industrial societies.[4] In short, they can detect no significant differences between the structure of opportunities in Europe and America.

Those German historians who have documented the intellectual and political reaction against modernity seem to have implicitly accepted the sociological dogma of universal cause and effect.[5] Others, clinging to the idea of German uniqueness, have maintained a healthy scepticism regarding the supposed homogenizing consequences of industrialization and modernization, but only by adopting a narrow focus on the persistence of traditional social patterns in such elitist institutions as the German officer corps or university.[6] While it is important that we should know, for instance, how many businessmen's sons attended universities, this is only a limited indication of the relative openness of German society and the nature of the changes that were transforming it in the late nineteenth century. Few historians have attempted to ask how modernization affected German social structure as a whole, or whether it was or had to be the same there as in other industrial nations.

This study begins that task by addressing itself to one of the most important questions that can be asked about social structure and social change: How rapid, widespread, and significant was social mobility? Its aim is to establish the actual dimensions of social movement in Bochum through an examination of occupational mobility, property mobility, and the accumulation of savings. However, it seeks not only to describe the objective structure of opportunities but also to suggest how these opportunities were perceived and grasped.

To determine the dimensions of occupational mobility in late nineteenth century Bochum, a random sample of 1,117 adult males (about one-tenth of the total adult male population) was drawn from the 1880 city directory. In each succeeding city directory up until 1901, changes in occupation, residence, and property holdings were noted; these data were then analyzed by computer.[7] Supplementing this study were two projects that attempted to determine the extent of intergenerational mobility in the town. The first involved comparing the occupations of 697 men who married during the course of one year, 1900, with the occupations of their fathers as recorded in the marriage register.[8] The second involved tracing and analyzing the occupational backgrounds of fathers whose sons apprenticed to one of the skilled metal trades at the largest iron and steel company in the town, the Bochumer Verein, during the period 1882–93. These occupations were the main element in the town's "labor aristocracy," and this study aims at determining exactly what types of young men had the best chances of entering it.

In addition, I have examined the role of secondary education in the mobility process; the social backgrounds of students at three local secondary schools have been analyzed at different points in time in order to determine which social groups were able or wanted to educate their sons, and whether education was becoming accessible to wider social strata. It was also possible to compare the later occupations of students at one of these schools, the Gymnasium, with those held by their fathers and thereby to suggest what function education served in defining social status.[9]

The General Dimensions of Occupational Movement

What were the main patterns of occupational mobility during the period under consideration? Tables 3.1 and 3.2 indicate degrees of mobility after ten and twenty-one years among members of the 1880 city directory sample.

From these figures two important images emerge. The first is of a society neither completely static nor highly mobile. By far the majority remained occupationally stable, while those who did move generally made very modest gains. Unskilled and semiskilled workers had the least chance of moving into higher positions; even after a twenty-one-year period only two in every ten had experienced any form of upward mobility and only one of these had been able to

Table 3.1 Occupational Mobility by 1890

	Absolute Number[a]	Percent
Unskilled and semiskilled in 1880		
Remaining unskilled/semiskilled	190	87.1
Rising to skilled/artisanal	15	6.9
Rising to nonmanual	13	6.0
Total	218	100.0
Skilled and artisanal in 1880		
Remaining skilled/artisanal	125	78.6
Falling to unskilled	18	11.3
Rising to nonmanual	16	10.1
Total	159	100.0
Nonmanual in 1880		
Remaining nonmanual	103	96.3
Falling to skilled/artisanal	1	0.9
Falling to unskilled/semiskilled	3	2.8
Total	107	100.0

[a]This includes those retired or invalided by 1880 or 1901; if a sample member was so listed in either of these years, his occupation was considered to be the one last recorded before he stopped working.

Table 3.2 Occupational Mobility by 1901

	Absolute Number[a]	Percent
Unskilled and semiskilled in 1880		
Remaining unskilled/ semiskilled	93	78.8
Rising to skilled/artisanal	11	9.3
Rising to nonmanual	14	11.9
Total	118	100.0
Skilled and artisanal in 1880		
Remaining skilled/artisanal	67	60.9
Falling to unskilled/semiskilled	17	15.5
Rising to nonmanual	26	23.6
Total	110	100.0
Nonmanual in 1880		
Remaining nonmanual	60	96.8
Falling to skilled/artisanal	0	0.0
Falling to unskilled/semiskilled	2	3.2
Total	62	100.0

[a]See note, Table 3.1.

abandon manual work completely. Indeed, the most common form of mobility for unskilled and semiskilled workers was not upward but sideways; for instance, after ten years almost 35 percent of the stable group had moved into other unskilled or semiskilled work. Skilled and artisanal workers were more mobile, but they faced the danger of falling into the ranks of the unskilled almost as often as they had the opportunity to rise into nonmanual positions. Members of nonmanual occupations also made some advances, as we shall observe later, but their most notable achievement as a group was their extremely low rate of downward mobility into manual work.

The second image is of a society in which the division between manual and nonmanual work is not merely a demarcation of status but a barrier. Movement occurred much more frequently on either side of that barrier than it did across it.[10] By 1890 only 7.7 percent, by 1901 less than 18 percent of *all* manual workers persisting in the town had been able to move into the nonmanual world. And the extent of exchange in the other direction was even smaller; after ten years only 3.8 percent, after twenty-one years about 3.2 percent, of the non-

manual group had been forced to descend to the manual
ranks. By 1901, then, few people in either group had experienced significant movement away from the position they had
held twenty-one years before. For the majority, stability and
continuity remained the dominant frame of social reference.

If the dimensions of occupational mobility were small in
absolute terms, they appear even more limited in comparison
to movement in a society generally considered to be open in
the nineteenth century. Mobility rates in Bochum were quali-
tatively different from those in several American cities that
have recently been studied. Worthman, in his analysis of
working class mobility in Birmingham, Alabama, found that
"after twenty years in Birmingham more than one half of the
persisting workers had risen to non-manual jobs."[11] In
Bochum, as we have seen, the comparable figure after twenty-
one years was only 18 percent. Richard Hopkins, studying
Atlanta, found that after a decade one of every five workers,
both natives and immigrants, had abandoned manual jobs for
white collar occupations; in Bochum it was one in thirteen.
Both also discovered significantly higher rates of upward
movement within the manual class. In Birmingham, after five
or ten years, one-quarter to one-third of the workers persisting
in most groups improved their occupational status, while in
Atlanta 50 percent of the native whites and 33 percent of the
immigrant unskilled workers rose to higher positions after a
decade. The only workers in Atlanta who showed lower
mobility rates than all workers in Bochum were blacks.[12] In
Boston, Stephan Thernstrom discovered that rates of movement out of the blue collar world into nonmanual employment
varied quite strikingly among various ethnic groups, but not
even the lowest rate for any of the four decadal periods he
studied matched the paltry 7.7 percent for Bochum's manual
workers in the first decade (1880–90).[13]

American workers undoubtedly moved more frequently
and faster up the occupational ladder than their German counterparts. Moreover, German workers also remained more
firmly attached to a particular line of work. Hopkins noted that
among all the groups in his 1870 sample who remained in
Atlanta for at least a decade, fewer than 10 percent had the

same occupation or continued to work for the same employer;[14] in Bochum after the first ten years, 62.4 percent of all unskilled and semiskilled workers were still in the same occupations, while among skilled workers and artisans that figure was 61.6 percent.

Our investigation of the main dimensions of occupational mobility in Bochum has revealed a general picture of the local structure of opportunity. Analysis of the career patterns of specific occupational groups within the overall status hierarchy can not only illustrate contrasts in that picture but also inform us in detail about the actual processes of mobility: What paths were open to what people? Which ones did they choose?

Unskilled and Semiskilled Workers

There were three main groups of unskilled and semiskilled workers in the sample: day laborers, miners, and unskilled factory workers. The experience of day laborers is important because they represented the absolute rock bottom of the manual world. The day laborer's main resource was his physical strength and willingness to perform almost any type of menial work that was offered: loading and unloading at warehouses or railroad yards, menial work in factories, odd jobs for householders. He lived in an environment of constant economic insecurity and maintained at best a tenuous foothold in the urban economy. This was reflected above all in low rates of persistence; 42 percent of the sample in 1880 were present to be counted in 1890, while only 17.8 percent remained in 1901.[15]

If, then, day laborers made significant advances, this would be an important indication that local society was relatively open. But, as Table 3.3 indicates, even though day laborers made some advances, in few instances could these be termed significant. No doubt the individual day laborer counted it as an achievement if he could exchange his insecure existence for the more regular and sometimes higher paid employment offered by the mine or factory. But this was at best a very modest advance. Even after twenty-one years in the

Table 3.3 Occupational Mobility of Unskilled and Semiskilled Workers (in Percent)

Occupation in 1880	In Same Occupation	Other Unskilled/ Semiskilled Work	Skilled/ Artisanal	Nonmanual
		Occupation in 1890		
Day laborers	33.3	54.8	2.4	4.8
Unskilled factory workers	72.5	8.9	11.8	4.9
Miners	69.4	10.2	0.0	6.1
		Occupation in 1901		
Day laborers	8.7	65.2	4.3	4.3
Unskilled factory workers	66.1	3.4	11.9	6.8
Miners	33.0	16.7	0.0	13.0

Note: In none of the cases does the total equal 100 percent since in each group workers had retired or become invalided by 1890 and 1901; these were not included. A separate trace of these people's careers indicated that their mobility patterns up until they became invalids or retired were similar to those of the main group in the sample.

city, few day laborers had managed to follow the path taken by Bernard Tiemann, who by 1901 ran a small business dealing in fruit, or Bernard Tüchter, who ended up as a skilled metal-worker at the Bochumer Verein: significant upward move-ment, into skilled or artisanal positions or into the nonmanual level, was the experience of only a small minority of day laborers.

The mobility patterns of miners and unskilled factory workers suggest that quite different possibilities confronted occupational groups even within the same stratum. Unskilled workers with aspirations for mobility could follow at least one of two paths. They could remain within the manual hierarchy in the hope of gradually rising to a skilled job and perhaps eventually entering the nonmanual world via a lower manage-rial or clerical post, or they could enter the nonmanual world directly as tradesmen. Factory workers almost exclusively followed the first course, while miners took the second. Why?

Did miners have greater expectations than unskilled factory workers? Did factory workers take the easier path? Granted that it was probably difficult for the average factory worker to accumulate the capital necessary for a small business, becoming a skilled worker was not all that much easier. The unskilled worker might learn the few skills necessary to tend a machine without financial sacrifice, thereby becoming semi-skilled, but few could afford to undertake the apprenticeship generally required for recognition of skilled status. Yet this path was appealing to many, for it had the psychological advantage of being not only familiar, but of offering relative safety and security. This type of advancement did not require individual initiative or the willingness to take risks, as did shopkeeping; it called for more passive virtues, chiefly loyalty to the company. Hence, if unskilled factory workers tended to advance within the factory considerably more often than they did outside of it, this was not merely an indication of their objective opportunities, but of which opportunities they preferred.[16]

Upwardly mobile miners, however, seemed to have concentrated all their energies on entering the nonmanual world by becoming small tradesmen. Was this a result of their greater expectations and opportunities? Certainly, miners, as we shall see, were able to accumulate more capital than other worker groups. But the evidence also suggests that miners were cut off from advancement within the manual hierarchy and that owning a small business was not their preferred, but their only escape upward. The structure of work in the mining industry did not present the same scope for significant advancement that existed in the metal trades. Distinction of status and function among workers in the mines were based more on experience than on formal training; these did not mean a great deal in terms of wages, and after the 1860s they meant even less in terms of skills.[17] As the mines expanded, new workers were needed and the owners hired "everything that applied and had arms."[18] It was possible to enter the lower levels of management in the mines, but that meant attending the Bergschule, and few miners in the sample followed that path. The miner could go to work in a factory, but unless he made that shift while still young (as few did) he was not likely to advance very far. Moreover, social prejudice against his occupational background and—if he came from the east—against his regional origins, probably closed other avenues of advancement into artisanal work.[19] In short, if miners wished to leave mining, their choice was virtually restricted to setting up a small shop selling beer or groceries, often to fellow workers in their own neighborhoods.[20] And since the miner had to move farther away from his original position in order to leave it at all, fewer were capable of doing so; while almost 19 percent of unskilled factory workers had made some advance by 1901, only 13 percent of the miners had risen at all. Those who did advance aimed at different goals than other unskilled workers, not necessarily because they had greater ambition or opportunity, but because they lacked more accessible alternatives closer to home.

Mobility Patterns of Skilled and Artisanal Workers

Mobility was a more common ingredient of the experience of skilled and artisanal workers, but since these men had status to lose as well as to gain, movement could be a dangerous as well as a rewarding proposition. Table 3.4 outlines patterns of mobility among this group of workers.

After the first decade, both skilled and artisanal workers showed considerable occupational stability. But both skilled metalworkers and skilled workers in the building and construction trades were more upwardly and downwardly mobile than artisanal workers. By 1901 the mobility of all four groups had increased, but whereas mobile artisans moved almost exclusively upward, skilled workers in the metal and building trades had experienced considerable downward mobility as well. Thus skilled workers had risen more quickly but suffered more losses in the long run than artisans.

Differences in the timing and extent of upward mobility may have had something to do with the fact that skilled workers in the factories and on the building sites were less satisfied with their positions than artisanal workers and hence

Table **3.4** Occupational Mobility of Skilled and Artisanal Workers (in Percent)

Occupation in 1880	Occupation in 1890			
	In Same Occupation	Other Skilled/ Artisanal Work	Unskilled/ Semiskilled Work	Nonmanual
Skilled metalworkers	71.4	0.0	9.5	14.3
Skilled workers: building and construction	72.7	3.0	12.2	12.0
Skilled/ artisanal: food, drink, and clothing	79.5	2.9	7.8	7.8
Skilled/ artisanal: wood, leather, luxury, etc.	80.6	0.0	6.4	9.7
Occupation in 1880	Occupation in 1901			
Skilled metalworkers	58.8	0.0	17.6	17.7
Skilled workers: building and construction	50.0	3.8	19.2	19.2
Skilled/ artisanal: food, drink, and clothing	70.4	0.0	0.0	14.8
Skilled/ artisanal: wood, leather, luxury, etc.	52.9	0.0	5.9	29.4

[a]See note, Table 3.3.

may have sought to improve their status more quickly and more often than artisans. But probably more important was the fact that these two groups followed different paths of upward movement that affected their relative rates of mobility. Artisanal workers concentrated on acquiring their own shops; that required capital and the time to accumulate it. Skilled metal and building workers may have dreamed of becoming tradesmen too, but generally they found advancement into lower managerial or clerical posts in industry. This meant they could rise more quickly, but as a group, they were less secure. Skilled workers who had not managed to advance into nonmanual posts found it much harder than artisans to maintain their status, especially as they grew older. Forced to accept unskilled work during an economic slump or no longer physically able to exercise their skills, many skilled workers found themselves downwardly mobile. Artisanal workers did not suffer that indignity quite so often, in part at least because, after living for twenty-one years in the city, considerable numbers of them owned their own shops and were their own masters.

Still, despite these differences, skilled and artisanal workers undoubtedly shared one important perception derived from their experience. Both could see examples of success in their own ranks; the skilled metalworker now foreman, the artisanal worker with his own shop. But they had also observed other, less heartening signs; skilled and artisanal workers who were now miners, factory hands, or even day laborers. The lesson to be learned was that mobility was a two-edged instrument, and that at least as much effort had to be expended in trying to maintain one's status as in improving it. As a group, then, skilled and artisanal workers undoubtedly were marked by caution, defensiveness, and modest ambition, qualities that best suited the needs of their exposed position on the boundary between the middle and working classes.[21]

Nonmanual Occupations

Only two occupational groupings in this category need concern us because they were the only ones exhibiting more than minimal improvement. Members of the sample with professions (lawyers, doctors, etc.) were 100 percent stable during this period, and others moved hardly at all. Lower civil servants, for example, remained totally stable in 1890, while by 1901 one of the nine still remaining had become a cleric.

Lower level white collar workers, on the other hand, were more likely to experience mobility in both directions. By 1890 several had suffered the indignity of becoming laborers, 8.4 percent in all. But in general this group was more likely to move sideways or occasionally upward; after ten years, 2.8 percent had become lower level civil servants, while 13.9 percent became tradesmen or merchants and 5.6 percent managed to rise into higher white collar positions. This still left 66.7 percent in their original positions. By 1901 the remaining members of this group had experienced even greater mobility, most of it in an upward direction; while 4.8 percent had dropped to become miners and 9.5 percent shifted into the lower ranks of the civil service, another 9.5 percent had become higher white collar workers and 14.3 percent were tradesmen or merchants.

The second group, tradesmen and merchants, also showed some movement, but only after a much longer period of time. By 1890 all but one had remained tradesmen or merchants; that single person now worked as an unskilled factory hand. Eleven years later, only nineteen members of the group still remained in Bochum; almost 70 percent were still in the same occupation, although some may have improved their position in the meanwhile. Of the remainder, one had become an innkeeper, one was an industrial entrepreneur, and one was still working in a factory.

Intergenerational Mobility

If rates of upward mobility were low within a single generation, did a higher degree of movement exist between generations? Were a sizable number of sons able to achieve a higher status than their fathers? By what routes could they hope to rise? Table 3.5 outlines the dimensions of intergenerational mobility among sons from manual backgrounds at the time of their marriage in 1900.

For all practical purposes, manual work in Bochum constituted an ascribed characteristic—no less than 87.8 percent of the sons of manual workers also worked with their hands. Many had made advances within the hierarchy of manual

Table 3.5 Intergenerational Mobility (in Percent)

	Sons' Occupations					
Fathers' Occupations	Same as Father	Same Skill Level	Total Stable (1 + 2)	Higher Skill Level	Lower Skill Level	Nonmanual
Miners	44.0	10.2	54.2	27.1	0.0	19.0
Unskilled factory workers	40.0	25.8	65.8	28.1	0.0	5.9
Skilled metalworkers	46.6	20.0	66.6	0.0	23.3	10.0
Skilled workers: building and construction	27.4	15.7	43.1	0.0	39.2	17.6
Skilled/artisanal: food, drink, and clothing	23.0	33.3	56.3	0.0	31.3	12.5
Skilled/artisanal: wood, leather, luxury, etc.	16.7	37.4	54.1	0.0	29.1	16.6

SOURCE: Rathaus Bochum, Familienbuch, 1900.

labor, but others remained stable or even experienced downward mobility. More sons of unskilled and semiskilled workers were able to advance into skilled or artisanal positions than had members of the intragenerational mobility sample from the same occupational group. But sons of skilled and artisanal workers had great difficulty simply avoiding downward mobility. Sons of artisanal workers in particular were considerably more downwardly mobile than were artisans in the sample.

There were too few sons from the individual occupational groups in the nonmanual category to warrant inclusion in this table. Sons from nonmanual backgrounds were often able to maintain the general status enjoyed by their fathers and, less often, to improve on it—54.3 percent in all—but no fewer than 46.6 percent had dropped into the manual category; 25.9 percent working in skilled or artisanal employment, while 21.5 percent were unskilled.

Clearly, this generation of Bochum's manual workers, like their fathers, must have perceived the idea of mobility through a prism of limited opportunity, modest expectations, and in some cases very great fears. Their main concern was probably security, defined by most as reaching or maintaining a position at the pinnacle of the manual class. On the other hand, the failure of so many white collar sons to retain the status of their fathers undoubtedly induced a similar concern with security among nonmanual sons. In both cases, sons and parents might well agree that it was better to remain close to home, at least socially, than to attempt any lengthy and possibly dangerous voyages.

Intergenerational Mobility: Apprenticeship

The shortest and most familiar route to advancement for the sons of manual workers was apprenticeship. In Bochum, where the economy was dominated by heavy industry, factory apprenticeship (usually to a skilled metal trade) was most common; fewer sons trained to become independent artisans. Factory apprenticeship opened the way for sons of unskilled manual workers to a better income and more stable employment than most of their fathers had been able to attain. It also promised greater social status; indeed, the very process of factory apprenticeship was a rite that set future skilled workers apart from and above other workers; at the Bochumer Verein, apprentices were required to give evidence of sound moral character and could even be dismissed for "unsittliche Lebenswandel." Moreover, apprenticeship had the advantage to the working class family of requiring a relatively limited financial sacrifice; at the Bochumer Verein apprenticeship lasted three to four years, during which the young boy earned a wage which could be added to the family income, his earnings were increased each year, and at the end a bonus was paid.[22] Even so, by no means all parents who started their sons in apprenticeship programs were able to see them finish. In 1898 the Chamber of Commerce complained that some working class parents, presumably in need of larger contributions to family income, were encouraging their sons to break their apprenticeship contracts and go to work at higher paying, although unskilled jobs in the mines.[23]

However, many families did manage to see their sons through to the end of their apprenticeships. Table 3.6, based on a trace of the occupations of parents of apprentices who

Table 3.6 Parents of Apprentices at the Bochumer Verein, 1882–1893

Unskilled Manual Workers	Percent
Miners	3.4
Unskilled factory workers	41.7
Others	4.4
Skilled and artisanal workers	
Skilled metalworkers	11.3
Others	5.9
Nonmanual occupations	10.3
Widows or working women	14.7
Others	8.3

SOURCE: WAFKH, 25000, Nr. 1 Lehrlinge, 1878–88; Nr. 4 Lehrlinge, 1889–95.

completed their *Lehrzeit* at the Bochumer Verein, shows that apprenticeship to a skilled metal trade was an important avenue of advancement for the sons of unskilled workers. But it was heavily dominated by the sons of unskilled factory workers, who represented no less than 41.7 percent of all the apprentices at the company; sons of other unskilled workers and particularly sons of miners were obviously underrepresented in proportion to their numbers in the total population. Miners' sons were no less successful than the sons of unskilled factory workers in rising into skilled manual positions, but they followed other paths into the building trades or artisanal work. Evidently unskilled factory workers were better placed to help their sons enter skilled metalwork and more interested in having them do so than were miners. This constituted an important difference of opportunity and experience between these two worker groups.[24]

Intergenerational Mobility: The Schools

Handwerker Fortbildungsschule

Apprenticeship did not have to mean the end of a working class child's opportunities to improve his status by learning. From the early part of the century, Bochum had a Fortbildungsschule. Originally a privately operated and sporadically run institution with loose connections to the Gewerbeschule, it had as its aim the general education of youths who had already left the Volkschule but later developed programs to help apprentices, both industrial and artisanal, to advance in their occupations. The curriculum included German, mathematics, drawing, and draughting, and in 1903 a voluntary *Fachklasse* teaching mathematics, mechanics, and other related subjects was added.[25] But from the beginning the school was poorly attended. In 1864 Mayor Greve complained that "despite the material aid which the city has given the school and the numerous efforts by a few well-meaning *Meister* . . . the school is pining away."[26] Lack of interest among parents and the opposition of many employers meant that few apprentices attended regularly. When a city ordinance of 1878 made attendance mandatory until the age of sixteen, several of the large local companies, including the Bochumer Verein, complied by stipulating attendance as part of the *Lehrvertrag* with apprentices. Although attendance increased considerably, the city administration still faced "an almost systematic agitation against the obligatory nature of the school." Eventually certain concessions, in the form of reduced hours of attendance, had to be made to employers like those in the baking trade, where "the practical exercise of the occupation requires no special education in the specific subjects taught at the school." Yet the school continued to meet with only limited response; again in 1892 the city government had to issue a second ordinance, warning that "parents and guardians may not keep their sons or wards from . . . attending the *Fortbildungsschule*. Rather they must guarantee to them the necessary time." Parents or employers who failed to comply were fined up to 20 marks, or faced three days in prison. Enrolment increased, and by 1900 the school was serving only slightly less than eleven hundred students. But it remained obvious that neither employers nor parents were particularly avid to have their sons and apprentices improve on the skills they had already acquired, and it is doubtful that the school helped very many young men to advance in their trades. Even as late as 1912, Director Grunewald was still urging local employers and masters to encourage their apprentices to take advantage of the programs offered by the school.[27]

The Bergschule
An alternative to apprenticeship was the Bergschule. The
Bergschule and the Bergvorschule had been organized in
Bochum in 1816. The Vorschule served to supplement the
education that the student had received at the Volkschule, to
introduce him to the basic elements of mining, and to act "as a
bridge to the Bergschule." Only a minority of those who
attended the Vorschule were likely to be accepted into the
Bergschule proper.[28] There, depending on the course of
instruction followed, a student could be qualified for lower or
higher managerial posts in the mines. Sons of manual workers
could conceivably attend the lower level course because it
allowed them time each day to work to support themselves.
But the higher course required "complete devotion of one's
energies and in general does not permit exercise of an occupation."[29] In either case, as the mobility study has indicated, the
proportion of miners' and other manual workers' sons using
this path of advancement was very small.

The Gewerbeschule
The royal provincial Gewerbeschule, established in Bochum
in 1851, was another potential social escalator for sons of
manual workers.[30] Its training in mathematics, science, and
technical subjects provided the necessary preparation for a
career in the lower managerial levels of local industry, or
further training at a Technische Hochschule. But sons of manual workers remained a distinct minority among its students:
as late as 1880, only eight of the forty-nine then attending the
school had manual workers as parents, all of them skilled
workers or artisans. The rest were from the middle and upper-
middle classes.[31]

The Gymnasium and the Oberrealschule
If worker parents had been seriously concerned and able to
help their sons out of the manual class, the surest step would
have been to send them to the Gymnasium or Oberrealschule.

Completion of nine years and the *Abitur* at the Gymnasium qualified the student for entry to a university, and even only six years carried privileges *(Berechtigungen)* which not only permitted shorter military service but bestowed important advantages both within and outside the civil service.[32] The Oberrealschule offered fewer direct privileges, but it too could be a path to social advancement.

But, as Table 3.7 indicates, relatively few sons of manual workers attended either school. Indeed, it was unlikely that many manual workers would have even considered sending their sons to the Gymnasium or the Oberrealschule in the first place. Apprenticeship was a more familiar alternative, requiring no unusual increase of expectations or motivation, whereas the secondary schools might well have appeared strange, even hostile. And even if a manual worker did decide

Table 3.7 Social Backgrounds of Entering Classes (in Percent)

Fathers'	Gymnasium				Oberrealschule	
Occupations	1876	1886	1896	1906	1895/96	1901
Unskilled manual	3.3	4.7	2.5	3.8	3.6	4.3
Skilled manual	5.5	1.2	11.3	6.7	15.5	15.3
Lower white collar workers and civil servants	26.4	24.7	28.8	24.1	26.4	30.6
Higher white collar workers and civil servants	3.3	17.7	5.0	14.4	4.5	5.8
Tradesmen, merchants, innkeepers, etc.	24.2	14.1	23.8	21.1	33.7	24.8
Professionals	4.4	8.2	7.5	13.5	3.6	2.2
Factory owners, industrialists	7.7	4.7	5.0	1.9	7.3	5.1
Others and untraceable	25.2	24.7	16.1	14.5	5.4	11.9

SOURCE: StAB, Städt. Hauptkasse, Schulgeld Hebeliste (Gymnasium and Oberrealschule).

that his hopes for his son were equal to this challenge, his income often was not. During the 1880s and 1890s a parent could expect to pay between 120 and 140 marks per year for six or nine years unless his child could obtain one of the rare free scholarships. This represented more than a tenth of the average annual earnings of a miner or a worker at the Bochumer Verein. Hence the few sons of manual workers who managed to stay in school long enough to take the *Abitur* probably came from unusual backgrounds, both mentally and materially.[33]

Indeed, the data presented in Table 3.7 indicate that the primary function of both the Gymnasium and the Oberrealschule was not to aid social mobility but rather to ensure status continuity. And evidence pertaining to the Gymnasium suggests that even within the nonmanual class, secondary education helped relatively few sons to significantly improve their social position. In 1910 the local Gymnasium decided to trace former students as part of its anniversary celebration. This information, coupled with the father's occupation drawn from the *Schulgeldlisten,* enables us to determine intergenerational mobility for three of the four different entering classes appearing in Table 3.7. Of the ninety-one students entering in 1876, 27.5 percent were by 1910 working in exactly the same occupations as their fathers, while 47.2 percent had remained at the same status level or were downwardly mobile. Most important, only 25.3 percent had experienced upward mobility; considerably less than half of the students who could have risen—students from the manual group and the lower and middle levels of the nonmanual group—did rise. More than half of those who did advance (thirteen) entered civil service jobs or became professionals. Gymnasium education was clearly indispensable to their success. But among the rest, education seems to have played little part in their advancement; most had become merchants by 1910.

The class entering in 1886 showed similar patterns. Of that group, only 18.8 percent had made any significant advances over their fathers' positions twenty-four years earlier. The class that entered in 1896 made the most advances overall; 27.5 percent (twenty-two out of eighty) were in higher positions than their fathers by 1910. But this still meant that less than half the students who could have risen did. Hence Gymnasium education aided only a minority, even within the nonmanual world, in achieving upward mobility.[34]

Savings and Homeownership

Savings were regarded by middle class contemporaries as security against poverty for the lower classes, but savings were also crucial to several forms of inter- and intragenerational mobility (for instance, acquiring a business or educating a son).[35] Table 3.8 indicates the proportions of workers among depositors at the main savings bank in the city. It suggests that workers were usually in the minority and that, between 1860 and 1895, their relative numbers declined. In short, the savings bank was and remained a middle class institution. And within the manual class, the per capita distribution of savings was one-sided; considerable numbers of master craftsmen were depositors, but relatively few factory workers or journeymen ever had accounts, and while miners had considerably more per capita, their numbers decreased between 1867 and 1895.[36]

However, manual workers who did save were often able to show quite significant increases in the size of their deposits; between 1856 and 1895 the average size of accounts among master craftsmen increased by 411 percent, accounts of miners by 321 percent, while factory workers and journeymen trailed with 147 and 86 percent respectively. By 1895 the average

Table 3.8 Unskilled and Skilled Manual Depositors at the Sparkasse

Year	Percent of All Manual Workers among All Depositors	Workers' Deposits as Percent of Total Deposits
1860	43.8	37.0
1870	52.6	31.5
1880	40.9	26.6
1885	33.6	28.5
1890	39.7	30.3
1895	38.5	29.6

SOURCE: Reports of the Sparkasse in StAB, VB, 1860–95.

account held by a master craftsman was over 2,000 marks, that of a miner over 1,100 marks, balances sufficient to help some members of these two manual groups to acquire their own shops or small businesses, a pattern of mobility already observed earlier in this study. But few factory workers or journeymen ever accumulated savings that exceeded the 1,000-mark line. These balances scarcely represented business capital. At best the savings accumulated by most factory workers and journeymen and many miners could only have facilitated the acquisition of another, more modest form of property, a home.[37]

Homeownership offered not only greater status in the eyes of the community[38] but provided a certain material advantage as well; once the mortgage had been completely discharged, the owner could then save the money he would otherwise have paid in rent. And in many cases, additional income could be earned by taking in boarders. Table 3.9 outlines the dimensions of homeownership in 1880, 1890, and 1901 among sample members still remaining in the city. The percentage increases should not mislead us; in most cases they indicate only that property owners were more likely to remain in the city than renters. The absolute increase of homeowners in each occupational group was not particularly large, although it is obvious that some people who did not own homes in 1880 had become propertied by 1890 or 1901. Among the ninety homeowners in 1901 for instance, 61.6 percent had rented in 1880, while 30.0 percent had still been propertyless in 1890.

These low rates of property accumulation reflected the difficulties most workers faced in procuring the necessary capital. It was almost impossible for a propertyless worker to borrow the money from a bank; the Sparkasse, for example, required collateral in the form of property already owned or the cosignature of two "responsible" citizens before it would loan money.[39] Nor could the worker turn to the company for which he worked as could employees at Krupp in Essen; local industrialists did not want their workers to own their homes but to rent company dwellings, and so they refused to give mortgage loans or other forms of help.[40] And neither the city

Table 3.9 Homeownership

Occupation	1880			1890			1901		
		Home-owners			Home-owners			Home-owners	
	Total	N	%	Total	N	%	Total	N	%
Miners	127	8	6.3	48	8	16.7	17	2	11.8
Unskilled factory workers	243	10	4.1	112	7	6.3	67	5	7.5
Day laborers	129	3	2.3	25	0	0.0	4	0	0.0
Skilled metalworkers	58	3	5.2	31	2	6.5	20	2	10.0
Skilled building and construction workers	61	11	18.0	26	10	38.5	16	8	50.0
Skilled/artisanal: food, drink, clothing	57	8	14.0	38	9	23.7	23	7	30.4
wood, leather, luxury	46	9	19.6	31	12	38.7	13	8	61.5
Lower white collar	81	8	9.9	33	8	24.2	23	6	26.1
Lower civil servants	30	2	6.7	15	3	20.0	13	3	23.1
Tradesmen, merchants	48	15	31.3	43	18	41.9	34	25	73.5
Innkeepers	13	9	69.2	15	10	66.7	7	5	71.4
Professionals	21	3	14.3	11	5	45.5	4	2	50.0

SOURCE: Data derived from the mobility inquiry.

government nor the cooperative housing movement offered the worker much hope. Many of the city councilors were also property owners who rented their houses to workers and did not want competition from public housing, while the cooperative movement served largely lower middle class interests and had accomplished little before the war in any case.[41] Inevitably, the average worker could not expect to acquire a home unless he saved for it.

Evidence from the mobility study suggests that among manual workers, homes were often acquired by committing the incomes of all members of the family to that one goal. Miners provide an instructive example. Several instances appeared in the mobility inquiry of a miner-father and his grown sons living in the same house. When the father grew too old or too sick to work, ownership of the property passed from him to one of his sons, while the parents and often the new owners' siblings continued to live in the house, officially at least as renters. This probably reflects an understanding between parents and their male children that, in return for making financial contributions to the acquisition of a home, each male family member was entitled to certain future benefits; one son was assured of becoming a property owner before his father died, the parents and sometimes the other children received a guaranteed roof over their heads.[42]

In many cases this family effort was rewarded by greater security; homeowning household heads were on the whole less downwardly mobile than renters. Not living on as narrow a margin between income and expenditure as renters, they were somewhat less vulnerable in economic crises. They could, for instance, afford to wait longer when unemployed before seeking a lower status job from which later escape might be impossible. And for a few, homeownership even seems to have opened up new possibilities. By 1901 homeowners were more often upwardly mobile into the nonmanual class than renters. Most of those who advanced did so by becoming small tradesmen, whereas mobile renters usually entered clerical or managerial posts. For some upwardly mobile homeowners, buying a house simply accompanied the acquisition of a shop, but in most cases the home preceded and aided the purchase of the business. Evidently, homeowners could afford to save the capital necessary for this form of mobility from their incomes, a possibility denied most renters.[43]

But property mobility may have eliminated other types of movement, particularly for the second generation. The children certainly benefited from the fact that the family had acquired a home (and in some cases, a shop) which they would eventually inherit; but such a long-term investment of the family's income often ruled out the possibility of occupational mobility for the children through apprenticeships or secondary education.[44]

Conclusion

Significant upward mobility in Bochum was neither wide-spread nor rapid. Rates of intragenerational mobility were low both in absolute terms and in comparison to those observed in America. The degree of occupational advancement between generations commonly resembled the prescription followed by a Berlin voluntary association in counseling orphans on the choice of a future career: "A descent of the child below the *Stand* of the parents is to be avoided if at all possible, but disproportionate ascent . . . is only to be furthered in special cases."[45] Other forms of progress—savings and homeowner-ship—were equally elusive.

Certainly, it can be argued that in any society, mobility patterns are ultimately determined by the objective structure of opportunities. Yet, in an analysis of social mobility in contemporary Germany, Ralf Dahrendorf suggests that structural factors are not the only, nor even the most important, determinants. Discussing educational opportunities, for example, Dahrendorf argues that

> there is much to be said for seeking one of the main causes of the inequalities of educational opportunity in Germany in the minds of those hardest hit by them, that is, with workers and peasants and with parents of girls, as well as with their children. Among all these people, an attitude of traditionalism prevails . . .[46]

Nor, according to Dahrendorf, is this "traditional" outlook confined to education. "Part of the same attitude is the failure to recognize any necessity to move more than a few steps from one's place in society." In short, it is people's values, and not just the shape of the social structure, that in large part determine mobility patterns. And these values, so Dahrendorf implies, do not derive from the structure or internal dynamics of contemporary German society; "the mentality of large social groups once again displays the faults that Imperial Germany and the industrial revolution have bequeathed to German society."[47] Germans failed fully to "modernize" their attitudes toward social mobility during the period of indus-trialization under the authoritarian Kaiserreich, and this legacy lives on in the consciousness of the citizens of the democratic Federal Republic.[48]

Does this argument not perhaps have some relevance to Bochum? The city was, after all, a new industrial town with an active, expanding economy and a growing population. Its industry needed more skilled workers than it could usually attract, and there were increasing opportunities for white collar employment. Its growing population presented new markets for small tradesmen, for building and construction companies, and for service industries. Yet few workers advanced along these paths. Since "self-made men" were a local rarity, since most upward mobility took the form of cautious advances between adjacent social groupings, then it might be tempting to argue that the cause was not just the inequities of the social system but the "backward" values of individuals who "refuse to be drawn into the venture of the road to the unknown . . . A mentality that rejects novelty and initiative."[49]

Values undoubtedly did play a significant role in shaping patterns of social mobility in Bochum. Yet I think that when the metalworker Steinmeyer warned his colleagues "to take care that our children think just as we do and that they also in the future become loyal and diligent workers,"[50] this indicated less his inability to "want mobility in the modern sense"[51] than his sensitivity to the environment in which most of Bochum's workers had to operate. While many workers may have carried with them into the industrial city some of the "traditional fatalism" thought to be characteristic of rural life, it is far more important that their experience in Bochum did little to encourage them to adopt more "modern" attitudes toward mobility and to take greater risks. Far from it; the insecurity and unpredictability of working class life made caution vitally imperative. Indeed, it is misleading to argue that workers' expectations and ambitions were "backward" with regard to the "real possibilities" industrial society had to offer them, since these possibilities included downward mobility and destitution as well as "success." If, then, many workers refused to take any risks and those who did were extremely cautious, seeking out the safest, nearest, and most familiar mobility routes, this was not a failure of perception but a necessary strategy for survival.

Indeed, it is likely that most workers did not define "success" as the ability to escape the working class but rather the capacity to gain and hold onto the more secure and better paid positions within it. And since the worker (or his children) did not necessarily have to leave the working class to count himself successful, individual ambition did not have to preclude or weaken a shared sense of collective identity with other workers. But these "small-scale versions of success"[52] could have quite the opposite effect, for they were clearly more available and accessible to some workers than to others. In the iron and steel industry, for example, there was a fairly extensive job ladder up which many unskilled factory workers and their sons could reasonably expect to rise. Mining, on the other hand, did not present the same possibilities. Consequently, workers in each industry would have felt quite differently about their futures and those of their children. Patterns of mobility within the working class thus had contradictory possibilities; they could fragment as easily as they might unite.[53]

four

Industrialists, "Mittelstand," and Workers

*. . . it is the urban elite . . . that most
represents the spirit of the city.*[1]

THE NATURE AND behavior of specific urban elites, while
perhaps not always reflecting some abstract urban "Geist,"
can nevertheless provide us with important insights into the
spirit of particular cities. Bochum is no exception in this
regard; there, heavy industry capitalists progressively came to
dominate and to shape the economic, social, and political life
of the community. At the same time, their behavior and consciousness was itself being formed by their relationship to the
new social system which they had helped to create. In both
senses of the term, then, they "represented" the "spirit" of this
particular city and it is therefore essential that we try to
understand them.

Bochum's Industrialists

First, who were they? Defining a local industrial elite can
never be a particularly precise task; in Bochum it is somewhat
simplified by the fact that social divisions were sharp.
Bochum's elite was correspondingly small and circumscribed.
Indeed, after looking through the records of the Chamber of
Commerce and the city council, the city directory and the
newspaper files for the period from about 1860 up to World
War I, one gets the impression that there were never more than

perhaps forty to fifty individuals who were thought to be and who regarded themselves as members of the local elite; by the end of the century, with the further concentration of big business, it can be argued that this number was smaller still.[2] At the very top of this local hierarchy, there undisputedly stood the representatives of heavy industry (at least from the 1870s onwards)—several local mine directors, the director of the Bochumer Verein, along with a handful of top level managers. Next, a group of smaller manufacturers and then finally a dozen or so of the wealthier merchants, many with close ties to local heavy industry. With the exception of the merchants, most of these men had been born outside Bochum. Old, native families did not involve themselves directly in industry until late in the century; it was outsiders who supplied the capital and technical and organizational skills that transformed Bochum's economic structure.[3] As far as they could be traced, the social origins of these "new men" have been outlined in Table 4.1. Here, I shall confine myself to presenting a handful of separate short sketches depicting the career patterns of different types of local industrial leaders and suggesting the changing patterns of recruitment to the industrial elite.

Representative of the early years of smaller scale and competitive capitalism in Bochum were men like Jakob Mayer in iron and steel and Wilhelm Endemann and Heinrich Grimberg in coal. Mayer, the son of a Catholic farmer, was born in a Schwabian village in 1813.[4] As a young man he moved to Cologne to learn watchmaking from his uncle, who was then experimenting with processes for the production of fine steel for watchsprings in order to end his dependence on the expensive, imported British product.[5] Mayer became interested in the problem and eventually traveled to England, where he worked in a Sheffield factory to learn the techniques of producing crucible steel. Returning to his native village, he made a usable steel but only in small quantities, and in 1838 he moved back to Cologne intending to build a factory in the suburb of Nippes. Rhenish businessmen took an interest in his project and in 1839 he was able to conclude a contract with Eberhard Hoesch; the two partners would establish a factory for steel production in Stolberg, Hoesch providing the capital

Table 4.1 Occupational Origins of Bochum's Industrial Leaders

Non-Manual Occupations	N	%
White collar workers	4	8.2
Civil servants	6	12.2
Professionals	6	12.2
Tradesmen, merchants, innkeepers	13	26.5
Landowners, farmers	1	2.0
Bankers	0	0.0
Manufacturers, company directors	9	18.4
Total	39	79.5
Manual Occupations		
Artisans and skilled workers	4	8.2
Semi- and unskilled workers	0	0.0
Agricultural laborers	0	0.0
Total	4	8.2
Unknown	6	12.2
Total	49	99.9

SOURCES: StAB, Küppers Nachlass, Bde. 5, 14, 15, 16, 17, 18, 22(3), 23a; StAB, VB, 1860–1912; Max Seippel, *Bochum Einst und Jetzt*; Karl Brinkmann, *Die Geschichte der Flottmannwerke*; Karl-Heinz Hemeyer, "Der Bochumer Wirtschaftsraum von 1840 bis zur Jahrhundertwende," Diplomarbeit Mannheim, 1959/60; *Vier Generationen. Vier Epochen. Hrsg. aus Anlass des 100 Jährigen Bestehens von Gebr. Eickhoff Maschinenfabrik und Eisengiesserei G.m.b.H.* (Bochum, n.d.); G. Hempel, *Bochumer Eisenhütte*; Karl Brinkmann, *100 Jahre Chemische Fabrik J. Chr. Leye*; Walter Bacmeister, *Louis Baare*; Franz Darpe, *Geschichte der Stadt Bochum*; *200 Jahre Tabakfabrik F. D. Cramer*; Walter Däbritz, *Bochumer Verein für Bergbau und Gusstahlfabrikation in Bochum*; Walter Bacmeister, *Hugo Schulz*; Franz Mariaux, *Gedenkwort zum Hundertjährigen Bestehen der Industrie und Handelskammer zu Bochum*.

and Mayer the skills. After two years, however, the partnership dissolved, Mayer deciding that it was necessary to move to the Ruhr, where the coal was better suited to his purpose,[5] Hoesch refusing to support an operation he could not personally supervise. In 1842 Mayer and his new partner, Eduard Kuhne, a Magdeburg merchant, opened a small foundry in Bochum.[6]

The new partners soon branched into several manufacturing areas, and within a short time they were competing, although often unsuccessfully, with Krupp for military weapons contracts. They had more success supplying the metalworking industry around Remscheid and Solingen; concentrating on producing high quality steel, they soon won a reputation for their products matching that enjoyed for so long by the English.[7] But despite these achievements, by the late 1840s the company faced acute financial difficulties generated by overexpansion and capital shortage.[8] By 1853 Mayer and Kuhne were scarcely able to pay their workers' wages, and in November of that year outside financiers transformed the enterprise into a joint stock company.[9] Mayer remained as technical director until his death in 1875, but his influence waned.

Like Mayer, Wilhelm Endemann and Heinrich Grimberg both came from *Mittelstand* backgrounds, although they were unusual among the city's early entrepreneurs in that both were natives of the town. Endemann, a Catholic, was born in Bochum in 1808. His father owned property in the town as well as a small distillery, an inn, and a bakery. After military service, Endemann attempted several ventures and finally settled on the lucrative local trade in coke. According to his own account, he managed by "constant restless activity" to expand his operations to over one hundred coke ovens by the middle of the century, and in the 1860s he became an important shareholder in several local mines.[10] Grimberg came from a similar background; son of a local innkeeper, he entered the industrial world by way of his marriage to the daughter of a local wire-rope manufacturer, in whose firm he later acquired a controlling interest. In the 1870s he began investing in mining operations, buying interests in the mining company Lothringen in 1872, Monopol in 1873, and Vereinigte General und Erbstollen in 1895.[11]

In iron, steel, and coal, the development of new forms of industrial and financial organization progressively displaced the older type of small entrepreneur-proprietor, replacing them with new men who managed larger companies owned by anonymous investors elsewhere in Germany. Louis Baare, who was installed in the newly created position of General Director of the Bochumer Verein by the bankers and merchants who had bought out Mayer and Kuhne, was the prototype of this new industrial leader. Louis Baare was born in 1821 in Minden. His father, originally from Lübeck, owned a decaying freight business and a tobacco factory. When Baare was seventeen his father died; the boy had to leave the Gymnasium and go to work to support his family. Despite these difficulties, he had risen by the age of thirty-three to a position as director of an office for customs affairs with the Hanoverian railway in Bremen, from which he was launched into his career at the Bochumer Verein. In 1854 he was installed as director of the company, and after initial difficulties, including conflicts with Mayer and the older company leaders, he managed to rationalize the organization of the firm and to initiate a series of new expansions. In 1859 the company entered the railway field with production of cast steel tires and wheels for locomotives, and in 1865 it added rails to its list of products. After 1889, under Baare's direction, the company began a classical pattern of vertical concentration, acquiring a competing steel company in Bochum, as well as interests in local mines and a coke works. Baare also gave the company a reputation for leadership in the area of *Sozialpolitik*; the company sickness and accident funds started by Mayer were expanded, pension programs introduced, and company housing provided for a large part of the work force.[12]

Baare's success at the Bochumer Verein gave him considerable influence and prestige outside the company; in the 1870s he "supplied much of the brain power and originated many of the bolder manoeuvres" undertaken by the Verein Deutscher Eisen und Stahl Industrieller in its fight to increase the protective tariff.[13] In 1884 he presented important proposals for the Reichsunfallversicherungsgesetz to Bismarck.[14] He served as chairman of the local National Liberal election committee and was an important force in city politics, a member of the Westphalian Landtag for twelve years (1884–96) and of the Prussian Abgeordnetenhaus. Baare was also named to the Volkswirtschaftsrat and the Prussian Staatsrat.[15] After a career of over forty years in Bochum, Louis Baare stepped down in 1895 to let his son Fritz take over as director of the company; two years later he died.[16]

In mining too, industrial concentration proceeded quite rapidly; even Endemann, who prided himself on being called "Herr Alleingewerke," was forced to enter a joint stock company in 1892.[17] And as local mines were progressively incorporated into large, outside-owned and -directed conglomerates, the representative figures in mining on the local scene became the mine managers. These men were recruited from somewhat different backgrounds than other members of the industrial elite. Until the middle of the century, state officials had administered the mines, the owners simply providing the capital.[18] The reform legislation of the fifties firmly placed both ownership and management in private hands, but the private owners found that it was advantageous to retain Bergamt officials, now retired, in administrative positions. Indeed, the title of Bergassessor a.D. became more important than any other qualification for top positions in mine management.[19] Hence most of the local mine directors had civil service backgrounds; Herman Pieper, director of the Vereinigte General der Grosse and Oskar Hoffmann had both been Bergassessoren.[20] Albert Hoppstadter, who took over Pieper's job, had been a Bergmeister, while Heinrich Heintzmann, director of the Hasenwinkel mine, came from a family that had supplied several generations of officials to the Bergamt.[21]

As early as the 1870s, then, in both mining and the iron and steel industry it was becoming progressively more uncommon for individuals to set themselves up in business; the efficient scale of production and the capital required were simply too large. But in the metalworking and machine building industries this opportunity was still open, and several men, mostly from artisanal backgrounds, some from Bochum, others born elsewhere, entered the lower ranks of the industrial elite in this fashion, Johann Eickhoff, for example, had started a small foundry in Duisburg in 1846, but when it went out of business in 1851 he came to Bochum to work as technical director in a foundry owned by a local iron dealer and his son-in-law, the banker Carl Korte.* By 1860 Eickhoff was able to start up in business again, and though he died in 1864, his business was continued successfully under the direction of his two sons, Carl and Robert; by 1914 they were major suppliers of a large variety of machine parts for the mining and foundry industries.[22] Albert Dreyer, descendant of a family of

---

*This foundry had been started with equipment from Eickhoff's Duisburg foundry.

farmers, master smiths, and local officials near Dortmund, had also come to Bochum to work as an engineer in someone else's iron foundry. And he too managed to achieve success in a relatively short time; by 1873 he and Heinrich Heintzmann had taken over the firm.[23] A third example, Heinrich Flottmann, unlike Eickhoff and Dreyer, was a native Bochumer. Son of a baker and tavern-keeper who had moved to the town in 1840, Flottmann was educated at the Royal Gewerbeschule in Bochum, then at the local Technische Hochschule. After the Franco-Prussian War, he and his brother-in-law bought a small local metal foundry which by 1900 was successfully manufacturing hammer drills and other equipment used in mining.[24]

The most obvious point to be made about Bochum's industrial elite was that it was becoming progressively more exclusive as the century wore on. Bochum's industrial leaders were indeed "new men," but in a rather limited sense. Some had transformed themselves from the sons of artisans or shop-keepers into small scale industrial capitalists, most notably in the metalworking and machine-building industries. Others, like Baare or the mine directors, had risen from the ranks of state bureaucracies to achieve even greater prominence. But there was no story of rags to riches ascent in Bochum; none of the industrial leaders, so far as I have been able to determine, were recruited from the ranks of the working class or the laboring poor.[25] Surely this was an important fact of social existence in the town and may help to explain a good deal of the community's social (and even political) history. In other contexts—the shipping town of South Shields (analyzed by John Foster), nineteenth century Birmingham where small scale production persisted in the metal trades, possibly some nineteenth century German textile towns—the relative fuzziness of lines between industrialists and other social groups, combined with the real possibilities for at least some skilled workers to enter the ranks of the industrial leadership, may well have produced a more open image of society.[26] But in Bochum the lines were more clearly drawn; no working class inhabitant and certainly very few members of the local *Mittel-*

stand, looking at Baare or one of the local mine directors, could reasonably feel that their chances of entering the industrial elite were very great.

Yet this was not the only sense in which the industrial elite was set apart from the rest of the community in Bochum. Like the *Grossindustrie* which gave them their position in the town, most of Bochum's industrial leaders had been imposed on the social structure of the community from outside. No matter how long they remained in Bochum—and some of them stayed more than one generation; Fritz Baare, for example, succeeded his father as general director of the Bochumer Verein in 1895 and Hermann Pieper took over his father's position as director of the mining company Constantin der Grosse—their primary identifications and concerns could never be the town itself, nor even the role of their industry in the town, but rather the way in which the town and its inhabitants responded to the imperatives of the German and world economy.[27] This meant that one of their main aims would be to ensure that social and political relations in Bochum conduced to their industry being able to compete effectively in the German and world economy, or at least that they did not hinder that possibility. Yet the very fact that the new industrialists were outsiders, responsible to investors who generally lived elsewhere and not to the community, might well frustrate that aim, or at least make it a difficult task.

A large part of the difficulties faced by the industrialists arose from the fact that they could not simply rule by fiat over the local community. Contrary "to the widely held view that from the start industrialists had the social and political power and prestige to match their economic force and that they controlled the towns," Herbert Gutman has recently argued, in an article on Paterson, New Jersey, that, at least for the first generation, the new industrialists' "power was not yet legitimized and 'taken for granted.' Surely powerful because of his control over 'things,' the factory owner nevertheless . . . met with unexpected opposition from nonindustrial property owners . . ."[28]

This opposition often made it difficult for the factory owner "to enforce noneconomic decisions essential to his economic welfare." Gutman shows, for example, that in two textile strikes and two libel suits against a socialist newspaper editor which occurred between 1877 and 1880, "important and powerful groups in the community refused to sanction and support the millowners" and indeed often gave positive support to the workers of Paterson and their spokesmen— shopkeepers extended credit during strikes and subscribed to strikers' relief funds, local courts displayed leniency toward striking workers, a socialist editor received demonstrations of "popular support" and special treatment from a sympathetic prison warden.[29]

The conflicts between industrialists and small property owners, so Gutman argues, may therefore provide one important key to the shape of class relations during the early history of industrializing towns. To explain this conflict he offers the following argument:

The new industrialist—especially if he came from elsewhere—was a disruptive outsider. He did not create an entirely new social structure, but he confronted an existing one. He found a more or less static city which thrived on small and personal workshops and an intimate and personal way of life. It was hardly ideal, but it was settled and familiar. Making goods and employing people differently, the industrialist abruptly disrupted this "traditional" way of work and life and, as a person, symbolized severe local dislocations. The older residents and the newer workers responded to these changes in many ways. But if the industrialist . . . violated traditional community norms or made unusually new demands upon the citizenry . . . his decision often provoked opposition.[30]

This is a suggestive analysis, and certainly one that may appeal to many German historians, for whom the importance of conflicts between "traditional" and "modern" values seem to be the central elements of the development, or rather misdevelopment, of German society during the course of industrialization. Indeed, given the fact that large scale industry was so rapidly superimposed on a society in which there were relatively large numbers of small property owners who, as Geoffrey Crossick has recently suggested, possessed a "traditional *Mittelstand* ideology . . . a distinctive consciousness in relation to industrial and commercial capital,"[31] we might expect that conflicts between big capitalists and small property owners would be even more severe than in the United States, and that their political ramifications would correspondingly be even more extensive. However, rather than simply assuming that there was such a conflict between the "traditional" values of small property owners in Bochum and the innovative mentality of the new industrialists, it might be in order to trace the history of the relationship of Bochum's *Mittelstand* to industrialization.

The "Mittelstand" in Bochum

Unlike some of the other Rhineland and Westphalian towns, Bochum had not developed a significant layer of large merchants and small capitalist entrepreneurs before the Industrial Revolution. Well into the 1840s and 1850s, local economic, social, and political life continued to be dominated by "petty shopkeepers, master artisans and innkeepers."[32] In 1842, for example, when the Bochum Landrat ordered a survey of prospective electors in preparation for the introduction of the new *Städteordnung*, he found that most of the 213 local residents who owned property worth more than 300 thaler were artisans, innkeepers, small merchants and shopkeepers. Similarly, among the 45 inhabitants who ran fixed enterprises producing an income of more than 200 thaler per year, the largest single group was tailors (8), followed by bookbinders, cabinet makers, watchmakers, and blacksmiths. Only a total of 3 men from both lists combined were listed as *Fabrikant*.[33]

Relatively homogeneous, rooted in the local community—as late as 1860 there were no fewer than 12 local merchants who had been doing business in Bochum for forty years or more and, of these, three had been there for no less than 170, 119, and 90 years respectively—and cut off from immediate and direct contacts with commercial and industrial capitalism, Bochum's preindustrial elite of small property owners might well have developed a strong sense of its own corporate and communal identity that would have made it critical of industrialization and industrialists. But if this was the case, we have little evidence of it.[34] To begin with, Bochum's prein-dustrial small property owners displayed a notable absence of "communal" consciousness—unlike the citizens of Mühl-heim and Essen, they actually voted against becoming a self-governing municipality in the 1840s on the grounds that the citizens were not able and did not wish to assume the tax burdens that self-administration would involve, preferring instead to continue being administered by the county offi-cial.[35] More important, Bochum's artisans, shopkeepers; and small merchants did not seem to have been particularly opposed to industrialization, at least not in the beginning. Indeed, in the early 1860s the city government, which was still dominated by local small property owners, actually removed the charge traditionally exacted from new residents (the *Bürgergeld*) on the grounds that "freedom of movement should be limited as little as possible and the worker's oppor-tunity to exploit his labor to his own advantage should not be spoiled."[36]

This is not to say, of course, that artisans, shopkeepers, and merchants were wildly optimistic about the potential benefits that economic growth would confer on their commu-nity. They watched anxiously in the next few years to see whether or not the new workers whom they were now freely admitting would cause serious problems for their community. In 1860, the city council observed with some relief that "the various disadvantageous consequences that had been feared from this migration had not occurred."[37] Four years later it also reported that it was "a happy sign for our local social relations that the working population is becoming more and more settled here, is founding families and seeking to acquire property."[38] In the early 1860s, then, it did seem to Bochum's small property owners that industrialization could be com-bined with relative social stability, or at least minimal social dislocation.

But if Bochum's artisans, shopkeepers, and merchants were tempted to support the social gamble that industrializa-tion seemed to involve, that was because they stood to gain considerably. Even though, in 1860 the city council registered the stereotypical complaint that local artisans were being hard

pressed by competition from factory production that possessed the advantages of "intelligence, capital, machinery and
all the technical aids *(Hilfsmittel),*" nevertheless it was clear
that industrialization offered considerable numbers of artisans, small shopkeepers, and merchants real opportunities to
improve their own rather threadbare existences.[39] Between
1856 and 1860 alone, for example, the number of master
shoemakers in the town rose from 29 to 51, tailors from 48 to
61, cabinet makers from 36 to 50 and by 1860 no fewer than 15
percent of the city's artisans were doing well enough to be
assessed for the *Gewerbesteuer* (Table 4.2).[40] And in the retail
trades, particularly those supplying the growing working
class clientele, there was a similar expansion. In 1861, for
example there were some 50 innkeepers in the town, one for
every 181 inhabitants, as well as 16 merchants and small
shopkeepers "who have the right to do a retail business in
brandy." Just six years later, there were

18 businesses selling brandy, 30 inns, 18 licensed bars in which
primarily beer is consumed and 15 in which primarily brandy [spir-
its], 6 other licensed premises and eating houses [*Speisewirtschaf-
ten*]; a total of 87 or one for every 143 inhabitants.[41]

Yet, if the initial stages of industrialization in Bochum
were generally encouraging to artisans, small shopkeepers,
and merchants, the decades that followed, particularly the
years of the Great Depression, were far more problematic. The
apparent prosperity achieved by the city's artisans in the late

Table 4.2 Assessed Master Artisans as Percentage of All Artisans

Year	Percent
1860	15.0
1866	16.0
1867	16.6
1868	15.7
1869	15.5
1870	17.1
1871	13.6
. . .	. . .
1884	8.9

SOURCE: StAB, VB, 1860–1871, and Adressbuch, 1884.

Table 4.3 Assessed Large Merchants, 1875–1884

1875	1884		
(Absolute Number Assessed)	No Longer Listed	Assessed as Merchants	Now Assessed as Small Traders
279	122	109	48
	(43.7%)	(39.1%)	(17.2%)

SOURCE: StAB, Adressbuch, 1874/75, 1884.

1850s, for example, was in reality built on rather weak foundations; during the optimistic fifties, which the city government later referred to rather caustically as a "Californian period," many of the city's artisans had borrowed money to go into business for themselves only to discover that they could not always earn enough, even in good times, to keep up with the repayment of their loans. In 1860 the city council observed that the Handwerker Hulfsverein, originally set up in 1850 to "give credit to needy *Handwerker* at low rates of interest," was in serious trouble because "loans are not punctually repaid." The fragility of artisan expansion did not tell immediately; indeed, by the mid-1860s the period of speculation seemed to be giving way to sounder and more solid growth. In 1864 the city council approvingly observed an increase of membership and capital in the Vorschuss Verein (which had replaced the *Handwerker Hulfsverein*), and by 1871 an unusually high 17 percent of the artisan population was now being assessed for business tax.[42] But in 1871, in reaction to war with France, the local economy contracted fiercely, squeezing many local artisans out of business. Unfortunately, we cannot trace their fortunes each year thereafter, but some further observations can be made. A trace of individual artisans in business at the beginning of the Great Depression in 1875 revealed that by 1884 some 44 percent had gone out of business entirely (Table 4.3).[43] Another 49 percent still operated shops in the city, but not all of them were necessarily as successful as they had been in 1875, since the 1884 city directory made no distinction between those who were paying business tax and those who were not. Indeed, 1884 was quite a bad year for the city's artisans; the proportions of them assessed for the business tax had dropped to an unprecedented 8.9 percent, largely as a result of an economic downturn this year. But in addition to the direct effects of economic depression, local artisans were also plagued by chronic credit difficulties; just five years later, the local newspaper reported the bankruptcy of the Vorschuss Verein, the artisans' main credit source. Due to mismanagement, its one hundred and thirty members faced the disagreeable prospect of repaying 30,000 marks in debts: "For the members this is an extremely unpleasant New Year's greeting [especially since] they had dreamed of such neat profits . . ."[44]

This does not mean, of course, that, even during the Great Depression, some artisans were not able to achieve rather considerable successes; apart from those who managed to hold onto their own small businesses for relatively long periods of time, there was a select minority that built on success in the artisanate to gain entry into the ranks of commercial and industrial capitalists; of the artisans traced from 1875 to 1884, some 5 percent did rise to become small or large merchants, and one man, an artisan plumber, gained the unique distinction of becoming a manufacturer (Table 4.4). And if they themselves were seldom able to enter the ranks of the city's industrialists, some artisans could at least hope that their sons would; we have already seen at least two such examples: Heinrich Trilling, son of a Bochum shoemaker, and Heinrich Flottmann, son of a baker and tavern-keeper.

But it is doubtful that these people were the main points of reference for the city's artisans, particularly during the Great Depression. Far more immediate and compelling were the examples of those who lived marginal existences on the

Table 4.4 Assessed Master Artisans, 1875–1884

1875 (Absolute Number Assessed)	1884				
	No Longer Listed	Still in Business	Assessed as Innkeeper	Assessed as Merchant	Assessed as Large Merchant
127	57	62	2	5	1
	(44.9%)	(48.8%)	(1.6%)	(3.9%)	(0.8%)

SOURCE: StAB, Adressbuch 1874/75, 1884.

edges of the artisanate or who dropped out of it completely. Extreme cases, like the 32-year-old master cabinetmaker, Johann Terbrüggen, father of two children, who on March 10, 1878, committed suicide "because of unemployment," according to the police, or a somewhat less dramatic instance, Carl Niermann, pastry cook in the nearby village of Hattingen, who in 1882 found he could no longer pay the school fees for his child to continue attending the Gymnasium. Moreover, when the court bailiff was sent to Niermann's home, he discovered there were no household items that could be seized and sold to pay the back school fees.[45] Then there were the hundreds of more anonymous individuals who each year, during the Great Depression, had to give up their businesses and with them the social status that attached to being an "independent" artisan. Indeed, the figures on additions to and subtractions from the business tax lists compiled by the city council reveal an amazingly high rate of business turnover each year. Between 1880 and 1896, the number of new businesses added to the tax list increased by some 16–37 percent annually, but at the same time, anywhere from 11 to 26 percent might be stricken from the lists (Table 4.5).

Like artisans, retail traders had also discovered new opportunities as a result of the industrialization of Bochum's economy and the growth of its population. Indeed, some branches of retail trade were actually created during this period by changes in marketing patterns and procedures, which often occurred at the expense of the old-style artisan shop where production and distribution to customers had been combined. But the experience of the Great Depression revealed to retail traders some of the fundamental contradictions that arose from their position with regard to industry—if indeed they had not already been aware of them. On the one hand, retail traders owed their very livelihoods to the growth and expansion of big business, yet on the other hand they were, with few exceptions, heavily dependent on working class custom, therefore extremely vulnerable to economic cycles in heavy industry that determined the levels of working class income and hence buying power. In 1877 the Chamber of Commerce, reporting on the effects of the Great Depression,

Table 4.5 Business Turnover from the Gewerbesteuer Assessments, 1880–1904 (Per 1,000 businesses assessed the previous year)

Year	Newly Assessed	Dropped from Assessment
1880	370	263
1881	211	223
1882	163	138
1883	239	187
1884	216	165
1885	253	193
1886	249	220
1887	173	182
1888	176	171
1889	181	150
1890	190	152
1891	193	151
1892	235	193
1893	205	117
1894	326	253
1895	341	132
1896	322	62
1897	356	157
1898	449	154
1899	457	129
1900	418	247
1901	451	251
1902	361	236
1903	369	162
1904	398	167

SOURCE: StAB, VB, 1880–1904.

made a specific point of remarking on this shared vulnerability of industrial workers and the artisans and small shopkeepers with whom they traded:

The great majority of the city and county of Bochum win their livelihood from the mining and iron industries. It is therefore easy to estimate in what manner the reduction of income of miners as a result of wage reductions in one form or another must influence, first the families of those immediately concerned, in second place also . . . the numerous small businesses and traders and from them also . . . wider circles.[46]

Again, some eight years later, the Chamber of Commerce argued that the considerable wage cuts that employers in the mining industry were at that time contemplating would have an "unhealthy effect on the living conditions of the miners and their families as well as the businesses and tradesmen whose well-being is dependent on the prosperity of coal mining."[47]

Small wonder, then, that during the Great Depression, working class poverty rapidly became the primary obsession of those artisans, shopkeepers, and small merchants who were able to articulate their sentiments through means of the institutions of municipal government.

By the late 1870s, the most dramatic symbols of the ravages of the Great Depression were the crowds of beggars and vagabonds choking the roads of rural Westphalia and gathering in the central squares of the cities to threaten middle class inhabitants. "We are surely not exaggerating in estimating at many thousands," the Chamber of Commerce observed in 1878, "the total number of those individuals . . . who are making the roads and settlements of Westphalia unsafe."[48] Local artisans, shopkeepers, and small merchants tried to respond to this problem through the Verein gegen Strassen- und Hausbettelei, a voluntary association, which by the 1880s was supported by the financial contributions of several hundreds of Bochum's citizens and had assumed the status of a semiofficial institution of municipal government. The Verein had originally been organized in the early 1870s to relieve journeymen on their Wanderung who had no trade Herberge in the city. By the early 1880s, however, it confronted the far more serious problem of relieving and finding work for thousands of transient, unemployed industrial workers. Although the Verein was concerned with aiding the deserving poor, it was at the same time anxious to ensure that professional beggars would "give the city a wide berth."[49] Originally this meant that the Verein had demanded some form of written certification of the transient's record, but by the early 1880s sheer weight of numbers made this impractical. Therefore, in 1882 the Verein introduced a work test. To receive aid, the unemployed were required to chop wood and later, since this was regarded as being too easy, to break stones. The Verein also eliminated money support completely; the unemployed migrant could expect to find only "a good night's lodging and food."[50] Tramps who might previously have been induced to work for the money to buy liquor would thus be encouraged to avoid the city. Finally, everyone who was granted relief was also required to seek work through the Verein's *Arbeitsna-chweis*. Unemployed workers who did not find jobs or who refused to take the work offered were required to leave the city.

By 1886 the city *Magistrat* could judge the Verein's policy a success: "The crowds of vagabonds that every evening infested the streets, insulted the citizenry and, in part, filled the prisons have disappeared."[51]

Local industrialists, on the other hand, could not bring themselves to be quite so sanguine in their judgments; although they agreed that the major problem for the "middle classes" was that "now the beggar from need and [the beggar] who is work shy and has lost his honor often are only with great difficulty to be separated," they did not think that the Verein had provided a complete answer, since the real issue was the elimination of vagabondage altogether and not simply discouraging beggars from entering the Bochum city limits.[52] To that effect, the local Chamber of Commerce suggested to the Regierung in 1878 that each worker be made to carry with him an *Arbeitsbuch* recording the details of his past life and employment. Once these work books had been decreed, local police could easily segregate the professional beggars from the worthy poor. The task then would be to rehabilitate these "sluggards and incompetents."[53] But for that purpose the present laws of the state were completely inadequate; indeed they made "vagabondage and idleness easier." In England, the Chamber observed, every justice of the peace could sentence beggars to hard labor for up to one month, and repeaters could be consigned to the same fate for longer periods, with doses of the lash as an added incentive to reform.

While protesting that they did not wish German judges to have such extreme powers, local industrialists nevertheless complained that current laws on begging did not go far enough; under the present system, the beggar was fined 15 marks or sent to jail for three days for a first offence then sent home; if arrested again, he faced a possible six weeks' sentence, but only after he had been arrested several times could he be put in a *Correctionshaus* where he was forced to work (in other prisons, the Chamber pointed out, he sat idle) and thereby become reaccustomed to regular labor. But, the Chamber complained, years often lay between the first arrest and final exposure to the reforming influence of the *Correctionsanstalt;* the present laws must be amended so that beggars could be committed to hard labor more quickly.[54]

Local industrialists argued that their proposed reforms "would further social discipline and order and thereby be very beneficial to the whole of industrial life."[55] The national government did not quite agree; while the proposal for a system of work books received the support of the Conservatives and the Center in the Reichstag Gewerbekommission, it was eventually defeated. Only workers under the age of twenty-one, who were still legally minors, were ever required to carry workbooks.[56]

Yet, if the state did not seem fully to share local industrialists' sense of the urgent necessity of disciplining and reforming the poor, local authorities certainly did. Although Bochum's city government could claim some success in keeping "immoral" vagrants away from the city, it still had to confront rapidly rising figures for relief of the poor; by 1880 the *Armenverwaltung* was warning that "from one year to the next ever higher sums [in poor relief] are required ... the *Armenkasse* has become in recent years of low incomes the regular means of assistance to worker families for every exceptional expense."[57]

The city government was willing to concede that this increase in poverty had direct economic causes. But, as the numbers of the poor rapidly mounted, the Armenverwaltung increasingly began to insist that the real problem was breakdown of morality among the working classes and weakening of the social controls by which morality had previously been enforced. In 1861, during an earlier economic downturn, the city government had reported that "the condition of public morals has not worsened" and that poverty had not increased, "rather it had receded."[58] But by 1877 the moral soundness of the working class seemed to have crumbled away:

Experience shows quite clearly that, when the first feelings of shame are overcome and the route to the *Armenkasse* has been traveled once, then [that institution] very rapidly comes to be seen as a convenient means of relief. The receiving of alms has become almost hereditary among some families and the same names are reappearing over and over again in the lists of the poor.[59]

As the depression deepened, so the moralistic emphasis intensified. By 1880 the Armenverwaltung was warning that "the disgrace of being a receiver of alms has totally disappeared; support from the *Armenkasse* is viewed as a rightful claim, the collection of which is sought on any pretext at all."[60]

Moral problems obviously demanded moralistic answers. The immediate response of the master artisans, innkeepers, and small shopkeepers who dominated the Armenverwaltung was to appeal to the force of community sentiment.[61] It was decided to print the minutes of the Armenkommission in the daily newspaper and to list the names and conditions of those receiving aid, so as to "put every inhabitant interested in the administration of poor relief in a position to give notice at the necessary place of any deceptions . . . in order that all expenses that were not absolutely necessary should cease."[62] Moreover, every applicant for support was to appear personally before the committee to show in detail why he should be granted relief. Yet local artisans, small shopkeepers, and merchants could not be content simply to ferret out immorality and deception among the working class. It was increasingly obvious to them that the lack of shame and self-respect that permitted the worker to turn to the Armenverwaltung "on any pretext at all" had caused him to grow poor in the first place. The prescription was obvious: Teach morality and poverty, or at least a good deal of it, would be prevented.

One way of attempting this moralization of the poor was to encourage social contact between the classes. In 1886, for example, Mayor Lange argued that even the city park could serve a moralizing function since there

all the different orders of society . . . pass their time and walk around and, as a result, against the brutalization . . . of morally depraved persons, an appropriate dam and barrier will be set which, so far as moral improvement is concerned, can only work to the good. Good examples produce good morals.[63]

Yet the force of good example communicated through informal social contacts between middle and working classes was
not a very satisfying or complete answer to the problem of
poverty, especially since such contacts were becoming more
and more infrequent and sporadic as the city grew and its
population became more mobile. If morality was to be properly learned by the working class, then this education had to
take place within the framework of formal institutions developed specifically for the purpose.

One of the most important of these institutions was the
savings bank. Savings banks were certainly not new to
Bochum; the local bank had been founded in 1838. But as the
city industrialized and was subjected to major economic
crises, the Sparkasse assumed a new importance in the minds
of both small property owners and local industrialists. Savings banks were, of course, designed to provide workers with
the opportunity to accumulate a cash reserve for those times
when, as a result of illness, accident, or unemployment, they
lacked a regular income to support their families. But far more
important than this was the moral function the bank was
expected to serve. The savings bank, so the city council
argued in 1860, was to be a school of morality providing
lessons in the "development of independence and character."
It would cultivate "a sense for saving and the understanding
of economy in terms of income and expenditure."[64] Poverty,
the city government suggested, was less the product of insufficient income than of the worker's inability or unwillingness to
utilize that income properly and with restraint. If the worker
learned not to waste his money in temporary amusements but
to save it for future emergencies, he would eventually enjoy a
sense of security and satisfaction that would content him with
his lot. Unlike their American counterparts, the supporters of
Bochum's savings bank did not expect that the institution
would help the worker accumulate capital for upward social
mobility or would increase his ambition for "success."
Indeed, they argued that savings banks would and should
have quite the opposite effect; they would be doing their jobs
properly if they simply nurtured in the worker "independence, frugality, love of order and honesty."[65]

Despite the relative modesty of these aims, Bochum's Sparkasse does not seem to have been very successful in acquainting workers with the joys of saving. The city government predictably attributed this to the fact that "money is so easily earned here [that] its worth is not appreciated and it is as easily spent out as it was earned."[66] Few proponents of the *Sparkasse* were prepared to concede that most workers had little to save in the first place, or to realize that when workers could save, they were more interested in such things as providing for a decent funeral by subscribing to burial clubs.[67] Instead, they called for a new form of savings bank, the Pfennigsparkasse, which supposedly would make it easier for workers to save. But, whereas the Sparkasse had originally been conceived of as a means both of providing real material security for the worker and at the same time implanting in his heart genuine moral virtues, the Pfennigsparkasse aimed more at dulling working class perceptions of social inequality and thus forestalling revolution. The Chamber of Commerce freely admitted that the size of the account a worker was likely to accumulate in the Pfennigsparkasse would hardly be large enough to keep him clear of poverty in hard times; nevertheless, if the worker had in the bank "something which he could call his own," then he would at least *feel* that he enjoyed security and was not simply living from hand to mouth.[68]

Bochum's industrialists certainly supported and encouraged these local attempts to moralize the poor: indeed, by the 1880s the Chamber of Commerce had become one of the more enthusiastic exponents of savings banks. Yet, at the same time, Bochum's industrialists took a broader view of the problem that caused them to promote responses not only at the local but also at the national level. The most immediate concern of local small property owners was to moralize local workers; industrialists certainly wanted that, yet they also wanted to discipline and reform the German working class as a whole.

This was clearly revealed by the industrialists' response to what seemed the most common symbol of working class destitution in the 1870s: the industrial accident which often cast a whole family on poor relief. Increases in mine and factory accidents were obviously not unrelated to the influx of unskilled and unwary migrants into Bochum during the 1860s and 1870s as well as the intensification of industrial work during the Great Depression. But local industrialists chose in the main to ignore this. Their attention focused much more on the moral than on the social or economic aspects of the crisis, which in turn led them to demand that the state help to redress what they regarded as a moral, as well as a material, disorder.

In earlier decades, many industrialists had provided programs of accident and sickness insurance for their workers, but by the 1870s they were being called upon to bear burdens for which they had never been designed. In a letter to the mayor of the city, Baare complained that his company accident claims had risen so sharply that for the last three years the Leipzig insurance firm that covered his workers had actually been losing money. Baare then appealed for municipal participation in a general insurance fund. Certainly Baare was interested in shifting some of the cost of workers' insurance onto the city government. But he also argued that the city government could play an important role, apart from any financial contribution, since its authority would discourage the "malingering . . . and the claims of individuals which were to the disadvantage of others."[69]

These themes became more explicit and more developed in a series of recommendations regarding the creation of an imperial insurance law submitted by Baare to Bismarck. According to Baare, the most pressing priority was the reform of the present legislation governing adjudication of accident cases, the *Haftpflichtgesetz* of 1878, which provided for litigation between worker and employer to determine who should bear the cost of an industrial accident in cases where no "amicable" agreement could be reached. This system, Baare suggested, was both morally and materially unsound. To begin with, it necessarily made workers and employers enemies because both had important conflicting interests in the outcome of each case. The worker was aware that the result of his suit would determine whether he lived the rest of his life as a pensioner of the company or a charge of the city Armenverwaltung. The company, on the other hand, could not afford to lose too many cases or it might go bankrupt.[70] This atmosphere poisoned relations between worker and employer: "Instead of quieting the passions of the worker and reconciling them to their position, the *Haftpflichtgesetz* . . . causes a sharpening of the oppositional position of the workers against the owner and the state."[71] In place of "mutual trust and goodwill," it substituted only "mistrust and hostility."[72] But more important, the *Haftpflichtgesetz* provided legal encouragement for lower class immorality. In Baare's opinion, though workers were generally at fault in most accidents, they often benefited from the sympathy shown them by the courts and by fellow workers called to testify. Knowing this, far too many workers were encouraged to "make their fortunes" at their employers' expense. Indeed, Baare claimed, it was not unknown that a worker would purposely mutilate himself for the sake of a pension, and it was a demonstrable fact that since the introduction of the *Haftpflichtgesetz* the accident rate had actually increased.[73] Under the present system, then, pensions served only as "premiums for fakers, idlers and loafers."[74] The new imperial insurance law would have to eliminate such abuses, as well as relieving industry of some of the financial cost.

Baare made four basic proposals to the chancellor; first, the cost should be split equally among industry, community, and worker; second, pensions should be limited to 500 marks; and third, workers who were not completely incapacitated by an injury should be required to continue working. The fourth point bore particular significance for companies like the Verein, which had created private accident and sickness funds for the benefit of their workers in order to foster their loyalty to the company. If they were completely supplanted by an imperial system, this means of disciplining them would be denied the employers. Therefore, Baare asked that where company-operated schemes provided comparable benefits to those envisaged by the imperial law, they would be allowed to serve as a substitute for it.[75]

Hence what Baare and other local industrialists were asking was that they should be aided by the government in controlling abuses associated with the old system, while ridding themselves of some of its cost, but without denying themselves the benefits of worker loyalty and tractability for which they had originally created their private support schemes.[76] Bismarck was not prepared to grant the industrialists' requests concerning the apportionment of costs, and he felt that Baare's ceiling on pensions was too short-sighted. In place of the 500-mark maximum, he proposed that pensions should be graded according to the worker's income. This, he argued "will be more useful for the employer, since it will join the higher classes of workers, that is, the most important support of every enterprise in the general security and thereby encourage striving for its achievement." On one point, the industrialists did get exactly what they asked for; company-operated accident and sickness funds were allowed to remain in operation.[77]

The Great Depression was a major test of the relationship between Bochum's industrialists and small property owners. It clearly showed just how vulnerable local artisans, shopkeepers, and small merchants had become, both as businessmen and taxpayers, to increases in working class poverty resulting from a major economic crisis in heavy industry. The most obvious result of this confrontation with working class poverty in the late 1870s was that it drew industrialists and small property owners together in a shared moral offensive against the poor. Although the vision of artisans, shopkeepers, and small merchants fixed primarily on the problem of poverty in Bochum itself, whereas local industrialists adopted a broader perspective, both groups came to share substantial areas of agreement with regard to the causes of poverty (working class "demoralization") and also its remedies (the "moralization" and disciplining of the working class).

Yet the poverty that resulted from the Great Depression also did a great deal to generate friction between Bochum's industrialists and small property owners. In the late 1880s, for example, Louis Baare was called upon in a city council meeting to "disprove the generally circulated (but false) opinion ... that a large firm like the *Bochumer Verein* lays heavy burdens on the city."

A city council member had charged that the Bochumer Verein was not paying enough taxes to the city to match the expenditures in poor relief made by the Armenverwaltung to unemployed, invalided and aged ex-employees of the company. Baare responded by calling on Bürgermeister Lange to show that the taxes paid by the Bochumer Verein "are in any case three times as high as the amounts paid by the city for support of former employees of the company," and Lange tried to reassure the councilors that "it is a triumph for the city that we have industry here. It is through the Bochumer Verein that the city has grown large."[78]

Yet these responses did little to dispel the underlying tensions that the charges themselves reflected. Certainly many small property owners must have been directly concerned with the question of who was going to pay for the increase of poverty that had resulted from the Great Depression, and they were undoubtedly angered to think that the Bochumer Verein might be evading its responsibilities to the community. But at the same time many of them were experiencing more fundamental doubts concerning their relationship to heavy industry. The fifties and sixties had seemed a time of promise—a period of growth from which both heavy industry and small property could benefit. The Great Depression, on the other hand, suggested that heavy industry was not always this beneficial. As the Chamber of Commerce put it in 1880,

While in the Ostseeprovinzen every possible means is used to attract industry . . . here, where for thirty years flowering cities have been created from poor villages, the attitude is much too readily accepted . . . that large industry is a misfortune. Here we are treated like milk cows and scarcely allowed room to graze.[79]

However, this anti-industrial attitude did not immediately produce much in the way of a critique of industrial capitalism beyond the charge that industry was not being properly "responsible" to the "community." What it did produce was resentment of heavy industry's growing economic dominance of the community and some attempts to resist that economic power being converted into political influence in city hall. For example, in 1878, when the Bochumer Verein for the first time publicly supported candidates for the municipal elections, the local *Bürgerpartei,* representing the "independent *Mittelstand"* of both confessions and political persuasions (National Liberal and Catholic Centre) reacted vociferously. One of them remarked that he would be glad to see the company's stock rise one or two hundred percent, but he would regard it "as an abnormal condition . . . if the *Bochumer Verein* should be too strongly represented in the *Stadtverordneten Collegium.*"[80]

Although the Verein was able to push its candidates through in the third class of voters, resentment of its influence continued. As late as 1888, the second class of voters (consisting primarily of artisans, shopkeepers, and small merchants) spoke out against "outsiders," a reference to the representatives of heavy industry.[81]

It was this rather vague and diffuse *Mittelstand* resentment that Johannes Fusangel tried to convert into a political platform in the late 1880s and early 1890s. Fusangel, a Catholic journalist born in Düsseldorf who had gained experience in Bavaria, where he became known as a "radical Catholic Prussian-hater," came to Bochum in 1884 to edit the *Westfälische Volkszeitung,* a Center newspaper.[82] Bochum was already sharply divided by the *Kulturkampf.* The Catholics, who in 1871 comprised some 61 percent of the population, formed so many separate clubs, according to Paul Küppers, that almost every profession and trade "divided itself up along confessional lines."[83] And in 1889 the local *Märkischer Sprecher* carried two advertisements that reflected the strength of Protestant religious identity among some elements of the town's population:

For an ironware business . . . a well-schooled apprentice of the Evangelical confession is immediately desired.

A young lady who has become ill needs an orderly maid, familiar with all household tasks and who is Protestant.[84]

By the end of the 1880s, according to Küppers,

the population divided in *Schwarz* and *Blau,* in Catholic and Liberal . . . Even outside election time [party allegiances] stipulate relationships and connections between people for which politics is not really even a question . . . *Blau* and *Schwarz* are the keywords which attract or repel—even so far as going to the pub is concerned.[85]

Fusangel certainly did not refrain from embroiling himself in these conflicts; indeed, as the anonymous editor of a pamphlet describing one of his many libel suits observed, Fusangel "provoked . . . a continuing press feud between the National Liberal and the Center newspapers."[86] In 1889 Fusangel was charged with having insulted both the Evangelical church and Luther. For that he was sentenced to fourteen days in prison. The very next month, he was sentenced to another three weeks in prison by the Schoffengericht for having slandered Louis Baare concerning his relationship to the Bishop of Fulda. Indeed, by the late 1880s, "the name of the editor of the *Westfälische Volkszeitung* had become a program."[87] But it soon became clear that Fusangel was not simply interested in "confessional politics." Between July 5 and December 17, 1890, he published a long series of muckraking articles in the *Westfälische Volkszeitung* that injected a strong class element into the local version of the *Kulturkampf.*[88]

In these articles, Fusangel made three basic accusations: first, that a large number of the richest local citizens, for the most part Protestant and National Liberal in politics and with close connections to the Bochumer Verein, had conspired to be underassessed for their income taxes; second, that "false economies" were being made in the relief of the poor and that recipients of poor relief were being subjected to abuses; then, finally, that the city administration was suffering from the fact that it had within its midst members who "belonged to" the Bochumer Verein and "that often times the interests of the city have to take a back seat to the interests of the *Bochumer Verein.*"[89]

As a result of these articles, both a civil suit and criminal charges *(Aufreizung zum Klassenhass)* were brought against Fusangel. That may have been ill advised since the trial itself gave Fusangel even more notoriety than his earlier articles; reports on the proceedings were carried by some fifteen hundred German and foreign newspapers and generated a ninety-page pamphlet summarizing the testimony which sold for 60 pfennigs under the title "Sensationell. Der Bochumer Steuerprozess" (1891).

Fusangel was very definitely trying to appeal to the "small men" of Bochum. In his first lead article (July 5), entitled "Allerlei Finanzkunste," he argued that "it is exactly the Mittelstand that is most significantly squeezed by taxes, whereas the rich are not treated in the same fashion." Another article was entitled "Gleiches Recht für Alles." The theme stressed in this and several of the articles that followed was that "whereas the Mittelstand and the poor people are taxed up to the very limit, those people who have a large income are assessed for only a portion of that income—this is a shockingly unfair situation."[90]

Although Fusangel at times seemed primarily concerned with eliciting the support of the Catholic Mittelstand—he made a point, for example, of showing that some Catholic artisans had been overassessed by a tax committee that was predominantly Protestant—the main thrust of his appeal was directed at securing the support of all the city's Mittelstand, Catholic and Protestant alike. These "kleineren Leute," Fusangel argued, were the "good citizens" who were being unfairly cheated and burdened by heavy industry. If not themselves the "community," the city's Mittelstand certainly were more responsible to the "community" than were the industrial leaders.

In an article discussing the poor, for example, Fusangel argued that

a large part of the cost of supporting the poor, which was formerly borne by the whole community, has now been pushed on to the shoulders of the Mittelstand, whereas big business and the rich, have been spared this burden.. . . . It can indeed easily be said that Baare has systematically and successfully represented the interests of the Bochumer Verein against those of the citizenry and for years has been trying to shift on to the citizenry the greatest possible portion of those costs which should have been paid by his firm.[91]

However, the threat to the local Mittelstand stemmed not only from the economic burdens heavy industry sought to impose upon it. Big business, so Fusangel argued, had introduced into the city values that were alien, indeed anthithetical to those of the *Mittelstand*. Heavy industry and the National Liberal establishment that supported it showed no respect, for example, for the artisan's personal "independence" and "honor." The example of the shoemaker Hoffmann was one case in point; feeling that he had been overassessed for his taxes in 1889/90, he went to *Bürgermeister* Lange to complain.

However, [Lange] told him that at his daughter's wedding wine was drunk and his daughter wore a silk dress, so that the shoemaker Hoffmann could well afford to pay these taxes. The witness [Hoffmann] declared, however, that not he, but a relative had paid for the wine and that while it was true that he had given his daughter a silk gown, a wedding was a once-in-a-lifetime thing; moreover, if there were a couple of bottles of wine in his cellar, that was because they had been needed for his sick wife.[92]

This victimization and humiliation of the shoemaker Hoffman was all the more infuriating, Fusangel suggested, when compared to the case of the local industrialist Knapp-stein who "under the cover of being a modest craftsman, understood full well how to make a lot of money, but without the tax commission knowing anything about it."[93]

But it was not only the artisanate who were denied personal independence and honor by heavy industry; it is, for example, striking that Fusangel's main criticism of the relationship between the Bochumer Verein and its workers was that

the leadership of the *Bochumer Verein* has abused the influence which the employer naturally has over the worker . . . [it] has marched its workers, under the eye of the foremen, to the voting stations and there has had them vote for candidates, to whom a *free* worker would never have *freely* given his support.[94] (my emphasis)

Similarly, what concerned Fusangel about poverty in Bochum was not so much the fact of its existence but rather that the poor were not being treated with respect and had been denied their rights as citizens. "*Bürgermeister* Lange keeps track of every egg and the remains of every ham, but the spirit which reigns in the *Armenpflege* has nothing to do with Christian charity." The relief of poverty, so Fusangel contended, was a right won through the citizen's payment of his taxes, yet, in Bochum, the poor were treated not like citizens but like criminals: "The *Armenpfleger* are also supposed to be police . . . Those receiving support are made to clean the city streets twice a week dressed in prison uniform."[95]

Fusangel's basic reason for publishing this long series of articles was to expose to the "community"—meaning primarily the local *Mittelstand*—exactly what heavy industry had done to the town. His main complaint seemed to be that the the wealthy and privileged were not properly fulfilling their duties as citizens and consequently were abusing the rights of others. "As a citizen [of Bochum]", his lawyer argued at the end of the trial,

[Fusangel] was rightly interested and concerned that all citizens should be taxed without regard to their party-political affiliations . . . in that sense he represented the interests of all the citizens, since every citizen had the same rights as Fusangel.[96]

Yet, Fusangel was not interested simply in defending or promoting the democratic political rights of the local *Mittelstand* and the poor against wealthy industrial capitalists—his articles and the questioning at his trial show that he was also engaged in attacking wealth per se. At one point, for example, Fusangel interrupted the testimony of a witness so that he could make it clear to the courtroom audience that what was being referred to as Fritz Baare's *Dienstwohnung* was in fact "a villa with a nice garden, electrical lighting, steam heating, elegantly furnished throughout." Such revelations undoubtedly served a dramatic purpose; by demonstrating the true wealth of Bochum's industrialists they emphasized their culpability in trying to cheat the city out of taxes. Yet, as Louis Baare suggested to Fusangel, after having been heavily cross-examined by the journalist, something more was involved; "I have the impression, that the very fact that I have a high income and receive various bonuses is being made an object of censure and criticism."[97]

Throughout the trial, Fusangel was indeed trying to show that the wealth heavy industry had created was itself objectionable, largely because of its moral implications. In the middle of the trial, Fusangel created an uproar by charging that for some years now the Bochumer Verein had gotten rid of their substandard railway products by illicitly affixing a government inspector's seal of approval. Once again, this demonstrated heavy industry's lack of concern for the common welfare; by its actions the Verein had endangered thousands of railway passengers. But Fusangel's revelations were also meant to show Bochum's *Mittelstand* that *Grosskapital* made its money by morally reprehensible means. No respectable artisan or shopkeeper would "cheat" in the way the Bochumer Verein had done.[98]

Similarly, Fusangel was at pains to show that immorality tainted all those who were touched by big industry's money and influence. What could be worse than the spectacle of Mayor Lange and the Guardians giving themselves "dinners in the poor house costing up to 50 Marks each of which are paid for from the poor relief budget." Fusangel's position with regard to industrial capitalism can probably best be characterized as Christian moralism heavily interlaced with *Mittelstand* self-righteousness which made their own usually straitened and difficult economic circumstances into a positive moral virtue. In the end, this meant that Fusangel's critique really did not go all that far. His invective was frequently bitter; "Baare is for me the prime example of mania for profit, of conscienceless exploitation and political tyranny."[99] But when it came to posing alternatives, Fusangel's suggestions were vague and relatively mild; both the poor and industrial workers should be "treated according to Christian first principles," and Christian charity should replace liberal acquisitiveness as the guiding principle of industrial society. Apart from this, however, there is little to suggest that Fusangel was fundamentally opposed to industrial capitalism in Germany as distinguished from what he took to be its more morally objectionable manifestations in Bochum.[100]

Yet, despite the obvious and considerable limitations of his critique, local industrialists regarded Fusangel as a considerable threat. Why? In his *Steuerprozess* articles Fusangel tried to articulate and arouse *Mittelstand* hostility to the industrialists. But even before this, Fusangel had already developed significant ties with some elements of the local working class. As early as 1886 he founded a "Rechtschutz-vereine für die bergmännische Bevölkerung in Oberbergamts-bezirk Dortmund" which had the aim of protecting and restor-ing the "hard-won rights of the miners," and he played an influential role in the 1889 miners' strike.[101] In 1887 he launched a press campaign in Bochum in which he charged that local industrialists were the incarnation of modern "eco-nomic" man, exploiting their workers ruthlessly. "Any rights of labor," Fusangel argued, "are recognized with extreme unwillingness by our industrialists. Whatever is given to the worker above and beyond his wages should, according to their opinion, be regarded as . . . a form of pure charity."[102] The worker used up all his strength in the service of the National Liberal big businessmen, but when he grew old, they told him, so Fusangel charged,

Go to the poorhouse, you ruffian, or die on the shit. We big business-men are not in a position to do anything for you . . . stop whining, old man, you're responsible for your own misery. Why didn't you become a General Director of the company?[103]

Fusangel thus represented to the industrialists the possi-bility that they might well have to face the simultaneous political opposition of disaffected elements within both the working class and the local *Mittelstand*. Indeed, there were signs to indicate that some members of the local *Mittelstand* were prepared actively to support workers against industrial-ists. In the confessional miners' unions formed in the 1880s, some of the leaders came from the ranks of the *Mittelstand*; the executive committee of the Christlich-Socialer Arbeiter-verein in neighboring Wattenscheid, for example, contained a master tailor, a baker, a city councilor, a barber, and two innkeepers. During the 1889 miners' strike, it was reported that some local shopkeepers were donating essential aid to the striking miners. And instead of responding to a violent con-frontation between troops and strikers at the railway station on May 9 by calling for more troops to protect lives and property, the "respectable citizens" actually petitioned for their complete removal. Moreover, a Center Party Reichstag election poster in 1890 made an explicit appeal for an alliance of "Artisans and Workers" against "Industry and Agriculture."[104]

The possibility of combined working class and *Mittelstand* political opposition would obviously have unsettled local industrialists at the best of times; but in the early 1890s that prospect seemed particularly dangerous because organized socialism, illegal and virtually invisible up until 1890, was rapidly beginning to create a public presence for itself in the Bochum area. The miners' strike in 1889 had already witnessed efforts on the part of "local agitators" of the Social Democratic Party to hold public meetings, and in 1890 the *Märkischer Sprecher* reported that "for the first time, the Social Democracy has voiced its intention to take part in municipal elections."[105] In 1884 the party had received only nine votes for its Reichstag candidate in the Stadtkreis Bochum and only 2.2 percent of the vote in 1887 in the Reichstagwahlbezirk (Bochum-Gelsenkirchen-Hattingen); but by 1893 its Reichstag candidate received 29.6 percent of the vote.[106] It is not surprising, then, that local industrialists felt that this was the worst possible time for Fusangel to be voicing his criticisms of industrial capitalism. For, in their minds, challenging the system, no matter in how mild a manner, laid the foundations for an oppositional consciousness among workers which could and probably would eventually lead them into the false paths of socialism. As the prosecuting attorneys put it at the end of Fusangel's trial:

From this conflict, there will be no gain for the Centre Party nor for any other party . . . the whole profits are going to fall into the hands of the Social Democracy. . . . the behavior of the accused is all the more culpable because those who have been attacked are employers. Think, gentlemen, how dangerous this way of acting is. Whoever has in these days read the Social Democratic newspapers will have seen that it is exactly the Social Democrats who will grab the spoils from the present trial. What impression must it have on a miner, for example, when . . . he becomes aware that his employer has been accused of perjury?[107]

While local industrialists did not deny that workers had some valid grievances, they seemed to feel that most working class dissatisfactions were not "real" but had been artificially incited by "outsiders" for their own selfish reasons:

not only the clericals [but also] . . . the democratic and extreme conservative press has, from party-political motives, often fallen short of the desired degree of objectivity and nonpartisanship in the discussion of the conditions of the workers. . . . As a result, the arrogance, the presumption and the greediness of the workers has systematically mounted.[108]

This was both irresponsible and dangerous because, local industrialists argued, the Socialists were always ready to step in, take the dissatisfactions that had been aroused by the rhetoric of the other political groupings, and then "diligently stoke" them up. The "poison of Social Democratic false doctrine" aimed at corrupting the "essentially healthy mining population" as a first step in an attack on "the existence of the state itself." Given time it would result in the "desired collapse of the social order."[109]

Given these views on the process of worker politicization and the role played in it by criticism from non-Socialist quarters, local industrialists can only have welcomed Fusangel's departure from Bochum in 1893, after he had suffered several more libel convictions.[110] This was their chance to bring disaffected elements of the local *Mittelstand* back into line politically, and thus to neutralize them as potential working class allies and leaders. Certainly many members of the local *Mittelstand* themselves felt that it was time to close ranks with industrialists against the threat of socialism. Consequently, local politics reached a definite turning point. As the *Märkischer Sprecher* reported in 1893,

in consideration of the fact that it is in the interest of the relationships of our city to dispose of municipal elections peacefully, there have taken place, in the last few days, discussions between the parties, and on the basis of these an agreement has been reached in such a way that, from the liberal side as well as from the side of the Center Party, it has been recommended that [a] joint list of candidates be elected.[111]

From that point onward, with some breaks, municipal elections were conducted primarily on the basis of uniting heavy industry and the local *Mittelstand* against the Social Demo-crats. The electoral agreement between Liberals and *Zentrum* lasted until 1902, when the Catholics, complaining that they were being given far too few representatives in the Rathaus, refused to support the candidates on the liberal list for reelec-tion.[112] But although the Haus- und Grundbesitzerverein and the Wirteverein put forward their own candidates in 1906, the threat from the Social Democrats was sufficient to reunite Liberals and Catholics in a common list.[113] In 1908 and 1910 this alliance split apart again; in the first year a group of reform-minded Liberals left their party to join with the Com-munal Economic Union, which advocated reforms in local housing, economic, tax, and school policies, while the remaining liberals, Catholics, and Social Democrats ran sepa-rate lists. The split in the liberal slate gave the Catholics a rare complete victory in the third class of voters. In 1910 liberal opposition to the provincial and national policies of the Zen-trum maintained the breach between the two parties, but by 1912 the danger of Social Democratic entry into the City Coun-cil pushed them back into another compromise list of candi-dates, which carried the elections.[114]

Yet, fear of socialism was certainly not enough to push all of Bochum's artisans, shopkeepers, and small merchants into a completely uncritical political and social alliance with the industrialists. Indeed, the persistent contradictions of the eco-nomic relationship between many members of the *Mittelstand* and heavy industry meant that their attitudes toward indus-trial capitalism remained ambivalent. Even though the period after 1889 marked an economic upturn that obviously bene-fited many artisans and small shopkeepers, their dependence on working class customers and hence their vulnerability to economic crises continued.

In 1902, for example, the Chamber of Commerce com-mented on a recent "decline in buying power . . . especially among the workers, who in some counties of our district make up 70–85% of the total population and whose buying power is therefore decisive for the state of business among small trad-ers." Similarly, in 1909, even though business for grocery shops had improved somewhat over the previous year those "which are predominantly dependent on working class customers have experienced the improvement to a lesser degree; this is especially true of shops in rural communities. They often suffer from the short time that the companies are working."[115]

Of course, small shopkeepers and artisans in Bochum did have other problems besides their vulnerability to the business cycle in heavy industry. Charges of unfair competition were as much a part of their litany of complaints as they were elsewhere in Germany. But, in Bochum, cut-throat competition was regarded by retailers not as something separate from, but rather the direct result of their heavy dependence on working class customers. This was particularly evident during economic downturns. As the Chamber of Commerce put it in 1902, when working class income and buying power declined, "it is always the cheaper quality of goods that are preferred and since the cheaper prices attract the great mass of buyers (cut throat competition thrives)." The rush to grab working class business by selling "cheap and nasty" was not, however, restricted to periods of economic recession. By the first decade of the twentieth century, small shopkeepers and artisans had to contend with the permanent presence of department stores such as the Warenhaus "Zum Bergmann" (Bochum, Bahnhofstrasse 30), which advertised: "furniture, single pieces, as well as whole sets can be acquired by everyone—regardless of their social status—with the easiest of credit payment systems, guaranteed good quality, from the simplest to the finest."[116]

These "so-called department stores," the Chamber of Commerce reported in 1902,

truly help to confuse the idea of quality and to discredit retail trade. Clearance sales have very much increased. Almost the whole year through you can find in the papers and posters that there are clearance sales at the department stores which go under every conceivable name and reason. . . . Inventory, Clearing-Out, Seasonal, Fire and Water Damage, Rebuilding, Moving, Remainder, Clearance Sales etc. . . . recently, the "Exceptional Day" [Ausnahmetage] seems to have become quite well loved, many businesses prefer to have Clearance Sales rather than periodic reductions of their prices.[117]

The same report then argued that this kind of competition inevitably forced small traders to follow suit simply to survive;

The better shops cannot escape; in the long run, they must join in this . . . mad hunt for customers . . . and the necessary means here are Clearance Sales, offering specific articles at cut rate prices and also free gifts . . . All the abuses that are to be seen in the department stores, are also to be found in many small shops.[118]

Given this already intense competition for working class customers, it was understandable that small shopkeepers would be less than charitable to either consumers' cooperatives or to company stores. In 1908, a bad year for retail traders, the Chamber of Commerce observed that

in the grocery, household goods and grease shops, business is relatively quiet compared to the general state of the economy. The market is suffering partially from a reduction of buying power among the workers who are most able to consume. [But] in a number of places, the competition of Konsumvereine is becoming more and more important and there are also, here and there, complaints about the sale of food by several of the [local] companies.[119]

The world of the artisan and small trader in Bochum thus continued to be extremely volatile, vulnerable, and unpredictable even after the Great Depression. Although small business turnover declined somewhat after 1896, the numbers dropped from the assessment lists each year still ran between 6 and 25 percent (Table 4.5). Some of these ex-proprietors were forced down into the ranks of industrial workers. But even if they stayed within the artisanal world working for another artisan rather than finding a job in a factory or a mine, their lives could often be economically more marginal and insecure than those of many skilled workers in industry; in 1901, for example, among a sample taken from the income tax register for the city's twelfth ward, only 18.3 percent of the three hundred ninety-three skilled metalworkers and 29.4 percent of the fifty-one skilled workers in other industrial occupations had incomes lower than 1,050 marks per year, whereas some 94.0 percent of artisanal workers fell into this category (Table 4.6).[120]

Indeed, the difficulties and discontent experienced by many artisans and small shopkeepers may well be reflected in the mobility patterns of their children. Rather than becoming artisans or small shopkeepers like their fathers, a not inconsiderable number of children from these backgrounds began to seek their futures in the public and private bureaucracies and the professions. The lists of students at both the local Oberrealschule and the Gymnasium reveal a particularly strong

Table 4.6 Income and Occupation, 1901

Income (Marks)	Unskilled Metal workers	Other Unskilled Workers	Skilled Metal-workers	Other Skilled Workers	Artisan Workers	Artisan Masters	White Collar
900–1,050	376	77	72	15	78		16
	(41.8%)	(49.0%)	(18.3%)	(29.4%)	(94.0%)		(23.9%)
1,050–1,200	472	72	154	28	4		8
	(52.4%)	(45.9%)	(39.2%)	(54.9%)	(4.8%)		(11.9%)
1,200–1,350	44	6	104	6			1
	(4.9%)	(3.8%)	(26.5%)	(11.8%)			(1.5%)
1,350–1,500	8		54				1
	(0.9%)		(13.7%)				(1.5%)
1,500–1,650			4	2	1		5
			(1.0%)	(3.9%)	(1.2%)		(7.5%)
1,650–1,800		1	3				6
		(0.6%)	(0.8%)				(9.0%)
1,800–2,100		1				1	4
		(0.6%)				(50%)	(6.0%)
2,100–2,400			2				4
			(0.5%)				(6.0%)
2,400–2,700							2
							(3.0%)
2,700–3,000						1	2
						(50%)	(3.0%)
Over 3,000							18
							(26.9%)
Total in sample	900	157	393	51	83	2	67

Note: Data derived from a sample taken from the manuscript tax schedule for the city's twelfth ward, an area of high concentration of incomes under 3,000 marks per year; StAB, Staatsteuerrolle, 1901.

component of children of tradesmen, innkeepers, and small merchants, from the mid-1870s onward.[121]

These persistent tensions in their relationship to heavy industry may well have pushed some members of the local *Mittelstand* into the orbit of right-wing politics. Bochum, like many other areas of Germany, had its anti-Semitic movement, which gained at least part of its support from local members of the *Mittelstand*. As early as 1883 the *Märkischer Sprecher* reported on several meetings of local anti-Semitic groups at which the newspaper editor, Kaiser, from Dortmund, appeared. And in the following year, local anti-Semites launched an attack on a prominent Jewish merchant, Philip Wurzburger, who was well connected with heavy industry circles. Important local industrialists, including Baare, Heintzmann, Mummenhoff, and Pieper responded by signing a petition against the anti-Semites. Moreover, some of Bochum's artisans were involved in the reactionary *Handwerker* movement; the 1890 program of the Deutschsoziale Partei, which called, among other things, for the restriction of *Gewerbefreiheit* and introduction of official examinations for master-employers, was drawn up in Bochum.[122]

Yet the picture is not quite that simple; during the 1905 miners' strike, for example, Sachse, the miners' leader, told an audience of workers that a Bochum merchant had given the Streikbureau a hundred marks. And again in 1912, Sachse observed that "thousands of shopkeepers and merchants embittered by the way the police are acting have given us sympathy and support." Gestures like these obviously did not mean that all shopkeepers felt genuine sympathy with the grievances of striking miners; but they do at least show that workers had the economic and social power to pressure some sections of the local *Mittelstand* to support them. In 1906, for example, the Social Democrats tried to get someone elected from the third class of voters in the municipal elections. The *Märkischer Sprecher* accused socialist workers of using "terror" in the elections to find out who voted for whom; "no wonder," the report continued, "that many shopkeepers who depend on the workers' trade vote red." The Amtmann of Bochum II Sud made much the same point, but in a slightly different manner, when he argued that socialism would be successful wherever "shopkeepers and small businessmen are [primarily] dependent on the workers and, naturally, the active resistance of the independent, small *Bürgertum* must be quite limited."[123]

There were also artisans and small shopkeepers who were deeply engaged in radical political activity, often as leaders. As early as 1876, the Social Democratic Wahlverein for the city and county of Bochum included five artisans and two innkeepers among its twenty-four members. In the 1890s and early 1900s, miners listened to speeches from men like the shoe dealer Heinrich Luckel, the printer Karl Klotz, and the master shoemaker August Kienholz. And between 1894 and 1907, the local Social Democratic agitators and leaders included several shoemakers and tailors, a cigar dealer and several small retail traders, one of whom had previously been a filesmith and another who had been a shoemaker.[124]

In Bochum, then, as in Paterson, New Jersey, the new industrialists, despite their considerable economic power, were not able simply to exercise an absolute rule over the political life of the city. And in both towns, it was the industrialists' relationship, not just to the working class, but to "nonindustrial property owners" that produced challenges to their political authority. Gutman's article thus draws our attention to an important dimension of class relations in the early industrial city, both in America and Europe.

Yet, if we try to apply Gutman's explanations for the conflicts between Paterson's small property owners and industrialists to events in Bochum, we run into some difficulties. Gutman suggests that these tensions arose primarily from a clash of values between the two groups. While the "nonindustrial capitalists" were certainly committed to "competitive private enterprise and the acquisitive spirit in their own dealings" they nevertheless "responded equivocally or critically to the practices of the new industrialists" because these activites often challenged the "traditional way of work and life" to which older residents were accustomed. Because they were known to be capable of and periodically did contravene these older community norms, local industrialists were unable to gain full "legitimation" as a local elite, despite the economic power they so obviously wielded. In the short run, then, their economic class position did not suffice to gain the "status" that was necessary for them to exercise political authority locally.[125]

But in the long run,

Class and status altered as the industrial city matured. The industrialist's power became legitimized. The factories and their owners dug deeper into the lives of the mill towns and became more accepted and powerful. The old middle class, and those who revered the old, precorporate town, lost influence and disappeared. They were replaced by others who identified more fully with the corporate community.[126]

While this may well have been the case in Paterson, it obviously did not happen in Bochum. There, conflicts between some elements of the local *Mittelstand* and the industrialists continued well past the early years of industrialization. An interpretation that sees these conflicts as the product of a clash between "old" and "new" values will be hard put to explain their persistence well into the twentieth century. By that time, Bochum had been an industrial city for more than half a century; the industrialists were no longer "new men"; they had in fact gained considerable local political power; and it might be assumed that sufficient time had passed for their power to have become properly "legitimated," for their "economic class" and their local "status" to fully coincide. Yet it is clear that significant elements of the *Mittelstand* continued to deny "legitimacy" to the industrialists. This cannot be explained simply as diehard traditionalism but has to be seen as a permanent feature of industrial society. A clash of values there may well have been (Fusangel's rhetoric certainly suggests that), but the values of the *Mittelstand* that gave them a framework in which to criticize industry surely derived less from the "preindustrial" period than from their own contemporary and quite contradictory relationship with heavy industry. This was not, then, a value conflict that would die away with time, after the first shock of industrialization had been absorbed and the older residents had passed on. It was a conflict which would be repeatedly reproduced by the dynamics of the new industrial society itself.

For the major point was that in order to become fully "legitimized" in the eyes of the local *Mittelstand*, heavy industry had to be able to ensure a degree of economic security to the artisans, shopkeepers, and small merchants who were so heavily dependent on it, which, in fact and in their experience, it quite obviously could not. Each period of economic crisis, whether that was in the late 1870s or the early 1900s, raised fresh challenges to the "legitimacy" of the industrial capitalists, in the minds if not always in the political behavior of significant numbers of the local *Mittelstand*. This could not be permanently obscured by any amount of political rhetoric or ideological manipulation (anti-socialism, for example) on the part of the industrialists. Nor was it in the industrialists' power to free the *Mittelstand* from their dependence on working class customers, their shared economic vulnerability with workers, their exposure to working class political pressure, or their cultural connections with the working class.[127]

And of all of this, the industrialists were most certainly aware. Indeed, by the 1890s, with the reemergence of socialism, the development of a populist Catholic opposition and the first general miners' strike in the region, local industrialists' confidence in their ability simply to dominate local society and run local politics the way they wanted must have been at a low ebb. Yet, if local industrialists could not completely control the industrial community itself, some of them at least might derive comfort from the fact that they possessed the power and the capital necessary to maintain their enterprises as virtually separate communities over which they could exercise a far more complete dominion.

The "Paternalism" of Heavy Industry

What local industrialists were most fundamentally interested in controlling was the cost of labor. Undoubtedly, all industrialists shared this basic preoccupation, but for heavy industry employers in the Ruhr it was a particularly compelling concern. The nature of Bochum's industrialization, which was based on capital-intensive heavy industry, made labor costs crucial to both mining and iron and steel production, either because they were such a large element in total production costs or because they played a significant role in determining the industry's ability to compete in world markets (or for both reasons combined; see p. 39f).

However, controlling labor costs was not simply an economic nor even a technological but a political problem. Employers operated on the assumption that they had the unquestioned, absolute power to set wages and determine the pace of work and general working conditions. But, by the 1890s, the employers' absolute authority over the workplace had already been challenged by some local workers and was at the same time threatened by the reemergence of socialism, which, while it had not yet developed a strong presence in the Bochum area, already existed as a national political force that could well make significant local inroads in the near future. Consequently, it seemed crucial to heavy industrialists that they strenuously resist all attempts by workers to infringe on the employers' "prerogatives." Up until the war, heavy industrialists refused, for the most part, to grant any significant degree of recognition to unions or to make concessions to strikers.[128] And they used whatever methods were necessary to root out dissidents and union organizers within their enterprises including firings, blacklisting, and paying bonuses to workers who informed on union members.[129] But even more than resistance and repression, employers banked on their ability to prevent grievances being articulated or workers' organizations being formed in the first place; in that task company welfare programs came to play a central role.

The Catholic newspaper editor Fusangel had argued that local industrialists were the incarnation of modern "economic man," exploiting their workers as they did any other raw material in the productive process. Workers were hired when needed, cast off when unnecessary. Labor was simply a commodity in the market economy, its fate determined solely by the relationship between supply and demand. Yet, in his eagerness to indict the economic "liberalism" of his heavy industry antagonists, Fusangel had overlooked aspects of their behavior as employers that deviated significantly from the picture he was painting. In 1878, for example, during a severe downturn in local industry, the Chamber of Commerce argued that many local employers had "made great personal sacrifices in order not to abandon their old *Arbeiterstamm* to unemployment."[130]

During the 1889 miners' strike, when production had to be cut back for lack of coal, Bochumer Verein steel workers were told they would not be laid off and were given short shifts or repair work. And during another miners' strike in 1905, the Westfälische Stahlwerke allowed its workers temporary aid for each shift lost (2 marks for married men; 1 mark for single), to be held back later from their wages. As soon as coal arrived from the Saar, the men were also put on short shifts.[131]

By these examples I do not mean to suggest that local industrialists were really charitable men who ran their mines and foundries like welfare institutions. What I do intend to show, however, is that local industrialists' attitudes and behavior toward their workers and the labor market was not as simple as Fusangel maintained because, along with the immediate market factors and cost considerations, long-range company interests as well as social and political considerations also played determining roles.

Certainly, labor market factors continued to be basic determinants of the worker's employment possibilities and prospects for job security; industrialists more readily fired those who were easily replaced, the unskilled members of the "floating population," whereas skilled workers, who were much harder to come by and for whom there was considerable competition among local companies, could well expect to continue working even when this cost the company money. Yet local industrialists did not respond exclusively to labor market considerations. Indeed, the development of company welfare programs is quite instructive in this regard. When industrialists initially decided in the 1860s to invest relatively large sums of capital in housing, insurance, and benefit programs, they may have been primarily interested in attracting and stabilizing a core element of skilled men.[132] But by the

1870s, local industrialists certainly felt that this *Stamm* of disciplined, trained, and productive workers must also include significant proportions of the unskilled if Bochum's industry were to compete effectively in world markets. As the Chamber of Commerce observed in 1878 during a period of very high labor turnover,

It is self-evident that with such a constant coming and going, a thorough training for the individual workers in their task is made extraordinarily difficult and that the productivity as well as the prosperity of the large works is severely affected. In this respect, the English and Belgian firms who enjoy a much more stable and well schooled work force have a great advantage over us.[133]

Of course, these are also market considerations; the point is that they operated in a somewhat different manner than those remarked on by Fusangel. Moreover, along with their "strictly economic" motivations, local industrialists also began to feel that stabilizing a sizable core of workers might well have extremely significant social and political consequences (themselves not without implication for labor costs, industrial profits and the ability to compete internationally). As Louis Baare told the Iron Enquiry Commission in 1878,

I have been in office for twenty-four years and a certain *Stamm* of masters and workers have been there even longer; consequently one enjoys a certain trust among the workers since they know that they will be treated properly. In this way I was in a position to combat the effects of Social Democracy.[134]

Under the combined pressure of each of these imperatives, industrial welfare programs were eventually extended to include a larger number of the workers in many local firms. At the Bochumer Verein, membership in the accident and sickness insurance funds was compulsory for all workers from the 1860s. By 1889 the firm had also built 1,045 dwellings which housed 6,000 of its fewer than 6,400 workers, complete with company store and even a day-nursery.[135] Indeed, in Bochum, as in many other Ruhr towns, the large companies built around themselves separate physical communities within the city.[136] Ultimately membership in that community came to depend not only on the employer's need for certain types and categories of workers as determined by the market, but also on moral and political imperatives, namely the loyalty the worker had shown or was prepared to demonstrate to his employer.[137]

This attempt to create a community both physically and morally insulated from the wider society was most clearly evident in the development of company housing. Initially, company housing was largely a response to pressing labor needs. Intense competition among Ruhr iron and steel companies for skilled workers combined with the inadequacies of housing in the city to produce a high rate of labor turnover. In 1864 the city council reported that despite numerous local opportunities for employment, some workers were being forced to move on since they could not find adequate shelter. In response to this problem, "the mines and foundries. . . . erected houses for their workers, especially for the good *Stamm*, often at great cost. . . ." However, this initial concern for the stabilization of skilled workers, though it always remained a central element in company housing policy, was soon overshadowed by a more diffuse desire to integrate the worker into the moral community of the enterprise. Heinrich Flottmann, proprietor of a local machine building firm, thought, for example, that company housing would prevent worker alienation in the city: "A worker who has a nice home near the factory is more bound to the company than one who works there for material reasons, but lives just anywhere and is basically rootless."[138]

Company housing was expected to be capable of performing such a crucial role in the industrialists' social policy for two basic reasons. First was the almost unchallenged attraction it held for workers seeking decent dwellings. Second and perhaps most important were the restrictive regulations governing occupancy. Like many other Ruhr industrial cities that had expanded so rapidly from the small or middle-sized country towns they had been at mid-century, Bochum experienced a chronic housing shortage. Those dwellings that were available, most of them converted artisan or merchant houses in the old city center, were usually small, cramped, dirty, and expensive. As early as 1864, the city government was attributing a wide variety of ills to residence in these quarters: "A large part of the sickness and early deaths [among the working population], the increasing inclination to spend much time in beer halls, the economic disorder of many workers' families as well as the increasing incidence of moral depravity are to be ascribed to this cause."[139]

Whatever the validity of these observations, it is undeniable that company houses, the first of which were just being erected at this time, must have appeared considerably more attractive than what was offered on the public housing market. By law, company-built homes had to be rented cheaper than comparable private dwellings, and for the most part they were better maintained.[140] It was quite natural, then, that there was "a great press on the part of workers" for such accommodations, and the company was able to turn this demand to its own advantage even at the initial stage of deciding who should live in these homes. As a rule, only the more "trustworthy" employees who had already been with the company for some time were allowed to rent them.[141]

The attractions offered by company houses over private dwellings were enhanced by the fact that up until World War I they had virtually no competition. To a large extent this was a consequence of the industrialists' control of the city government, the other most logical sponsor for worker housing. Industrialists in the city council managed to restrict local government efforts to rather ineffective police measures aimed against overcrowding and other flagrant abuses.[142] The local *Mittelstand* was inclined to support this position if for no other reason than that they were not interested in raising their own taxes to fund public housing projects. Hence even the most innocuous proposals for city government involvement in housing were guaranteed virulent counterreactions. In 1883, for instance, the Armenverwaltung suggested that the city build an *Obdachlosenasyl* to provide temporary shelter for homeless inhabitants. The *Asyl* was immediately branded in council meeting by industrial leaders as

just a form of humanitarian nonsense designed to give the advantage to the Social Democrats and to hurt the mine and foundry owners in their most essential interests . . . If the city were to start giving free places to live to distressed persons, the workers, who have up until now been diligent and orderly, would, as a result of this bad example, soon forget their own duty to pay their rent and demand that they too receive free lodging from their employer.[143]

Though this attack did not block erection of the *Asyl*, it did ensure that the institution never became more than a "temporary shelter" in which were housed only the lowest failures from urban society: "convicted persons, notorious drunkards, and other morally defective individuals" as the *Magistrat* described them in 1900.[144]

The near monopoly of sanitary, low-cost housing that local industrialists enjoyed meant that many workers faced a difficult choice. If they wished to retain their freedom to change jobs at will, they and their families would have to put up with generally undesirable accommodations in privately rented houses. But if they wanted to improve their family's environment by renting a company house, they would have to submit to considerable restriction of their occupational freedom. For the worker who rented a company home discovered when he read his rent contract that his job and his home were not separate and independent of each other. For example, if he was fired or if he decided to quit, a worker at the Bochumer Verein was required to vacate his company-owned dwelling *on the same day*. But if he wished only to move elsewhere while continuing to work for the company, he had to provide at least three months' advance notice. And what he would not find in the rent contract, but would surely be made aware of either by his employer or his fellow workers, was that should he engage in a strike, he could usually expect immediate eviction.[145] Through such regulations, the company attempted to make it difficult, if not impossible, for workers living in company houses to seek employment with other firms or to organize protest against low wages or bad working conditions.[146]

Other restrictions aimed not only at stabilizing fathers but also at recruiting their sons. At the Bochumer Verein, for instance, a restriction requiring tenants to take in only boarders who worked for the company was held to apply to sons as well. When the young man reached employable age he faced

the choice of continuing to live with his family and working
for the Verein or of leaving home to seek a job elsewhere,
which, perhaps, neither he nor his parents were ready to
countenance. Some sons of Bochumer Verein employers who
attempted a third alternative, working for the competing
Westfälische Stahlwerke (which paid higher wages) while
still living at home, were soon discovered by a company
official and their families threatened with eviction if the sons
did not either come to work for the Verein or move out.[147]
These pressures for family continuity might of course serve
the interests of the workers themselves, since they aided in
transferring job security from one generation to another; but in
the main they were designed to serve the company's and not
the worker's interests; for they enabled employers to recruit
significant numbers of new workers from families they knew
could be held responsible for the good behavior of their sons.

This must have appeared a particularly important advantage viewed against the general background of extremely high
turnover among most young workers at the company. Company housing for families of workers could indeed promote
both residential stability and company loyalty, but it had little
effect on the thousands of young single males who drifted in
and out of employment at the Verein during any given calendar year. Since most of these young men had migrated to the
city alone and had only themselves to consider, they could
afford to quit their jobs when they felt wages were too low,
company discipline too harsh, or when they simply wanted a
change. If, however, employers could not or did not want to
stabilize this floating population, they could at least segregate
it both from other workers and from other townsmen. This
seems to have been one of the main functions of the *Kost- und
Logirhaus,* a barracks-like building erected by the Bochumer
Verein in 1873 that by the early 1890s sheltered over twelve
hundred single workers in one hundred fifty rooms where
four, eight, and twelve workers slept in small individual cubi-
cles.[148] Just a few of the regulations governing conduct in the
Kost- und Logirhaus serve to indicate its purpose in controlling and segregating young workers: "Addiction to alcohol-
ism and quarrelsomeness will not be tolerated"; "Climbing
over the *Kost- und Logirhaus* enclosure is punishable by a 3

Mk. fine"; "Outsiders are allowed in the building only with the permission of the administrator"; "Outsiders are not allowed to lodge with inhabitants"; "Every inhabitant must present himself in his assigned room by 11 P.M. under penalty of a 1–3 Mk. fine."[149] Thus while company housing had endeavored to create a community of work and residence from which "all foreign elements are fundamentally excluded," the *Kost- und Logirhaus* aimed at preserving that community by segregating transient young workers from it.[150]

Like industrial social policy in general, company housing involved a fundamental compromise. In return for a certain measure of security the worker was expected to forfeit the right to seek higher wages by means of collective action, or even the opportunity to improve his condition by moving to another company.[151] Yet not even the industrialists expected that the material advantages offered by industrial social policy were alone sufficient to induce most workers to accept the conditions of this contract. The industrial enterprise had not simply to be the source of his employment, his home, and his security against accident, illness or old age; it also had to become the focus of his affections.

To engage the worker's moral and emotional commitment, the industrial enterprise had to be presented to him not merely as a productive unit, but in some sense as an integrated, organized social system. A basic step in this process were symbolic acts emphasizing the personal relationship that was supposed to exist between employers and workers. Thus Baare ate regularly in the workers' canteen, a symbolic compensation for the general absence of personal contacts between management and labor that characterized such a massive operation as the Verein. In smaller firms such activities seemed somewhat less contrived, though they were no less indicative of internal tensions in the factory and of similar efforts at obscuring them. Flottmann used various means, including the formation of a company singing club, to convey the impression that employers and workers were mutual elements in an "indivisible community" of work.[152]

These notions of "community" were given greater form and substance at the company anniversary celebrations. To the Bochumer Verein celebration in 1894 were invited two hundred ninety-eight *Beamte*, masters and workers who had been continuously employed with the firm for between twenty-five and forty years.[153] In an introductory poem, Emil Rittershaus provided the assembled workers with the basic ideological and moral justification for the long years of service that had brought them to this celebration. By contrasting their high-minded devotion to the company with the materialistic self-seeking that seemed to Rittershaus to characterize many workers elsewhere, the assembly was made to feel that whatever they might have lost in material advantages had been redressed by their moral superiority. They were not infected by the

> . . . spirit of selfishness, a raw
> lust of the senses which passes through our time
> There grins the face of envy, there hatred clenches fists
> For blows. . . .
> As if there were nothing more important . . . than treasures of
>   gold.[154]

Loyal workers at the Verein should know that wealth was indeed the least desirable of all worldly achievements because it was both ephemeral and morally corrupting: "Riches seduce into idleness and idleness in every land and every order of society is always the father of need, vice and shame." Any worker who, inflamed by his greed and dissatisfaction, believed that "improvement and salvation" could be achieved through revolution was only deluding himself. The workers gathered at the celebration had, by their years of devotion to the company, shown that they understood what was lasting and meaningful in life: diligence, loyalty, and steady application to the task at hand.[155]

Rittershaus told his audience they could indeed expect to achieve "success" in their lives, but the qualities of "diligence" and "loyalty" that he cited as the necessary prerequisites to this success indicated the narrowness of his vision. What Rittershaus meant quite simply was that the worker who devoted his life to his employer (in this case the Verein), who served him honestly and efficiently, could in the end expect to be rewarded with security and possibly modest advancement

within the ranks. The rich man's purse and the beggar's sack
might well not lie more than a hundred years before the same
door, as Rittershaus claimed in his labored rhyme, but he was
certainly not prepared to argue that at the end of that time they
would simply have changed places. Rather, the thrust of Rittershaus's warning was that, should they abandon morality,
both rich and poor could be cast down into abject degradation.
The message for the worker was clear: If even the rich could
lose their wealth through immorality, how much more vulnerable then was the worker, with his very modest measure of
security?[156]

From Ritterhaus' depiction of the traits of character and
morality that set the anniversary celebrants apart from other
workers, the theme of the subsequent poems and songs turned
to the unique nature of the enterprise itself. The most consis-
tent image was that of the Verein as a sort of pseudo-familial
group. As each member of the family played his ascribed role
in showing loyalty to the family, so too each loyal worker was
expected to dedicate himself to the company, as a family
surrogate. In the song "Dem Ältesten Jubilär," the company
was depicted as a white-haired family patriarch, himself the
"oldest anniversary celebrant" in whose service the assembled company had "bent their backs and bleached their
hair."[157] Another song was devoted to family history, estab-
lishing a sense of continuity with the past through individuals
who had been important in the company. The achievements of
the founders were described in somewhat the same tones that
might have been used to honor family ancestors. And whereas
in the earlier song the company itself had been symbolized as
the family head, now that role was transferred to the General
Director, Baare. The family image was completed by thanks to
Baare and the original founder, Mayer, for having made the
Bochumer Verein a "home" for its workers;

And a home has grown here for thousands
Who remain loyal to the Bochumer Verein
For this thank this gallant pair.[158]

The family metaphor was an apt expression of what
industrial leaders hoped the Bochumer Verein and companies

like it would become, for it conveyed the proper blend of affection, loyalty, obedience, and renunciation of self-interest that they intended to inculcate in their employees. Yet it was not the only theme that pervaded the ceremonies that night. Complementing the family image was also a suggestion that the body of anniversary celebrants belonged to a select club where differences of status were submerged in the general dedication to the welfare of the company. The form of the celebration, with all ranks mingling together in a convivial atmosphere, singing and drinking toasts, conveyed this image implicitly. The presence in the audience of a number of "Jubilär-Kandidaten" who had not yet attained the twenty-five years of service required for entry but who hoped to do so, stated the same theme explicitly.[159]

But the implication of both images was the same; the body of celebrants was represented as a heterogeneous yet cohesive social unit, a community of affection and mutual obligation within the enterprise, an ideal to which all workers could and should aspire. On entering it they entered a charmed circle where social relations were regulated by morality and duty, where security and contentedness were assured, where alienation and conflict were abolished.

Conclusion

The "paternalistic" control of their workforce that heavy industrial companies like the Bochumer Verein tried to exercise has usually been regarded as either an anachronistic hangover from the preindustrial world or simply evidence of the big capitalists' inability and unwillingness to accept fully "modern" and more "rational" industrial relations.[160] This judgment, it seems to me, is based on the assumption that there is an intrinsic logic in the nature of industrial production that requires employers eventually to realize that it is "rational" for them "to accept labor as a valid source of input to the process of framing the structure of the workplace."[161] Judged by this yardstick, Bochum's heavy industrial employers would certainly have seemed "backward." Yet, as I have attempted to demonstrate in this chapter, local heavy industrialists had quite compelling and logical reasons that derived both from their present and future economic interests and from the contemporary German political context (and not from their inability properly to learn the "rules of the industrial game") to use company paternalism as a way of controlling labor costs by preventing workers from organizing and striking.[162]

Not only did heavy industrialists have the reasons, they also had the means. While smaller industrial companies, like those in metalworking and machine building, were equally (indeed even more) concerned with controlling labor costs, they did not have the same kinds of resources to support extensive "paternalistic" programs.[163] Thus, rather than describing company paternalism as a specific form of German "backwardness," we might prefer to view it as a specific form of capitalist rationality appropriate to the development of heavy industry in the German context.[164] But, while we may well be able to argue that company paternalism was an attempt at "social control" made both rational and feasible by the interests and resources of German heavy industry, that does not tell us whether or not it worked.[165] It is time, then, to turn to the behavior of workers in the two branches of local heavy industry to find an answer to that question.

five

The Foundations of Worker Protest: Miners and Metalworkers

WEDNESDAY, MARCH 13, 1912, the third day of a miners' strike in the city. An hour and a half before the end of the shift, a crowd of young men and women gather before the main gate of the Präsident mine. As the midday shift comes up to go home at about eleven o'clock, they are greeted with catcalls from the crowd. The strikers try to get at the working miners as they leave but are held off by the police. Then, as the nonstrikers and their police guard move off down the Dorstenerstrasse, the young men in the crowd follow them almost to the center of town. When the police guard leaves to return to the mine, the crowd storms after the workers into the Heinrichstrasse. The working miners try to escape; one seeks refuge in the entrance hall of the Kortum café. The crowd of youths does not follow him but remains outside in the Kortumstrasse. Mounted police are summoned by phone and within a few minutes have "cleaned the streets."[1]

As the police repeatedly intervene in the clashes between strikers and strikebreakers, the crowd also begins to turn its anger directly on them. By Thursday, vicious neighborhood wars between strikers and police have broken out in various districts of the city.[2] Along the Dorstenerstrasse and at the Hannibal mine in Marmelshagen, there are violent confrontations between police and strikers. In Hamme, where the police break up a street demonstration with rifle butts and saber hilts, a number of strikers retreat behind the churchyard wall and bombard the police with rocks. On Friday, there is renewed violence in the northern part of the city; police accompanying nonstriking miners to work are fired upon from the windows of several houses. Three persons with revolvers are being sought.[3]

But physical violence is not the only means by which strikers try to intimidate strikebreakers. Miners who continue to work also face ostracism from the miner community: "From several sources it has been reported that miners who are still working are exposed to attacks in their neighborhoods, even in their homes."[4] Along the streets, all the windows are filled with women and children shouting insults. Children form the first row in every crowd and vigorously deride the strikebreakers. And some of the women take even more direct action; on Friday, March 15, a number of wives of Polish miners attack another group of women bringing food to their husbands who are still in the mines. The food containers are taken away, emptied out and then made dirty "in a manner which cannot be repeated." Faced with this kind of communal rage, miners might find it easier to stay at home and lose wages than risk being cut off permanently from fellow workers, friends, and their families.[5]

The most obvious meaning of the violence assocated with the 1912 strike was that it reflected the relative weakness of support for that particular walkout. (Table 5.1). Striking miners had to physically and verbally coerce strikebreakers to join the strike precisely because it was relatively unpopular. By contrast, this kind of violence seems to have been much less common in the 1889 and 1905 strikes because the great majority of miners supported them and walked off the job spontaneously. In that sense then, it is correct to argue that the violence in 1912 reflected a weakness in the solidarity of miners during that strike.

But that is not the only, nor the most important lesson to be drawn from the experience of 1912, for even in that relatively unpopular and divided walkout, miners displayed a much stronger sense of their identity as an "occupational

Table 5.1 Strike Participation (in Percent)

1889			
Mine	May 7	May 8	May 9	Up to May 10
Dannenbaum				73
Julius Philipp				82
Prinz Regent				95
Hannover I, II				76
Präsident			100	95
Bochumer Gesellschaft				
Pit I	100			
Pit II		100		

	1905								
	Jan. 15	Jan. 17	Jan. 21	Jan. 24	Jan. 26	Jan. 30–31	Feb. 1	Feb. 3	Feb. 11
Hannover I, II				75	73	78	67	62	0
Amt Bochum									
Sud				82	79				
Nord				79	78				
County of									
Bochum		71							

	1912[a]						
	March 11	March 12	March 13	March 14	March 15	March 16	March 18
Präsident	6(12)	14	51				
Hannover I, II	9(6)	12		47			
Hannibal I	7(6)	13		87			
Hannibal II	6(6)	12		43			
Lothringen	few(21)	47					
Dannenbaum	2(12)	40	55(33)	61			
Prinz Regent	42(27)	78	80(100)	100			
Julius Philipp	20(27)	77	84(87)	88			
Friederika	11(12)	37	49(67)	68			
Constantin I, II	5(6)						
Constantin III	40(29)						
Constantin VI, VII	8(8)						
Deutsch-Luxembourg		63	65	69	73	53	63

	March 19	March 21
Deutsch-Luxembourg	56	"Hardly any"
Bergrevier Sud Bochum		37
Bergrevier Nord Bochum		11

SOURCES: Bericht des Oberbergamtes Dortmund, May 10, 1889 to Oberpräsidium Münster, Staatsarchiv Münster, reproduced in Wolfgang Köllmann, ed., *Der Bergarbeiterstreik von 1889*, p. 70; daily reports on numbers striking in StAB, MS, 1905 and 1912.

[a]Two figures are given for some days since total numbers reported working at individual pits varied.

community" than workers in the metal producing and finishing trades, which comprised the other major branch of local
industry. Compared to miners, the level of solidarity and the
record of protest among metalworkers was weak indeed. The
major strikes before the war were miners' strikes; there were
three general walkouts among miners in 1889, 1905, and 1912
involving many mines and thousands of workers in the whole
Ruhr, as well as numerous localized and partial strikes.[6] But
there was no record of any strike in the mammoth conglomer-
ate of foundries, rolling mills, and metalworking shops owned
by the Bochumer Verein during this same period. Metalworkers' strikes were largely confined to the smaller local firms,
and even when they did occur they seldom included more
than one category of worker in a given shop, nor did they
spread from one plant to another.[7] In 1872, for instance, filemakers at the Mummenhoff and Stegemann file factory struck
over wages; the company employed less than one hundred
men at the time, no other workers at the firm walked off the
job, and no other local metalworkers took up the strike. Again
in 1901 the same firm was struck; this time by six polishers
protesting wage reductions.[8] Three years later at another local
metalworking firm four workers went on strike for unspecified
reasons. In 1905 ninety rollers at a local steel mill also walked
off the job but were not joined by their fellow workers. And in
1909 fifteen molders at the Westfälische Stahlwerke struck
over wage reductions and poor working materials; their
attempt to spread the strike to other workers in the plant
failed. Finally, another strike by the same category of workers
in 1911, fifty of them this time, lasted just two days and was
also ignored by the other employees.[9]

The relatively higher level of solidarity among miners
was not, however, reflected only in their strike behavior. Miners also formed trade unions earlier and participated in them
more often than most local metalworkers. In 1890 the Bochum
police reported that there were already two local branches of
the Verband zur Förderung der bergmännischen Interessen in
Rheinland und Westfalen in the city with 306 members, or
about 15 percent of the local work force. Four years later, a
Gewerkverein Christlicher Bergarbeiter was also formed. And

by 1907 in Amt Bochum Sud, which included three neighboring mining villages, no less than 64 percent of the local work force belonged to the Deutscher Bergarbeiterverband alone.[10]

Local metalworkers, on the other hand, did not have a branch of the German Metalworkers' Union (DMV) until 1892; initially it had a membership of only fifty workers or about 1.0 percent of the work force in the metal trades.[11] The city's Christian metalworkers organized later still, in 1902, when a local branch of the Christlicher Metallarbeiterverband Deutschlands was formed. Subsequent efforts to increase the numbers of organized metalworkers were not all that successful; by 1907 the Free Trade Unions in the city counted only between 8.6 and 15.7 percent of local metalworkers as members, while a year later in the neighboring village of Weitmar, where the Westfälische Stahlwerk employed several hundred men, only twenty-seven belonged to the union.[12] Clearly, then, we are dealing with significantly different degrees of solidarity and militance among miners and metalworkers—how do we explain these differences?

Explanations of Protest

Historians and social scientists have often interpreted worker solidarity as the product of certain shared conditions of working class life: geographic and social uprooting, economic misery, social and technological change. The purpose of the following section is to use Bochum's miners and metalworkers as test cases of each of these explanations to discover what elements of working class life and experience in this industrial city were crucial, what merely contingent to the generation of worker protest. If any of these explanations are correct, we should expect to discover that Bochum's miners were more uprooted, more economically deprived, or had undergone greater social and technological change than the city's metalworkers. If, however, we find that the terms "misery," "uprooting," or "change" describe the experience of both worker groups, we must look past the simple notions of collective experience they convey for some more fundamental substructure of worker protest.

Uprooting

Proponents of the "uprooting" theory of protest argue that the source of working class disturbances can be found in the disruptions experienced in migration from rural to urban areas and from the agricultural to the industrial economy:

The wrenching from the old and the groping for the new in the industrializing communities create a variety of frustrations, fears, uncertainties, resentments, aggressions, pressures, new threats and risks, new problems, demands and expectations upon workers-in-process, their families and work groups . . . beneath the exterior is always a latent protest seething and simmering.[13]

Among European social historians, the "uprooting" theory has had several influential exponents, the best known being Louis Chevalier, who has written two major works on Paris during the first half of the nineteenth century.[14] As George Rudé has rightly observed, there is in Chevalier's work no explicit formulation of a theory of urban lower class protest, but his assumptions and their implied consequences are quite clear. Chevalier sees the city as a living organism and his concern is to describe and define what he calls its "biological foundations." This has led him to a distinctly one-sided and pathological picture of the city. In his work, statistics on migration, ages, occupations, births, deaths, and marriages shade into and are often overshadowed by indices of breakdown in the urban environment: crimes, suicides, violent assaults, prostitution, beggary, starvation, and disease. During the course of half a century, Paris, according to Chevalier, is progressively infiltrated by an uprooted population from the provinces who crowd into dismal, unhealthy, and dangerous quarters of the city raising the rates of crime, poverty, and disease. Working classes and dangerous classes become progressively indistinguishable. This much is explicitly stated by Chevalier. Also implied, though nowhere deliberately spelled out, is the notion that, accompanying the crime and disease, are also increases in social protest and revolt. Chevalier's argument emerges in his paraphrase of Balzac's statement that "crime swelled under the impact of popular revolt, blended with it and took on its shape." Crime and social protest fuse; the collective outburst becomes a collective "settling of accounts" between uprooted outsiders and the settled population.[15]

Chevalier's interpretation has been the most powerful, but by no means the only argument for the "uprooting" thesis. Girard has described Paris in the nineteenth century in a similar vein.[16] And though some of his work implicitly contradicts Chevalier's assumptions, David Pinkney has nonetheless argued in support of the French historian's case.[17] Nor are the echoes of the uprooting theory restricted solely to writings on early nineteenth century French history; they can just as easily be heard in Dorothy George's description of eighteenth century London and A. J. P. Taylor's comments on the revolutions of 1848.[18] Twenty years ago, Val Lorwin also suggested that the working-class occupations in Europe most prone to radicalism were those that were least stable and most isolated from "normal" social life.[19]

Until quite recently, German historians have not contributed a great deal to this discussion, since few of them have demonstrated interest in the history of the modern city or popular protest. Wolfgang Köllmann, one of the few West German historians who has systematically investigated the growth of German cities in the nineteenth century and the processes of internal migration that caused this expansion, presents a somewhat ambivalent judgement. On the one hand, Köllmann suggests that "the isolation of the individual and the depersonalization of relationships" that accompanied movement to the city "provided the impulse for the new independence and self-assertion which made changes of social position possible." Yet, Köllmann also emphasizes the "growing dualism between social mobility and social antagonism" that "was from the first inherent in the urbanization process."[20] One of his studies specifically addresses itself to the connections between population movements, the growth of cities, and the "social problem," and concludes that internal migration relieved pressure on the land only to concentrate social disruption in the city.[21] Like Chevalier, Köllmann does not specifically link these "social problems" and the migration that caused them to social protest, but such a connection is undeniably implied.

Recently, however, a number of American and English historians have explicitly challenged the uprooting theory in their works on France, Germany, and Italy. In France, Charles Tilly and George Rudé have discovered that urban disturbances did not coincide with peak periods of city growth and migration, that at least until the 1860s disturbances more often characterized older cities and older, more stable sections of cities than the newer, more mobile urban centers, and that it was the older residents rather than the "uprooted" new arrivals who were most likely to participate in social protest. Rudé has added to this discussion a further logical objection to Chevalier's hypothesis, arguing that "the social instability and uprooting that were conducive to acts of individual violence were probably not conducive to any but the most elementary forms of collective activity."[22] In a tentative introduction to the same problem in Germany, Richard Tilly concludes that "scattered information about various instances of disorders in nineteenth century Germany suggest a pattern much different from that implied by the 'dislocation' thesis; namely that well-established, but threatened, groups are the most prone to violent protest."[23] Finally we can note the recent work of Louise Tilly on Milan, a city that was industrializing late in the century and that attracted large numbers of new migrants. Similar arguments to Chevalier's were advanced by at least one group of nineteenth-century Italian observers to explain the 1898 rebellion called the Fatti di Maggio. Yet, by carefully comparing nativity distribution of workers arrested in the revolt with those in the specific trades to which they belonged, Tilly finds little room for an uprooting theory of protest.[24]

We have already determined that labor protest in Bochum was far more common among miners than among metalworkers. Was this a result of miners being substantially more uprooted? To answer that question we must first decide how uprooting shall be measured. The most obvious indicator is the proportion of migrants to natives in a given group and its relative stability in the city. Groups with high proportions of migrants and groups that are extremely transient can be regarded as uprooted. These are the workers we should expect to be most commonly engaged in protest if the uprooting theory is correct. Yet nativity and turnover figures are only crude indicators of uprooting. Contemporaries also discerned a number of characteristics of working class groups that they felt separated the stable and integrated worker from the floating outsider, and to a significant degree these characterizations were realistic. Young single men were more uprooted than their older married fellows; hence, large proportions of young men in a specific occupation would indicate a strong influence from uprooting. Yet even after marriage, the worker with kin or property in the city was likely to be more integrated into the local community than one who married an outsider or who never bought a home. If our investigation shows that, judged by each of these measures of uprooting, miners conformed more closely to the stereotype of the alienated outsider than other manual groups in the city, then we have reinforced the explanations of protest advanced by Chevalier, Lorwin, and others. But if not, then we must agree that the criticisms of the uprooting thesis offered by the Tillys and Rudé are justified, although we may not necessarily accept their revisionist interpretation.

The published census returns for 1907 show that migrants were indeed most heavily concentrated in mining; 83.8 percent of miners had been born outside Bochum compared to 68.7 percent in metalworking and 72.2 percent in machine building (Table 5.2). However, this is scarcely convincing proof of the uprooting theory, since it serves only to empha-

Table 5.2 Nativity of Workers in Mining, Metalworking, and Machine Building (1907 Census)

	Native Born	Near Migrants	Far Migrants
Mines and foundries	16.2	47.0	36.8
Metalworking	31.3	29.0	49.7
Machine building	27.8	36.3	35.9

SOURCE: *Statistik des Deutschen Reiches*, Bd. 210/2.

size the fact that the great majority of the work force in all three trades was composed of migrants. Moreover, far migrants, whom we might suppose would have experienced the greatest dislocation, were most heavily concentrated in metalworking, not mining. More important than both of these observations, however, is the fact that the published census returns obscure the relationship between nativity and skill levels. In mining, where skill differentials were not pronounced, this is not a serious difficulty. But metalworkers were in fact divided into at least two distinct subgroups, the skilled and the unskilled. While the record of men marrying in 1900 reveals that skilled workers in the metal trades were primarily drawn from Bochum and the five surrounding counties, it also shows that unskilled workers actually came from outside this region more often than miners.[25] If, then, uprooting was the cause of miners' protest, why did it not generate collective outbursts of similar intensity, frequency, and scope among the unskilled workers in Bochum's metal trades?

Movement and uprooting did not of course end when the worker reached the city. Among the industrial towns of the Ruhr there was a constant exchange of thousands of workers. Therefore transience was an important element in uprooting, for the transient worker was not likely to experience any but the most superficial forms of integration into the local community. Yet rather than indicating that miners were uniquely transient, Table 5.3 emphasizes the similarities among miners, unskilled factory workers, and skilled metalworkers. For, with the exception of day laborers, these three groups were considerably less stable than any of the city's other workers.

Table 5.3 Persistence Rates of Sample Members (in Percent)

Occupation	Remaining from 1880–90	Remaining from 1880–1901
Miners	38.6	18.9
Unskilled factory workers	42.0	24.3
Skilled metalworkers	36.2	29.3
Day laborers	32.6	17.8
Skilled builders	54.2	42.6
Artisans: food, etc.	68.4	47.4
Artisans: wood, etc.	67.4	37.0

SOURCE: Data derived from mobility study.

Among miners, unskilled factory workers, and skilled metalworkers there were of course noticeable differences in persistence rates. In the first decade, miners were actually more stable than skilled metalworkers, while unskilled factory workers showed the lowest rate of out-migration. By 1901, however, miners were more transient than either unskilled factory workers or skilled metalworkers. Yet it can reasonably be questioned whether such small variations in persistence rates serve even partially to account for the quite remarkable differences in occupational solidarity that we have observed among miners and metalworkers. Indeed, we must pay attention to the qualitative as well as the quantitative aspects of transience if we are to grasp the significance of geographic mobility in the formation of collective consciousness. For as Richard Tilly has observed, geographic mobilty did not necessarily cause a high degree of uprootedness in a social sense if it occurred within a framework of occupational or social continuity (Tilly cites the example of the journeymen's *Wanderschaft*). As I argue later in this chapter, because of the nature of their work and the structure of their neighborhoods, transient miners experienced greater social continuity and subsequently were less socially uprooted than either unskilled or skilled metalworkers, who were somewhat more geographically stable.

However, regional origins and rates of turnover are only rather crude indicators of uprooting. What we are really seeking to discover is the extent to which various groups of workers were or were not integrated into the local community. Obviously this sense of belonging depended on many factors other than simply where one had been born, or even how long one remained in the city. For instance, contemporary observers regarded all young unmarried workers as being far more unsettled than older men with families. Free of the responsibilities and integrating bonds created by a wife and children, and financially emancipated from the discipline of parents (if indeed he even had parents living in the city), the young male worker could "be at home wherever the best earning opportunities were offered."[26] Young workers were unsettled in a social sense as well; standing on the fringe of "respectable" society, they had less regard for authority than their older, married peers. In 1892, for instance, the Chamber of Commerce complained that "it is exactly the young workers who are the most easily seduced by the Social Democratic agitators, and who, especially in strikes are always pushing to the forefront."[27] There is of course a logical contradiction in this stereotype; if young workers were the least tied to a particular job and community, why should they have been interested in collective protest at all? Presumably they could best hope to improve their situation by simply moving to a better job elsewhere.[28] But even if we leave this objection aside for the moment, we can still question whether this middle class stereotype provides a convincing explanation of worker protest. For according to this argument, workers in occupations with a high propensity to protest should characteristically be younger with proportionately fewer married men than the more passive workers in other occupations. Yet as Table 5.4 indicates, these assumptions are quite false. Young, single miners may indeed have injected fire into miners' strikes, but in order for their protest to have been as widespread as it was, it must have involved large numbers of older, married men as well, since they dominated the occupation.

Far from fitting the stereotype of the young, unattached, unsettled, and therefore radical worker, the miner was generally older than his counterparts in the metal trades and was more likely to be married. Hence the presence of young unmarried men in an occupation in large numbers was not strongly associated with an inclination to protest, despite the misgivings about this group harbored by middle class observers.

Of course, by itself marriage did not provide a blanket guarantee of integration into the local community, Brepohl

Table 5.4 Distribution of Young Men and Married Men in 1907 (in Percent)

	Men Aged 11–25 Years	Married Men
Mines and foundries	28.5	61.2
Metalworking	51.9	42.3
Machine building	43.1	46.6

SOURCE: *Statistik des Deutschen Reiches*, Bd. 210/2.

Table 5.5 Intermarriage with Women Born in the City (in Percent)

Occupation	All Migrants	Migrants Born Outside Bochum Area[a]
Miners	22.7	17.7
Unskilled factory workers	17.6	14.6
Skilled metalworkers	42.0	35.9

SOURCE: Calculated from Rathaus Bochum, Standesamt Bochum, Familienbuch, 1900.

[a]Counties of Bochum, Gelsenkirchen, Recklinghausen, Essen, Dortmund, and Hattingen.

has argued that many migrant families long continued to experience an overwhelming sense of disintegration and alienation in the industrial cities of the Ruhr.[29] I would suggest, however, that marriage could be an important step toward local integration depending on the nature of the kinship relations it created. If the migrant worker married a woman born in the town, he gained a set of relations who might now perform some of the economic and social functions of the kin he had left behind in his village or hometown.[30] The man who married a fellow-migrant or who sent home for a bride was denied this entry into local society. Indeed, both he and his bride might well remain relatively isolated from the community until they could build up new social relationships. And whatever ties they eventually formed might well be neither as strong nor as significant as those created by ties with local kin. Hence the extent of intermarriage between migrants in various manual occupations and women born in the city is a more refined measure of relative integration and uprooting. If migrant workers were noticeably less able to form kinship bonds with local inhabitants by marrying a native-born woman, then we might assume that marriage was not as significant in mitigating their sense of being uprooted as it was for other workers.

Table 5.5 indicates the proportions of migrant miners and metalworkers who married native-born women in the year 1900.

Rates of intermarriage between migrant men and native-born women obviously varied quite remarkably from one occupational group to another. Migrants in the skilled metal trades faced the fewest barriers to intermarriage, undoubtedly as a consequence of their superior position in the city's working class. But surprisingly, migrants employed in mining married native-born women more, not less, frequently than migrants in unskilled factory work. This was true whether we consider all migrants or only those born outside the six surrounding counties. Hence if (as I have argued) the rate of intermarriage with native-born women was a significant indicator of relative uprootedness, then we should expect unskilled factory workers, not miners, to be the least integrated into the local social structure even after marriage. Yet it was miners who were the most active in local labor protest, which further increases doubt that "uprooting" and protest are directly connected at all.

The migrant worker who married a local woman gained access to the social network of the settled community members. The worker who acquired property created the possibility of himself one day becoming a member of that settled community. Whereas only one-fourth of those in the mobility study who rented dwellings in the city remained there for twenty-one years or more, almost one-half of the homeowners were still there at the end of this period. Their stability helps account for the euphoric rapture with which the seemingly mundane aspects of homeownership were greeted by the city's middle classes. The worker who owned his home, it was suggested, was involved with "his family, in his neighborhood, in [his] surroundings and occupation," which made him "morally higher and . . . also stronger" than his unpropertied counterparts.[31] In short, property was an effective antidote for uprooting.

Given these assumptions, it was natural that middle class observers should have been greatly disturbed by the changes they observed among miners after the middle of the century. Around 1850, it has been estimated, most Ruhr miners owned their own homes and small garden plots.[32] The influx of new migrants in the 1860s and 1870s, along with the progressive industrialization of mining enterprises, changed this. As early as 1873, the city government in Bochum complained that "agriculture and gardening within the city limits are continuing to lose importance not only because the land is being built on for industrial purposes but because . . . the miners, who earlier used their free time for cultivating the land, feel that, in light of present high wages, such effort is not worthwhile."[33]

Of course, the main reason that many miners no longer worked the traditional small garden plots was that few of them could now afford to buy property of their own. By 1876 no more than eighty, or fewer than 9 percent, of the nine hundred eleven men working at the local mine *Constantin der Grosse* owned their own homes. And by 1893, though property ownership among all Ruhr miners was somewhat higher, it had still barely reached 15 percent of household heads.[34] In the passage of a few decades, miners did indeed seem to have become rootless proletarians. Yet that impression was substantially correct only insofar as it contrasted the condition of miners in the late nineteenth century with what was presumed to have been a golden past. Judged on their position relative to other workers, however, miners came off better. As Table 5.6 indicates, miners actually owned homes more frequently than unskilled factory workers and skilled metalworkers.

The "uprooting" theory of protest argues that it was the unintegrated, the alienated, the outsiders who generated collective disturbances during the period when workers were moving into the cities. But on several counts, the uprooting theory has proved a poor guide in helping us explain why miners were in the forefront of labor protest in Bochum, while metalworkers were more passive. In most cases, miners did not fit the stereotype of the "uprooted worker" as well as some other types of manual laborers, and at no time were they the main or only candidates for the role. Certainly protest in

Table 5.6 Homeowners in 1880

Occupation	Percent
Miners	6.3
Unskilled factory workers	4.1
Skilled metalworkers	5.2

SOURCE: Data derived from mobility study.

Bochum did not erupt from the ranks of the most stable and settled segments of the population, as Tilly and Rudé argue for Paris and France, but neither was it a product of the most marginal and least integrated groups in the city, as Chevalier's hypothesis leads us to expect. In fact, neither the uprooting theory nor its recent revisions can provide us with the instruments of analysis we need to understand the bases of labor protest in Bochum. Where else should we look?

Misery

On May 5, 1889, an anonymous letter to the Dortmund newspaper *Tremonia* offered these comments on the miners' strike that was then paralyzing the Ruhr coal industry: "Living costs, rent and taxes continue to rise . . . the coal industry has made fundamental gains—therefore the miners also want to earn more than they have until now. . . . That is the gist of the matter."[35]

Interpretations of worker protest like this one have appealed to many historians. Their simplicity is their strength. Worker protest appears as a straightforward reaction against material deprivation. Workers who suffer the greatest material deprivation will be the most militant, while more affluent workers remain passive. Workers strike when wages are low or falling, when the cost of living is high or rising or when inflation outstrips increases in income.[36] Yet the simplicity of this argument is also its main weakness. In its one-dimensional portrayal of workers as men motivated solely by their economic condition it does violence to a far more complicated social reality.

The available information on local wage patterns in the mining, foundry, and metalworking industries certainly does not support the assumption that misery caused protest. Tables 5.7 through 5.9 compare shift wages for the three main classes of miners with workers in a wide variety of skilled and unskilled occupations in the foundries and metalworking shops for the years 1878, 1889, and 1910. At no time did miners appear at the bottom of the local wage structure and in many instances they were comparatively well paid. In 1878, for instance, there were at the Bochumer Verein's blast furnace alone, no less than six different categories of workers who received less money than the lowest paid adult mineworker. Miners' wages equaled those received by many categories of unskilled workers at the blast furnace and even approached those of some skilled men (Table 5.7).

By 1889, the year of the first major miners' strike, the highest paid mineworkers, who constituted some 50–60 percent of the work force, frequently earned more than some categories of skilled workers in the local foundry and metal-working industries (Table 5.8). Certainly all miners, except for the small percentage who were under the age of sixteen, were a considerable distance away from the bottom of the local wage structure.

By 1910 the average shift wage of a miner at the coal face was 5.37 Marks (Table 5.9). Though skilled and even some unskilled workers in the Bochumer Verein's foundries and

Table 5.7 Pay Scales in 1878 (Marks)

Bochumer Verein—Blast Furnace			
Skilled workers			
smelter	3.45		
fitter	3.05		
smith	3.40		
Unskilled and semiskilled workers			
slag transporter	2.50	lime and iron ore breaker	3.75
ironstone/lime loader	2.85	rail cleaner	1.40
worker at furnace mouth	2.88	machinist at blower	2.62
tool carrier	2.00	machinist at furnace throat	
wagon greaser	1.30	hoist	2.62
heating apparatus servicer	2.60	machinist at coke transporter	1.60
coke stoker	2.60	boilerman and stoker	2.50
iron breaker and loader	4.00	Average overall wage	2.93
scrap collector	1.50		
Mines			
coal face workers	2.66		
other underground workers	2.13		
workers above ground	2.24		
young workers	1.05		

SOURCE: StAB, Küppers Nachlass, NI 23a, p. 61, and *Die Entwicklung des Niederrheinisch-Westfälischen Bergbaues in der zweiten Hälfte des 19. Jahrhunderts.* XII. *Wirtschaftliche Entwicklung,* Teil 3 (Berlin, 1904), p. 79. Miners' wage rates are for the Oberbergamstbezirk Dortmund.

workshops sometimes earned more (often considerably more) than this, miners were still by no means the worst paid local workers. Indeed, their shift wages compared favorably with those of many skilled workers and exceeded those received by many other unskilled laborers. For instance, coal face workers did earn less than smiths in Hammerwerk I and II and less than some of the unskilled operatives in the Bessemer and Thomaswerke, but their wages were higher than those of skilled fitters and turners in the repair shop and skilled smiths in the axle-turning shop.

Thus miners were far from being the poorest paid workers in local heavy industry; in fact, their wages were relatively high. If they were able to work a full number of shifts in a given year, their average annual income could often exceed that earned by workers at the Bochumer Verein, even though the work force there included a high proportion of skilled workers, not present in the mines, whose relatively higher

Table 5.8 Pay Scales in 1889 (Marks)

Blast Furnaces, Rolling Mills		Mechanical Workshops, etc.	
Skilled workers		Skilled workers	
smelter	2.88	fitter	3.17
roller	4.04	smith	3.62
rough roller	4.15	turner, borer	3.34
fine roller	3.43	tinsmith	3.20
		varnisher	3.29
		molder	4.26
Unskilled and semiskilled		Unskilled and semiskilled	
coke and ore transporter	2.86	hammerman	3.23
coke burner	3.81	riveter	3.60
yard worker	2.42	helper	2.55
loader	4.20	apprentice	1.23
apprentices and underage workers	1.66		
Mines			
coal face workers	3.42		
other underground workers	2.60		
workers above ground	2.57		
young workers	1.12		

SOURCE: Koch, *Die Bergarbeiterbewegung*, p. 141. Figures for Regierungsbezirk Arnsberg. Miners' wage rates from *Die Entwicklung des Niederrheinisch-Westfälischen Bergbaues*, p. 79.

Table 5.9 Pay Scales in 1910 (Marks) Bochumer Verein

Bessemer and			*Repair Shops I, II, and III*		
Thomaswerke			*Skilled workers*		
Unskilled and			fitter		4.90
semiskilled			turner		4.70
helper		4.05	smith		5.05
machinist, crane			*Unskilled and*		
operator		4.75	*semiskilled*		
converter man		(5.25)[a]	machine worker		4.56
ingot mold/melting pot			*Axle Turning Shop*		
man		(5.25)	*Skilled workers*		
Iron and Steel Foundry			smith		5.00
Skilled workers			turner		(6.00)
smelter		5.60	fitter		(5.80)
molder	(6.13)	5.75	*Unskilled and*		
mold core maker		4.60	*semiskilled*		
Unskilled and			helpers		3.90
semiskilled			machine workers		(5.78)
casting cleaner		4.50			
helper		4.15			
Hammerwerk I and II					
Skilled workers					
hammersmith		I (9.00)			
		II (7.50)			
other smiths		I (6.30)			
		II (5.10)			
Unskilled and					
semiskilled					
hammer helpers		I (5.50)			
		II (4.96)			
furnace workers		I (5.45)			
		II (5.35)			
helpers		I 3.88			
		II (4.00)			
Mines					
coal face workers		5.37			
other underground					
workers		3.98			
workers above ground		—			
average shift wage		4.54			

SOURCE: *Die Schwereisenindustrie*, pp. 336–37, and Koch, *Die Bergarbeiterbewegung*, p. 150.

[a]Figures in parentheses indicate piecework rates.

incomes inflated the average. In no less than nine of the twenty-four years between 1889 and 1912, miners earned on the average more than their counterparts at the Bochumer Verein (Table 5.10). And in eleven of the remaining fifteen years, miners' average incomes came within a hundred marks of those at the Verein.

If then, material deprivation was the source of miners' protest, why did it not result in similar disturbances among other workers in the iron and steel industry and the metalworking and machine building trades who received similar or even lower remuneration for their labor? Koch is undoubtedly correct when he argues that in the years before the first miners' strikes in 1889, "the economic situation of the miners was extremely unfavorable and their income barely sufficed for the most necessary items of life." And no doubt the trade union

Table 5.10 Average Annual Income (Marks)

Year	Miners	Workers at Bochumer Verein
1889	941	1,018
1890	1,183	1,058
1891	1,217	1,074
1892	1,120	1,115
1893	946	1,057
1894	961	1,081
1895	968	1,090
1896	1,035	1,127
1897	1,128	1,165
1898	1,175	1,205
1899	1,255	1,252
1900	1,332	1,287
1901	1,224	1,267
1902	1,131	1,206
1903	1,205	1,216
1904	1,208	1,255
1905	1,186	1,271
1906	1,402	1,328
1907	1,562	1,415
1908	1,494	1,451
1909	1,350	1,378
1910	1,382	1,426
1911	1,446	1,463
1912	1,586	1,465

SOURCE: Compiled from Koch, *Die Bergarbeiterbewegung*, pp. 148–50, and Däbritz, *Bochumer Verein*, Statistischer Anhang.

leader Kuhne accurately reflected popular sentiment when he told his audience of strikers in 1912 that "wage reductions in recent years [have] caused bitterness among the miners."[37] Yet this does not explain why miners struck while other workers remained relatively quiescent.

Structural Change, Skill Dilution and Status Deprivation

"Terms like misery," sociologist Neil Smelser contends, "are too general as explanatory concepts. They cannot explain why misery erupts into disturbances only now and then, and only in certain directions and not others.[38] Smelser suggests instead that worker protest must be understood against the background of the fundamental changes that characterize the transition to a modern industrial society—a process he terms structural differentiation. Structural differentiation occurs, according to Smelser, when "one social role or organization . . . . differentiates into two or more roles or organizations which function more effectively in the new historical circumstances. The new social units are structurally distinct from each other, but taken together are functionally equivalent to the original unit." Structural change has a great potential for disruption and the creation of disturbances since it creates new values and activities that challenge traditional ones and because the process itself is uneven, leaving gaps in society that temporarily forestall reintegration. Individuals can respond to these discontinuities with anxiety, hostility, or fantasy, and each of these individual responses may be represented in a collective social movement.[39]

   In his book on the Lancashire cotton industry, Smelser shows how protest among cotton workers was a response to structural changes in the industry and in society. As long as cotton remained a domestic manufacture, the main economic and social functions were retained within the same social unit: the cotton workers' family. The shift to the factory did not immediately break the nexus between economic activity and kinship since adult operatives were still able to recruit their helpers and apprentices from among their own family members. Consequently, although material deprivation was often intense during this period, cotton workers remained relatively quiescent. The introduction of new inventions in spinning and weaving upset this balance, since they required more helpers than could be recruited from among kin. This marked a growing separation between the family and work, made more severe by the new strains it put on relationships within the family. The family also became both less independent and more vulnerable in the society at large. It was against these changes, Smelser argues, that cotton operatives protested and not simply against "immiseration."[40]

Structural differentiation does, of course, ultimately result in a new integration of society. Workers in a mature industrial economy no longer have to deal with the fundamental disruptions of their world that confronted cotton operatives in early nineteenth century England. Yet change continues to affect workers. Innovations in factory technology or the organization of production can produce significant reorientations of the worker to his work, to his fellow workers, or to the other members of the community. Mechanization may, for instance, reduce the amount of skill or manual dexterity required for the performance of a task, and when this happens the worker may lose not only the money but also the status that went with the old skills. Even changes that do not dilute skills may cause disruption and be greeted with protest from workers. Arensberg notes the example of older workers in an American paper mill who went on strike when management introduced a new incentive scheme, reversing informal patterns of authority among workers on the job that had been derived from relationships away from work.[41]

It is tempting to see the protest of Ruhr miners as a collective response to just such a combination of changes. Adelmann, for instance, contends that miners were much better organized than iron and steelworkers largely because the miners' consciousness of their traditional rights made them extremely sensitive to the changes by which they were deprived of them.[42] And Koch concludes that it was the general "social decline of the *Bergmannstand*" in the second half of the nineteenth century and not outright "misery" that accounts for their militance.[43] To understand what these authors mean, we must briefly survey the main changes that occurred in the mining industry from about 1850 on as they affected the position of the worker.

There is absolutely no doubt that the social and economic position of the miner was fundamentally transformed between 1850 and 1900.[44] Before midcentury, the miners' economic, social, and legal roles in German society were undifferentiated from each other. To be a miner was not simply to earn a living digging coal, but to exercise a calling with special privileges and distinctive moral qualities and responsibilities: "The efforts of a miner," ran an ordinance of 1824, "must be directed to the loyal execution of his exceptional calling, and through good moral conduct, orderliness, industriousness and obedience towards his superiors to the winning of respect for his estate."[45] The miner's calling and his estate were, of course, primarily the creation of the Prussian state, which in the eighteenth century had begun to "raise the *Bergmann-stand* above the level of the common population"[46] by freeing miners from certain taxes and military service, by creating special assistance in cases of accident, sickness, and death, and above all, by directly regulating miners' working conditions, hours, wages, seniority, and hiring and firing. The power of the state was used to endow the miner with a semblance of that honor and respectability (*Ehrbarkeit*) that had traditionally been denied occupations like the one he followed.[47] Miners were organized in state-controlled guild-like institutions called *Knappschaften* to foster their corporate spirit and had distinctive uniforms, bands, parades, and special holy days to emphasize their exceptional status.[48]

His occupation therefore provided the miner with an "integrated" role in German society, for in it were combined economic, social, and legal functions. Yet suddenly in the 1850s this integration was threatened. Responding to what Smelser would call "dissatisfactions" with the traditional structure of mining that impeded economic development, the state withdrew from mining, handing over direct control to the individual mine owners. In the process, the miner's traditional rights and security were undermined. His economic fate now depended on the conditions of the market, and the old notions of the honor and dignity of his occupation did not travel well into the industrial world. Expansion of the industry prompted massive migration to the mines of the Ruhr, and few of those coming had any previous experience of mining:

Shoemakers, tailors and agricultural laborers became so-called mining men and were soon entrusted with work for which neither their individual capacities nor their experience and training suited them. The miners who had been trained properly under the old system . . . soon became a minority among the irregularly composed modern *Bergarbeiterstand*.[49]

As management shortened, or even abolished, the traditional step-by-step training periods, work in the mines became not only less skilled but also considerably more dangerous. Accident rates rose; but when the injured or sick miner came to claim assistance from the *Knappschaften*, he found that this institution, once regarded as the basis of his "esteemed position" in the working class, was now in the hands of his employers, with whom he would have to argue for every benefit he received.[50] Each of these developments made miners who had lived and worked under the old system sharply aware of the injury that had been done to their status by legal and economic change. From once having been a *Bergmann*, he had now descended to the role of *Bergarbeiter*.[51] Paradoxically, the only form of change miners were spared during this period was exactly the one that, given the nature of their work, might have helped improve their condition. Mechanization was slow to spread in the German mining industry, and as late as 1900 most Ruhr coal was still won by hand with an advanced version of the primitive *Ruhrhacke*. By 1914 only 3 percent of German coal production used the new mining machines compared to 10 percent in England.[52]

But changes in the local iron, steel, and metalworking industry were equally disruptive. After 1850 the technology of steel making and metalworking underwent a series of important innovations that directly affected the positions of both skilled and unskilled metalworkers. It is unnecessary here to reiterate these changes in detail; we need only observe that their general consequences were, on the one hand, to substitute a series of simplified tasks performed on machines by unskilled and semiskilled men for the all-round skills of the artisan metalworker and, on the other, to replace the physical exertions of unskilled laborers with machine power.[53]

In the early iron and steel industry, the making and working of products required considerable manual dexterity, experience and understanding of materials. For example, the production of puddled steel was a skilled and demanding job involving a good deal of intuition about when the ball of molten iron was properly cooked.[54] The men who performed such tasks were artisans: at the Bochumer Verein, Mayer had recruited artisan metalworkers from the traditional centers of the metal trades.[55] Even within the industrial factory they continued to work as artisans employing all-round skills and enjoying considerable autonomy on the job. But technical and organizational changes introduced in the 1860s and after began to undermine the position of many skilled metalworkers. Most important was the introduction of new methods of making steel, particularly the Bessemer and Siemens-Martin processes, which virtually eliminated puddling and with it the skilled and expensive puddlers. The Bochumer Verein had erected its first puddling furnace between 1854 and 1857; but in 1865 a Bessemerwerk was completed and in 1874 a Martin-stahlwerk went into production.[56] During the same period, the new management introduced organizational changes that deprived the skilled metalworker of his former autonomy on the job, destroyed old ties between masters and apprentices and created a new rationalized hierarchy extending from the worker up through the foreman and engineers to top-level managers themselves.[57]

However, technological and organizational changes in the iron, steel, and metalworking trades did not foster a strong sense of oppositional solidarity among all skilled metalworkers, because it affected different categories of skilled men at different times and in different ways. Indeed some skilled workers were left virtually untouched by technical change until the early twentieth century. The fine skills of the puddler and the sure hand of the roller were progressively supplanted by new processes and mechanization. And the work of the planer, the borer, and certain lathe operators became increasingly simplified and routinized. But other metalworkers, particularly vice-hands, machine erectors, smiths, and smelters continued to perform relatively skilled jobs. Entry to these trades still required a certain training—apprenticeships lasted three to four years at the Bochumer Verein—and men working in them retained a larger degree of autonomy on the job, commanded good wages, and were dignified by old craft occupational names such as *Schlosser*, even when these no longer described the functions they performed in the factory.[58] Since they were almost always in short supply they could afford to be independent; in 1902, for instance, the Chamber of Commerce observed that even though a recession had forced employers to lay off large numbers of unskilled men, "the valuable and better workers are scarcely touched. These are held onto by every company at great cost."[59] Such workers obviously possessed a certain sense of occupational pride and dignity. In 1910, for example, the German Metalworkers Union reported that among the abuses that offended skilled metalworkers at the Bochumer Verein were the management's use of foul language and of the familiar "Du" when speaking both to young and old workers.[60]

Among the unskilled metalworkers technological innovation had similarly divisive results. On the one hand, mechanization of some production processes, particularly those involving the handling of materials, resulted in the elimination of many unskilled jobs. The early steel industry had employed armies of manual laborers to unload ore and coke from railway cars, to charge furnaces, and to pour ingots by hand. But the new processes, especially the Bessemer process, worked so much faster and produced so much more steel that only machines could keep up with them.[61] Yet at the same time that mechanization was depriving many unskilled manual laborers of their livelihood it was also providing others with new possibilities for promotion. Wherever formerly skilled tasks were being broken down into a series of simplified operations and these operations in turn mechanized, new positions as semiskilled machine tenders opened up that unskilled laborers could fill.[62] Obviously this change served to hinder any developed sense of solidarity among unskilled men; at the same time it made solidarity across skilled/ unskilled lines virtually unthinkable since the unskilled laborer was now a potential competitor for the skilled man's job.

Moreover, unlike many of the skilled men, unskilled laborers were recruited primarily from the ranks of rural and urban laborers. Compared to their past work experience, unskilled jobs in the local metal trades may have been an improvement. Until they formed new expectations, it was unlikely that these men would engage in collective action aimed at improving their situation.[63]

Yet, if we make this quite valid observation concerning unskilled factory workers, we must at the same time challege the idea that miners were protesting against disruptions of their traditional occupational structure. For like unskilled factory workers, the majority of miners were new recruits. By the mid-nineties only 37 percent of Ruhr mineworkers were themselves sons of miners, and possibly even fewer of the fathers had worked underground before the reform laws.[64] Most miners were inexperienced recent arrivals or sons of immigrants from the rural areas of the east and from the Rhineland and Westphalia. As we have seen, they were actually one of the main causes (or at least, symptoms) of the occupation's social decline. Yet these new workers protested along with natives and older miners. By 1905, for instance, 88 percent of the men at the local mine, Constantin der Grosse, were Ostdeutschen, and most of them joined in that year's walkout.[65] How could these men be protesting against changes they had never experienced?

The objections I have raised to each of the three main theories of protest would seem to have exhausted all possibilities of explaining why miners engaged in collective disturbances when other workers remained relatively quiet. Yet the fault lies not so much in the theories themselves but in what they seek to explain. Misery, uprooting, and change can all create grievances experienced individually by workers, but there is no guarantee that these grievances will be expressed collectively if they are all that binds the group together.

Indeed it is not difficult to see how some of these conditions of working class life, rather than building solidarity, isolated workers from each other. Richard Tilly has suggested that "people had to possess a sense of common identity and a certain amount of familiarity with the views and probable reactions of others before they were likely to engage in collective violence" and argues that "this common experience was not necessarily only that of deprivation itself."[66] Concerned as they have been with the early nineteenth century, the Tillys, Rudé, and other students of protest have been able to identify this sense of community only as it resulted from the shared experiences of relatively stable and settled social groups: the lower class inhabitants of a village or small town, or the artisans of an old neighborhood in a large city.[67] Miners, like many industrial workers, were neither stable nor settled, but their experience created a similar sense of "community," what I have termed "occupational community," which was the basis for their protest. Lacking this same experience, other workers were unable to achieve the solidarity which would have made collective action possible.

The Foundations of an Occupational Community

The sense of occupational community grew out of the total experience of workers in a specific branch of industry, but its first foundations were laid on the structure and nature of the work itself. As. E. J. Hobsbawm noted some years ago, mining is an industry in which "the habit of solidarity suggests itself naturally."[68] Even in the pre-reform period, the functional divisions among workers in the mines had been comparatively simple. The beginner started as a *Schlepper*, hauling wagons around in the mines, or as a building and repair worker. From there, usually after about two years, he entered a training period in which he learned how to win coal from the face. Finally he worked as an independent hewer.[69] Most workers went through all these stages, so they were familiar with the tasks and conditions each involved. The reform laws and industrialization, far from complicating this situation, actually simplified it by reducing training periods and hence lowering the skill barriers between workers.[70]

Of course, workers in the mines did receive different wages and were indeed paid by different methods. The haulers earned a set daily wage, while the hewers were paid according to the amount of coal produced.[71] This method of paying hewers no doubt fostered solidarity among them, since the piece rate was usually paid for group and not individual production. Hewers had to work well together or they would all suffer. Haulers could afford to be more independent, although their job also required cooperation. Perhaps most important was the fact that, despite these variations in the method of payment, the spread of wages underground was not as large as in an iron and steel mill or a machine building shop. During the whole period the ratio of the highest wage in the mines to the lowest rarely exceeded 1.5:1, whereas in the Bochumer Verein it could be 2.3:1.[72]

The wage structure and the division of labor underground made solidarity possible and even desirable, but danger made it essential. Miners needed to cooperate among themselves, not simply to perform their work but to safeguard their lives.

> The baker bakes his bread alone
> And so too the carpenter joins the chest without help
> But the miner on all his paths
> Needs brave and loyal comrades.[73]

Solidarity was certainly not a natural consequence of the work structure in the iron and steel industry. Indeed, the division of labor in the blast furnaces and the machine shops tended to fragment rather than unite the work force. The most obvious and formidable barrier separated the skilled from the unskilled metalworkers, and skilled men had a vital interest in maintaining this separation. Once a number of semiskilled men tending machines could be used to replace one skilled metalworker, the basis of the skilled man's position in the factory would be destroyed. On the other hand, the unskilled worker's prospects of advancement were entirely dependent on just such a process of skill dilution. Thus these two groups undoubtedly confronted each other with active and continuous hostility.[74]

This should not suggest, however, that skilled workers were themselves a cohesive group. Functional differences, widely varying pay rates and methods of payment, and, in large factories, isolation from fellow skilled workers, split these men into a number of small groups and subgroups. Even the workers within one trade—turners, fitters, or smiths, for instance—often worked under such a wide variety of conditions and were so isolated from each other on the job that any developed sense of occupational solidarity was rendered impossible. Let us take as an example the skilled smiths at the Bochumer Verein. As Table 5.11 indicates, workers in that occupation were employed in at least six different shops, performing different work and being paid (either by shift or piece rates) wages which ranged from a low of 5 marks to a high of 9 marks.[75]

Given this structure of work, solidarity was most likely to develop only when members of the same trade worked closely together and experienced similar conditions, for instance in a small and specialized factory. The striking filemakers at the Stegemann works fit into this pattern. But the development of a broader sense of solidarity among skilled metalworkers as a group, or even among skilled workers in the same trade working in a large factory, faced serious hindrance from the barriers imposed by the structure of the work itself.

Unskilled metalworkers were an even more fragmented group. Though they were not separated from each other by differences in training, they were split up into a seemingly endless variety of job classifications. In 1912 the German Metalworkers' Union complained that in German blast fur-

Table 5.11 Skilled Smiths at the Bochumer Verein, 1910

Number	Shop	Shift Rate	Piece Rate
3	Axle-turning shop	5.00	
4	Wheel-turning shop II		5.70
7	Switch-building shop		5.25
8	Blast furnace repair shop	5.25	
10	Hammer mill I		9.00
20	Hammer mill II		6.30
12	Hammer mill I		7.50
18	Hammer mill II		5.10

SOURCE: *Die Schwereisenindustrie*, p. 331.

naces alone there were no less than sixty different occupational categories, in steel works ninety-four, and in rolling mills no less than one hundred twenty-four, although "for the most part it is mainly a question here . . . of pure manual work, that every unskilled worker can carry out."[76] The report suggested that all these workers should simply be termed unskilled, but changing the name assigned to these tasks was not likely to have produced solidarity among the workers who performed them, since each category was associated with a minute but, to the worker, important difference in pay. At the Bessemer converter in the Bochumer Verein, for instance, there were usually four to five "converter men," each of whom was paid a different rate.[77] Instead of creating solidarity this "awakes the bad instincts of the men and creates envy, self-seeking, jealousy and other excrescences. The fifth man naturally is anxious soon to become fourth man and uses every means to reach this goal. The fourth man has perhaps the same ambition and so on."[78] The unions were quite aware of what this meant and endeavored, though without notable success, to instill in unskilled workers a sense of solidarity that the structure of their work had denied them:

Foundry workers must, without regard to their momentary position in the production process, always be conscious of the fact that they all suffer under the same yoke of capitalistic exploitation and that this yoke will not alter to their benefit by achieving a better paid post, rather . . . emancipation from their hard work is only possible through unanimous cohesion in a strong organization which is in the position energetically to represent the rights of all foundry workers.[79]

The structure of the miner's work created the foundations for his occupational community, but were not these foundations weakened by the variety of experiences the miner confronted as he moved from one job to another? Miners were, after all, extremely transient, more so than both skilled and unskilled metalworkers. But movement from one job in the mines to another, or from one town to the next, did not create discontinuities of experience. Indeed, even though he might change jobs often, the miner's work environment altered only insignificantly. Though working conditions and discipline might change from one mine to the next, the structure, the nature, and the dangers of work did not. And since the mineworker's specific function largely depended on his experience, he was likely to work at the same job wherever he went. All this no doubt made even the most transient workers aware that they shared common experiences and common interests with other miners not simply in one locality but in a whole district. Indeed, transience, far from reducing worker solidarity, may thus have strengthened it.[80]

For both skilled and unskilled metalworkers, on the other hand, movement did often represent a break with past experience. Changing jobs might lead the skilled metalworker from a mammoth enterprise like the Bochumer Verein to a small machine building shop, or in the other direction. As early as 1880, the size range of local metalworking enterprises ran from one employing only twenty-nine men to the Bochumer Verein with over four thousand. In the same year the smallest local mine had one hundred forty-eight workers, while the largest had only 1,689.[81] The conditions and nature of the work varied accordingly. Skilled journeymen metalworkers knew, for instance that in large plants they might only be producing one or two types of products, whereas in smaller factories they would have to be more versatile and for that reason often favored the latter for the practical experience they could gain there.[82] An unskilled worker might leave a job as a stoker in one place and sign on elsewhere as a helper or machine operator. His lack of specific skills not only made job changing relatively easy, but also meant that each move could bring a different work experience.[83] The varieties of experience that transient metalworkers confronted when they changed jobs was a far more important impediment to occupational solidarity than movement itself. Already divided among themselves within each factory, metalworkers were at the same time isolated from the experience of their counterparts in other factories even within the same locality.

Shared work experiences were crucial elements in the formation of occupational community, yet the sense of community included more than the work situation alone. In their neighborhoods, miners extended the bonds that had been forged among them at work and cemented that solidarity which every miner experienced not only in strikes but in his everyday life. Miners' neighborhoods both represented and maintained occupational solidarity because in them miners and their wives and children were unlikely to come into frequent or close contact with anyone who was not also a miner or a member of a miner's family. Miners' neighborhoods did not of course approach the total occupational homogeneity of the isolated mining village,[84] but they did segregate miners from other workers in the city sufficiently to give occupational community a clear geographical expression. As Table 5.12 indicates, miners were usually clustered in a limited number of wards of the city in which large numbers of other workers were seldom to be found. Almost 72 percent of the miners in the sample lived in only four of the city's wards; in the first, second, and third in the north near the *Präsident* mine, and in the seventh, near the smaller mines to the south in the Ruhr valley. Here, with some exceptions, miners had few other workers for neighbors; indeed, clusters of streets within individual wards were inhabited almost exclusively by miners and their families. Metalworkers, on the other hand, lived in far more heterogeneous districts; in only one ward,

Table 5.12 Occupation and Ward Residence, 1880 (in Percent)

	Ward											
Occupation	*1*	*2*	*3*	*4*	*5*	*6*	*7*	*8*	*9*	*10*	*11*	*12*
Miners	29.1	14.1	15.7	5.5	4.7	2.4	12.6	3.1	5.5	3.1	3.9	0.0
Unskilled factory workers	6.2	3.7	0.8	1.2	2.1	2.5	3.7	8.6	14.8	5.8	11.1	39.5
Day laborers	10.9	13.2	7.0	5.4	7.8	1.6	3.9	17.8	10.1	6.2	10.9	5.4
Skilled metalworkers	6.9	5.2	6.9	3.4	13.8	10.3	3.4	13.8	17.2	10.3	6.9	1.7
Skilled building workers	11.5	3.3	4.9	1.6	4.9	4.9	13.1	16.4	13.1	18.0	3.3	4.9
Artisan: food, etc.	8.8	8.8	15.8	1.8	21.1	7.0	10.5	5.3	3.5	12.3	3.5	1.8
Artisan: wood, etc.	10.9	6.5	6.5	10.9	10.9	17.4	6.5	17.4	4.3	4.3	4.3	0.0

SOURCE: Data derived from the mobility study.

the twelfth, were unskilled metalworkers isolated to any extent, mainly as a consequence of company housing, which dominated this area. Elsewhere, however, both skilled and unskilled metalworkers congregated in wards that also had high concentrations of other types of workers.

As a consequence of these patterns of residence, metalworkers were far more likely than miners to have other workers for neighbors. If we compare the distribution of day laborers, skilled building workers, and artisans in the wards where miners lived most frequently and in those most commonly the residence of metalworkers, we can see this quite clearly (Table 5.13).

Patterns of neighborhood segregation changed little before the war. Miners continued to live near the mines in the north and the south of the city, while metalworkers found housing near the Bochumer Verein and the smaller factories clustered around it in the city's western and central districts. Mass transportation did little to change these residential patterns; the first streetcar line was not opened until 1894, and as late as 1911 one observer commented that "Nowhere do special cars . . . run between home and workplace and no account is taken of the change of shifts in the timetable. This no doubt serves to explain why everywhere the worker lives close to his place of work".[85] Internally, miners' neighborhoods maintained greater continuity than those favored by other workers (Table 5.14). Despite the deficiencies of the local transport system, many workers did move from one ward to another in search of better or cheaper housing or when they changed jobs. Though miners did leave the city altogether more often

Table 5.13 Distribution of Day Laborers, Skilled Building Workers, and Artisans in Miner and Metalworker Neighborhoods, 1880 (in Percent)

	Neighborhoods	
Occupation	Miner	Metalworker
Day laborers	35.0	59.8
Skilled building workers	32.8	65.5
Artisan: food, etc.	43.9	54.5
Artisan: wood, etc.	30.4	58.6

SOURCE: Data derived from the mobility study.

Table 5.14 Ward Persisters, 1880–1901 (in Percent)

	Persisting to 1890		Persisting to 1901	
Occupation	Same ward	Another ward	Same ward	Another ward
Miners	71.4	28.6	66.6	33.4
Unskilled factory workers	54.9	45.1	45.8	54.2
Skilled metalworkers	47.6	52.4	23.5	76.8
Skilled building workers	72.7	27.3	65.2	44.8
Artisan: food, etc.	46.2	53.8	51.9	48.1
Artisan: wood, etc.	48.4	51.6	47.1	52.9

SOURCE: Data derived from the mobility study.

than many other workers, those who settled there tended more than most manual laborers to stay put in their neighborhoods and not to venture into other districts of the city. This relative stability meant that some miners had lived together for quite a long time.

Moreover, the relative homogeneity of the mineworkers' neighborhoods was preserved over the years by the fact that a miner who stopped working in the pits and took up another form of work generally left the old neighborhood as well whereas it was more common for other workers who changed their jobs to remain where they had previously been living. This meant that the occupational complexion of miners' neighborhoods was more constant over time than those where other types of workers lived. For miners then, the link between occupation and neighborhood was both strong and enduring.

The collective experience of work underground and life together in the neighborhood forged a sense of solidarity among miners. Marriage was both a test of that solidarity and a possibility for its reaffirmation and renewal. A miner who married outside his circle of fellow workers acquired new relatives and new friends, thereby exposing himself to experiences of the industrial world different from his own. A miner who married a miner's daughter kept the circle closed. Yet obviously, it was impossible for all miners to marry women from the same occupational backgrounds simply because there were never enough of them. What we need then is a measure of tendency; some means of determining what role occupation played in influencing marriage patterns. The "Intermarriage Index" provides such a measure: if the Index is found to be 50, then we can assume that occupational background played no role in the choice of a marriage partner.[86] Deviations in either direction indicate that occupation did play a role; if the Index is less than 50 this indicates a definite avoidance of intermarriage with the group concerned, whereas an Index over fifty shows a positive attraction. The stronger the deviation, the more important the role of occupation. The index of intermarriage of miners with miners' daughters was 124, with daughters of unskilled factory workers 64, and with daughters of skilled metalworkers 71.[87] Marriage therefore confirmed rather than challenged the miner's sense of belonging to an occupational community.

Much more so than for unskilled or skilled metalworkers, then, the miner's residential and marriage patterns reinforced the solidarity that was created, in the first instance, by the structure of his work. Since the miner's personality and his occupation were so intimately associated, it was predictable that grievances experienced individually would be expressed in collective protest. The nature of this protest is the subject of the following chapter.[88]

six

Miners' Strikes in 1889, 1905, and 1912

NO SOURCE AVAILABLE to the historian is likely to reveal all that he or she wants to know about the attitudes of ordinary people, how they responded to their work, how they perceived the society in which they lived, and what they expected to get from it. But, as Peter Stearns has recently and, I think, correctly argued, "The best starting point in determining what workers wanted is a summary of the goals and methods of strikes."[1] This argument is particularly applicable to the Ruhr miners.

Strikes were the earliest forms of collective protest among miners. There had already been two miners' strikes in the Ruhr valley (one in 1872, confined largely to the Essen area, and a second more important walkout in 1889)[2] before miners began to seriously organize trade unions. Indeed, the organization that was later to become the most important trade union, the Alter Verband, actually grew out of the miners' strike in 1889 and the lessons its failure had taught miners.[3] Knappenvereine, Rechtsschutzvereine and other miners' organizations had indeed been formed much earlier in the 1860s and 1870s; Bochum had an evangelical workers' club in the early 1880s along with a Catholic Rechtsschutzverein started by the editor Fusangel, while neighboring Amt Wattenscheid already had a Christian-Social workers' club in 1882 and Amt Bochum Sud a Christian miners' club in 1885.[4] However these were not, strictly speaking, modern trade unions whose primary function was to represent the workers' interests on the job and create solidarity for collective bargaining, but rather multi-functional clubs devoted to promoting sociability, providing mutual assistance and nurturing moral and religious sentiments.[5] The miners' club formed in Amt Bochum Sud in 1885, for instance, aimed at promoting "moral and general education, as well as Protestant religiosity among the faithful, support in sickness and death," while the East Prussian evangelical workers' union in neighboring Hofstede strove to further religion, morality, loyalty to the Kaiser and Reich, education, and mutual assistance.[6] Only after the 1889 strike and the emergence of the socialist Alter Verband did most of these workers' clubs see the need of exercising the functions of a trade union.[7]

But neither the activities of trade unions nor the opinions expressed by trade union leaders, many of whom were not miners at all, can uncritically be accepted as pure expressions of rank-and-file sentiment.[8] Of the three strikes here under consideration, only the last and least popular in 1912 began and was conducted under union auspices; even that one was opposed by the confessional unions. In 1889, as one strike leader put it, "the strike came like a sickness overnight."[9] Leaders of the existing workers' organizations looked on it as a mistake and obviously had little if any control of the strikers; on 17 May, for instance, the Protestant Arbeiterverein in Bochum pleaded with its members to think of the results of a long strike for their families, for the workers in the local factories and elsewhere, as well as for German trade, and finished rather pathetically by reminding its members,

that you stand on the foundation of evangelical confession and that you run the risk of contravening the commands and the laws of the state! Show the world that our miner is still the same upright [brave] miner, the same peace-loving worker, the same pious Christian that he has been for centuries.[10]

Although the 1905 strike was supported by the Alter Verband, the union's leaders were obviously not prepared to go as far as the rank-and-file themselves. When the men walked off the job at the Bruchstrasse mine in neighboring

Langendreer, the Socialist Reichstagabgeordnete and miners' leader Sachse warned that the strike must remain local since there was no chance of success for a general walkout, "which would only forfeit the sympathy of the 'Bürgerstand.'" But within three days of that statement, sixty mines employing about eighty thousand men in the Ruhr valley had been struck. On the other hand many leaders of the Evangelical Workers' union did not support the walkout at all, no matter how limited it remained; on the twenty-sixth the Evangelical Arbeiterbund met in Bochum to find "a practical way out of the present confusion surrounding the strike." Editor Quandel, founder of the Arbeiterbund, told his audience that he "did not reject the use of strikes in principle, but they must be justified and have some prospect of success," conditions he obviously did not think applied to this walkout.[11]

Although the 1912 strike was directly provoked by one union, the Alter Verband, it was bitterly opposed by another, the Christliche Gewerkverein.[12] However, the decision of rank-and-file miners to participate seems to have depended far less on their union loyalties than on their individual opinion of the strike and the intensity of pressures to join in from men already off the job. At a meeting on March 14, the Socialist editor Pokoing from Düsseldorf assured his listeners that the number of strikers was growing daily and that the "Christian" miners were joining the strike in bunches, despite their leaders' warnings to remain uninvolved. He also noted that at a special conference the Christliche Gewerkverein had decided to allow members who had already joined in the walkout to continue striking. Yet only four days later an observer at the mine Carolinenglück reported that many members of the Alter Verband were already returning to work and that by Tuesday there were enough men on the job at Carolinenglück, Engelsburg, and Präsident so that two shifts could be run.[13] Even in this, the most controlled of the three miners' strikes, union discipline was fragile and the element of spontaneity continued to be extremely important.

Participation in a strike reflected a relatively intense commitment to protest, since the risks involved were greater than in joining a union. When miners walked off the job they were not only forfeiting their wages but running the risk of losing their jobs; since German law forbade unexcused absences from work for more than four consecutive shifts, employers could and often did discharge strikers. In 1905, for example, a number of local mines sent firing notices by mail accompanied by this explanation:

Since you have remained away from work for more than four shifts you are hereby discharged according to section three of the work rules. Any claims for back wages can be registered at the central office. Otherwise, you are hereby warned that from today on you are forbidden ever to enter the mine yards again.[14]

In 1912 another local mine threatened any worker who did not return by the following Sunday with automatic dismissal.[15] And all miners realized that even if they were not fired they might be fined or punished in various ways once they did go back on the job. Thus, in each of the three strikes, a central demand was that the miners' delegates "not be disciplined" once the men had returned to work.[16] Moreover, the men living in company homes were vulnerable to other forms of employer retaliation since their rent contract automatically ended when they stopped working. In 1905, for example, at some mines in Langendreer, it was reported that "the striking miners who live in company homes have until February 1 to get out." At the Dannenbaum mine, a number of strikers had already been evicted.[17]

Finally, all miners faced either the complete or partial reduction of the sickness and accident benefits afforded them by the Knappschaften when they stayed off work for more than three shifts. In 1905 the striking miners were told that they would be stricken from the list of those employed "so that we can take appropriate measures with regard to sickness insurance liability."[18] In 1912 the Knappschaftsverein warned that "all miners who have been members for five years can retain their eligibility through payment of fifteen *Pfennige* per week." But those men who had been members for less than five years, "are separated when they stop work for over a week and cannot revive their eligibility if they are over forty years of age. If, however, they are under forty then their eligibility will be revived again after another year's membership."[19]

If, then, relatively large numbers of miners were prepared to take all of the risks that going on strike involved, as they were in 1889, 1905 and 1912 (see p. 161), we must assume that the grievances that motivated them were of considerable importance and widely shared. They therefore warrant detailed consideration.

The Strike Demands

What did miners expect to achieve by their protest? What grievances were sufficiently important to cause them to risk a strike and the sufferings that it involved? The best way to answer these questions is to look closely and carefully at the strike demands that the miners themselves presented.

The 1889 strike began with a walkout of the haulers for higher wages but very rapidly developed into a widespread protest among all classes of miners for considerably more complex aims. A letter from the miners at Zeche Präsident on May 7 demanded a 20 percent increase in the contract price paid to hewers for winning the coal, an eight-hour day, including the ride to the pit bottom and the ascent and, finally, delivery of the wood (pit props) to the working site itself. On May 9 a mass meeting of five thousand local miners advanced all three of these demands and also called for a ban on overtime and abolition of the fines for wagonloads of coal that were rejected by the overseer for being impure. But, as the miner Bauer argued, not all of these demands were equally important to the strikers; "The eight hour shift is the cardinal issue of the whole strike; we cannot give it up under any circumstances." Most of his audience seemed to agree; when a young miner suggested that overtime shifts should still be permitted he was firmly shouted down.[20]

On May 13 several more grievances were added to those already raised. The miners now demanded that workers who had no previously arranged contract should be paid a normal shift wage of 4 marks whenever flooding, bad air, or other stoppages interfered with their work. They also asked that shifts be changed each week, that oil for their lamps and blasting materials be provided at 5 marks per shift and at cost respectively, and that satisfactory wash houses be erected at the pit head. Finally, miners demanded that a traditional perquisite of minework, house coal, continue to be provided them at a specified cost, indicating that many employers were no longer doing so.[21]

Yet it was the length of the work day that interested miners most. When Sachse, one of the strikers' representatives, met with the Kaiser in Berlin on May 14 he told him, "We are demanding only what we have inherited from our fathers, namely the eight hour day. Increases in pay are far less important to us . . ." When the strike ended in failure some days later, miners were still clinging to their hopes for a shorter work day; a report of May 24 observed that now the miners had modified their request to an eight-and-a-half hour shift including the trip down and back up.[22]

It was a conflict between workers and management at the Bruchstrasse mine in neighboring Langendreer over increasing the trip to pit bottom and thereby the work day that provoked the next general strike in 1905. At a meeting of two to three hundred miners in Langendreer, Alter Verband representative Sachse protested the lengthening of the descent and ascent and told the workers they must now begin fighting for a nine-hour day, then the following year for eight and a half hours, then the year after that for eight hours. By January 11 the walkout had spread to the Dorstfeld, Borussia, Margarethe, Prinz Regent, Dannenbaum II and III, and Hercules mines. Here, other but closely related grievances had aroused the miners: "The first and foremost of the complaints . . . concerns the *Wagennullen*," the overseers' practice of not counting all wagonloads of coal that were "impure," (i.e., contained stones, etc.). The miners at these pits wanted some legal means that "would permit an exact, constant test of the *Wagennullen* by a controller appointed by the workers."[23] Complaints were also made about the length of the trip to pit bottom and the mine overseers were charged with mistreating the workers.[24] Miners at these pits were also angry about the way they were paid—every month instead of every week or two weeks—but did not seem as concerned with how much they were earning: "The question of wages is of secondary importance."[25]

Local meetings on the twelfth and thirteenth at the Präsident, Dannenbaum, and Friederika mines raised similar demands and unveiled other grievances. For instance, these miners charged that they had been forced to pay 65 pfg. for the *Hackensteile*, their digging implement, which previously had cost only 35 pfg. In addition, they complained that pit props were often of poor quality, sometimes completely unsuitable and frequently were stolen from already dug-out sections. The miners also claimed that, although the local work force had grown considerably in recent years, the pit head baths had not been expanded to keep pace with it: "Men are standing head to head." Often the water was too hot, then too cold so that their health suffered. Moreover, even though it directly contravened the *Bergpolizeiordnungen* and obviously outraged the older miners' sense of propriety, the boys under eighteen and the older men were forced to wash together in the same room.[26] Finally, in an unusual display of solidarity that overrode ethnic prejudices, the miners also complained about the unsanitary living conditions that young, single Poles and Italians were forced to endure in the company dormitories.

At the Julius Philipp mine in Querenburg, the workers demanded that they be allowed to choose their own carters to haul house coal, since those supplied by the mines often charged up to 2 marks per delivery. Three days later, a meeting of the same miners gave their approval to the mine director's promise to set up a family sickness fund, to sell house coal to workers and invalids for 2.25 marks, to make no claims for damages against workers who had stayed off the job for more than three shifts, and to end the monopolistic agreement with the carters for house coal deliveries. The miners then agreed to go back on the job but warned that if they were required to do more than the normal amount of work, or should unusual amounts of coal be shipped (which would weaken the bargaining position of the other miners who were still on strike), then they would stop work again and contribute one third of their pay to the strike fund.[27]

On January 13 a meeting of miners from the whole Bochum area synthesized these variegated local demands into a ten-point strike platform. The meeting called for the nine-hour day to be introduced in 1905, eight and a half hours in 1906, and the eight-hour day later on. The *Wagennullen* was to be abolished and wagons henceforth to be paid by weight alone under the inspection of a controller hired by the workers themselves. Hewers were to be given a minimum wage of 5 marks, haulers 3.80 marks, and horse drivers and brakemen 3 marks, with a worker committee being set up to rule on wage disagreements and help administer the accident and sickness fund. House coal was to be supplied at cost, the Knappschaften were to be reformed according to the plan advanced by the workers' unions, the Oberbergamt was to be called in as arbitrator, and no fines or penalties were to be levied against the strikers once they had returned to work.[28]

Seven days later in Bochum, another general meeting heard the chairman of the Christian Gewerkverein, Kuhne, repeat their demands for an eight-hour day and call for the abolition of overtime shifts except when absolutely necessary. He approved the idea of having a wagon inspector, but warned his audience that it would make little difference if the controller complained when the overseer rejected a load, since the section leader would simply accuse him of trying to hold up production. It would be far simpler, he suggested, just to have a minimum wage of 5 marks so that the hewer would be protected against unfavorable working conditions. The workers' committees were absolutely essential, Kuhne argued, because now, when a worker went and complained about his contract to the Berggewerbegericht, he was usually fired the next day. As to the *Wagennullen* and the fines, Kuhne suggested that the mines and not the miners should worry whether the coal was pure enough. Finally, Kuhne raised a new grievance that revealed how the miners' sense of oppression at the hands of their employers had extended beyond the work situation itself: "it is sad," Kuhne remarked,

that the bosses feel they must combine the rent agreement with the work agreement . . . we don't want this compulsory arrangement, we demand to be allowed a month's notice on our accomodations.[29]

In 1889 and 1905 it had been the rank-and-file who had spoken and the leaders who had attempted to combine their disparate grievances into a coherent regional strike platform.

But in 1912 the strike had a completely different tone, for it was clearly the least spontaneous and least popular of the three major work stoppages. The strike was the final outcome of a campaign launched by three of the workers' unions two years earlier. In the fall of 1910, the Alter Verband invited the other miners' unions to support a joint demand for higher wages. The Christian Gewerkverein refused on the grounds that this was simply an excuse for the Alter Verband to swallow up the other unions. Two more meetings in 1911 and 1912 ended in a similar impasse. Finally the Alter Verband, the Hirsch Duncker Gewerkverein, and the Polish union agreed to send a petition to the employers by themselves. It demanded wage increases, abolition of the *Arbeitsnachweis* (the employers' labor exchange), and called for an eight-hour shift and improvements in the Knappschaften. The Zechenverband responded to the petition by saying that wage increases could be expected if business remained good and got better, but warned that it had no authority to speak directly for the mineowners on wage matters. Therefore, on February 19, 1912, the three unions sent these and other demands directly to the individual mines. Since, as Koch argues, the unions must have known their demands would not be accepted, this action made a walkout inevitable.[30]

From the first day of the strike, the grievances of rank-and-file miners were pushed into the background by the welter of charges, counter-charges, and mutual abuse that union leaders leveled against each other. At meetings held by the evangelical Arbeiterbund and the Christian Gewerkverein on March 8, 9, 12, and 13, union leaders warned that the socialists and the Alter Verband meant to absorb the Christian unions and that the strike had been fomented purely for "political reasons" to divert attention from the socialist defeat in the recent Reichstag elections. "I ask you Christian-National miners," implored the secretary of the Christlicher Gewerkverein on the twelfth, "is there a purpose to this strike (Shouting from the audience for several minutes; No!) Should we strike here while elsewhere miners are working?"[31]

Naturally, the Alter Verband and the socialists responded to these charges by claiming that the Christian unions did not represent the true sentiments of the rank-and-file. At a meet-

ing on the fourteenth, the socialist editor Pokoing observed
that many Christian miners were actually joining the walkout
despite their leaders' warnings and accused the Gewerkverein
of "moral bankruptcy" for not supporting the strike. Yet the
Alter Verband leaders could themselves make no better claim
to speak for the ordinary miner, since in only one of their
strike meetings did they discuss the workers' actual grievances in any detail. At that meeting on the seventeenth, the
chairman of the Alter Verband told his audience that

If the mine bosses had satisfied our demands we would have peace.
What we must have now, unconditionally, is an immediate ten per
cent increase and a later increase of five per cent along with an end
to the overtime and "side-shifts" which are endangering our health,
a reduction of the time between wage payments and removal of the
Knappschaft deductions, at least with regard to the children's allow-
ances that have been newly created by the Imperial insurance
scheme.[32]

But by the seventeenth it was already too late; the strike
leaders had spent too much time denouncing each other and
too little articulating the demands of the rank-and-file. By the
eighteenth, "many members of the Alter Verband" were
observed going back to work at the Carolinengluck mine, so
that there and also at Engelsburg and Präsident, "from Tuesday on it has been possible to run two shifts." By the nineteenth, even the Alter Verband leader, Loffler, was forced to
concede that "the actions of the police and the swindles of the
Christians with the employers has reduced the number of
strikers from 230,000 to 172,000 [in the Ruhr valley]." After
much "soul-searching," the regional strike conference finally
asked the miners to return to work.[33]

The Meaning of the Strike Demands

Time, Money, and the Intensity of Labor

The situation that provided a unifying theme for the miners'
strike demands was the ongoing battle between the employer
and the worker for the latter's time and effort. Miners were

first of all concerned with the growing amount of unpaid time they were being asked to spend on the job. As the mines grew deeper, the length of the descent to pit bottom, as well as the ride back up, increased considerably (at some mines it was already more than half an hour by the 1880s) as did the distance from the entry shaft to each team's coal face.[34] The miner was asked to contribute the time and effort involved in these journeys for nothing, since he only started to earn his daily wage when he actually began digging coal. Moreover, many employers began to demand that their men appear for work long before they could actually be lowered into the pit. According to Bergamt regulations, the miner was expected to appear for the descent one half-hour before the shift began, but mines with large work forces and inadequate winding gear found it impossible to get all their men below ground in just thirty minutes. Therefore, "alongside the officially decreed beginning of the descent, an earlier, unofficial time is enforced by brutal coercion."[35] This meant that some miners had to stand around waiting while others were being lowered to pit bottom. And since any miner still above ground by 5:45 (the shift began at 6:00) would be sent home and lose a day's work, "the men come earlier and earlier, everyone wants to be the first one at the descent so that he will not lose a shift . . . as early as three-thirty men appear for the trip to pit bottom." Nor could the miner expect to get out of the mine any faster than he had entered it. At the end of the day, "the men must . . . often wait for a long time without being paid. First, so and so many wagons of coal must be lifted out; only then can the miner ascend." As a result, by 1905, "for many workers the eight hour shift has become ten hours or more."[36]

Unpaid demands on the miner's time were, however, not restricted to the descent and ascent; they also intruded into his work at the coal face and affected both his income and the pace of his work. Miners worked in *Gedinge,* that is, they contracted as a team to produce a certain amount of coal for a given price.[37] All other tasks besides winning coal were either unpaid or else were paid at a lower rate, so that miners were obviously interested in keeping time spent on such work to a minimum. Thus they argued that pit props for shoring up dug-out areas should be brought directly to them rather than having to waste their time fetching them. There also seem to have been incessant conflicts over how much timbering should be done, in which miners, despite the danger, often argued for less than the overseers wanted. Miners also complained about the overseers' practice of rejecting all wagons of coal containing stones, earth, or other impurities since this also meant that they were forced to work more and harder without getting paid for their additional labor.

Under these combined pressures from employers, the pace of work underground had noticeably intensified since the 1860s and 1870s:

Whereas in the old days when the miner came down into the pit he started off by looking around for this and that and by exchanging a pleasant word here and there . . . today everybody hurries . . . to the coalface to begin work.[38]

But it was not simply the passing of older routines of work and sociability that miners lamented; longer, more arduous hours underground seriously taxed the miner's physical strength and endurance. In 1889 the Knappschaft elder, Sacker, warned that extra shifts below ground ruined the miner's health, while the miner Weber observed that, as the pits grew deeper, they also became hotter and more dangerous. In 1905 miners' delegate Sachse connected the increasing length of the descent, and thus of the work day itself, to the rising incidence of invalidism among miners and to the fact that the average age at which a miner became an invalid had now been reduced to forty-six. In a later meeting, Kuhne, chairman of the Christian Gewerkverein, agreed with Sachse's opinion, adding that since the mines were now much deeper and hotter than thirty years before, there should be no overtime unless absolutely necessary. Ten or twelve years ago, Kuhne warned, the rate of illness was already 54–56 percent per year; in 1901 it had risen to 61 percent and in the last few years had climbed still higher to 71 percent. Moreover, Kuhne argued that miners were becoming invalids even earlier than Sachse had suggested; whereas sixty years earlier the average age of invalidism was fifty-one, it now had dropped to forty-four. Confronted with this evidence, many miners could feel that their long hours underground made them something less than human beings; as one socialist speaker at a meeting in 1908 put it, "We do not live to work, but rather we work in order to live; if it is true that Man is a higher being than the animals, then Man should not be used like a work horse. Under present conditions, life is simply a torture for the worker."[39]

Wage Demands

Miners raised wage demands in all three of these strikes. In 1889, they called for a 20 to 35 percent pay raise. In 1905, along with immediate wage increases, they demanded a guaranteed minimum wage for all classes of workers, since, under prevailing conditions, many were not earning enough. And, finally, of course, the 1912 strike concentrated primarily on the wage question.[40]

What can these wage demands tell us about the consciousness of Ruhr miners? Recently, Peter Stearns has suggested that strike demands can be ranked according to their degree of "sophistication." The least sophisticated wage demands, for example, aim solely at regaining ground lost to wage cuts or possibly to inflation. On the other hand, the most sophisticated wage demands will be "genuinely offensive," reflecting a readiness on the part of workers to demand as much for their labor as the market will bear as well as their willingness to compensate for dissatisfactions experienced on the job by means of progressively higher economic rewards and a better standard of living. Defensive wage demands thus reflect only the worker's desire to protect previously achieved standards, whereas offensive wage demands reveal "a real attachment to material progress."[41]

Certainly, none of the three miners' strikes under consideration here seem to have been responses to the fact that miners' incomes were being directly threatened or undercut. Both the 1889 and 1912 strikes occurred after income had been steadily improving for some time. And the 1905 strike followed a sharp, but only partial relapse of income, which had already recovered from a far more serious low reached in

1903. Moreover, miners do not seem to have been responding primarily to losses from inflation. Throughout most of the period, food prices seem only to have kept pace with income; in general they did not outrun it. Indeed, the years before the 1889 strike, when income was rising, were actually marked by a decline in the cost of pork and beef on the local market, although wheat, rye, and potatoes—all important working class foodstuffs—showed definite increases. Potato prices in particular showed sharp increases from 1887 to 1888 but were already dropping down to their 1886 level in the year of the strike itself. The sharpest rises during the period occurred between 1890 and 1892, when wages were also rising rapidly. Pork, beef, and butter prices remained fairly steady from this point onward, although potato, wheat, and rye prices tended to fluctuate more. Considerable food price inflation was reported in 1911 and again in 1912, but income increases were still usually great enough to offset the effects of inflation.

In any case, the size and buying power of the miner's income, while obviously crucial to the working class budget, was not the only important factor to the miner himself, because in mining the size of income did not always, or even usually, reflect wage rates. During much of the nineteenth and early twentieth century, when miners increased their income, this was more likely to have resulted from working more shifts per week, month, or year, or from having worked harder during a given shift, than from being paid more for the same amount of work.[42] Miners' wage demands, then, rather than representing a separate set of grievances or aspirations, arose from and were intricately interwoven with the issues of work length and intensity that we have already discussed.

In assessing his material situation, the miner had to balance out two factors against each other. On the one hand, miners obviously had to be interested in the total amount of their income. But, at the same time, given the arduous, dangerous, and already pressured nature of their work, they were also concerned with how long and how hard they had to work for a given amount of income. The most fortunate situation in which a miner could find himself was to be earning high enough piece rates that he could actually afford a degree of relief from the rigors of his work. As the Chamber of Commerce complained in 1899, during a period of prosperity,

This improvement of the living standard of the worker is a very happy phenomenon in the present boom period; however, a large percentage of workers are not [properly] utilizing this quite favorable business cycle, higher wages are inducing them to cut back on time worked, so that, repeatedly, shifts are missed and . . . Monday is a complete holiday. [Consequently] complaints are being heard about declining productivity in mining.[43]

Similarly, the British Board of Trade reported, in a 1908 survey of German towns, that

The "played shifts" [gefeierte Schichten] are the despair of some of the collieries in busy times. By way of illustration, in one large mine 8.52 percent of an aggregate of nearly 500,000 shifts [i.e. the number of shifts multiplied by the average number of men] were "played" in 1905, and after making allowance for all sick leaves and leaves of absence, the great majority were regarded as unjustifiable abstentions from work. The losses in wages was nearly 10,000 M.[44]

Conversely, miners were likely to regard themselves as less fortunate to the extent to which this trade-off between earning additional income and gaining relief from work in the mines became more and more difficult. Indeed, it is not surprising to find that not only the 1889 strike but also the 1905 and 1912 walkouts followed periods of several years in which the possibilities of making this trade-off had progressively diminished.

The 1889 strike followed on a quite long period in which miners' wages had dropped remarkably and their work intensity increased considerably. Although miners' total annual income began to rise significantly, especially after 1886, this was primarily the result of miners being allowed to work more shifts per year and not the consequence of significantly improved piece rates. Indeed, as late as September 1887, the *Gedingelohn* of coal face workers was reported to be 2.70–3 marks on the average, while *Schlepper* were earning 2–2.10 marks. By the end of April 1889 (the month before the strike), average wages for hewers had indeed risen to between 3.20 and 4.60 marks, while for *Schlepper* they ranged from 2.30 to

3 marks.[45] Yet, all these figures were still lower than the over-all averages for 1874, the last year before the onset of the Great Depression.[46] Miners had thus endured a prolonged period in which they had been required to work progressively harder and longer for daily wage rates below pre-Depression levels. In the period before the strike, their total income began to improve, but they gained less of an advantage in terms either of reducing work intensity and working day(s) or improved wage rates (which amounted to different sides of the same coin). Now, in the 1889 strike, they demanded improved wage rates so that their other major demand—for a reduced working day—could be met without their losing out in terms of total income.

Roughly similar conditions seem to have set the stage for both the 1905 and 1912 walkouts. In 1900, for example, a coal face worker earned on average 5.16 marks per shift and gained a total yearly income of 1,592 marks by working some 308.5 shifts per year (Table 6.1). However, in the years that followed, piece rates were reduced as managers tried to cut costs and increase productivity, so that miners found themselves work-ing harder for less money per shift. Even in 1904 and 1905, when shift rates had begun to improve again, the miner was still in a relatively worse position than he had been in 1900; to earn the same annual income as he had in 1900, he would have had to work at least twenty shifts per year more than at the turn of the century. For the men who joined in the 1912 strike, the reference point was 1907, a year in which shift wages had reached 5.98 marks on average for coal face work-ers who earned 1,871 marks by working 312.9 shifts. From that year onward until at least the first quarter of 1912, low-

Table 6.1 Number of Shifts Necessary for Miners To Work To Earn Same Income as in Base Year

Base Year 1900 = 308.5	Base Year 1907 = 312.9
1901 = 319.6	1908 = 319.3
1902 = 348.4	1909 = 351.0
1903 = 343.1	1910 = 348.4
1904 = 333.1	1911 = 337.1
1905 = 328.9	1912 = 259.5

ered piece rates meant that miners could not have earned the same income without working harder and without working considerably more shifts per year.[47]

It is difficult, then, to categorize miners' wage demands as either "defensive" or "offensive" in terms of the way Stearns uses these categories. Wage demands were not presented by miners simply to restore a previously achieved standard of income, nor, on the other hand, were miners primarily interested in compensating for "job dissatisfactions" (lengthening hours, increasing work intensity) by higher wages. What miners wanted was to reduce those "job dissatisfactions" without losing income, and to do that higher wage rates were necessary.[48]

It could, of course, be argued that the 1912 strike, in which for the first time wage demands became the dominant issue, demonstrates a basic change in the nature of workers' grievances and/or demands, a new willingness to accept "job dissatisfactions" and to compensate for them by demanding higher pay. Yet the 1912 strike was also the first real union-organized walkout, and this undoubtedly affected the nature of the demands advanced. Tilly and Shorter have recently suggested that in France,

strikes waged over job control issues tended to fail more often than strikes in general, and a lost strike could devastate a struggling union. Bureaucratization meant for union leaders a greater concern for preserving the integrity of the organization. . . and leaders who thought this way would avoid explosive authority issues that could shatter the union into fragments.[49]

But this in effect meant that it was the employers rather than the rank and file or even the union leaders who played the dominant role in defining what questions were and what issues were not open for discussion. Keith Burgess argues that in British mining this meant that "the focus of collective bargaining centered on the wage" since "other issues were rarely accepted by the owners as subject to joint negotiations" even though there is evidence of continued rank-and-file discontent relating to these issues.[50] Ruhr mine operators were even less willing to negotiate with striking miners than were their British counterparts; but, as Albin Gladen and Stephen Hickey have recently pointed out, the one area in which Ruhr employers might make concessions was wages.[51] Undoubtedly, this influenced the kinds of demands the unions decided to advance in 1912. Yet the relatively weak support given to that strike suggests that, in this instance at least, the unions may not have been speaking directly for the men.[52]

Other Grievances

Apart from their grievances concerning the length of the work day, the conditions under which coal was won, and wages, miners also raised demands that their customary perquisites be retained or restored. Chief among these was the demand that house coal continue to be supplied to the miner at traditionally low prices.

House coal was important to the miner not just as the last remnant of a once-privileged status, but because it was an essential element of his "domestic economy." Well into the twentieth century, an important part of the subsistence of many miners' families did not depend on cash; wages were used to pay rent and to buy staples such as flour, coffee, spirits, and clothing, but the family also raised animals (usually goats, pigs, and rabbits) as well as vegetables on the small plot of land attached to their house, and used the coal provided by the mine for heating and cooking. Even some of the most urbanized miners continued to maintain these habits, as the 1907 livestock census in the city clearly reveals.[53] Obviously, the mines' decision to abolish the house coal privilege or to charge market prices for it seriously disrupted the delicate balance on which the livelihood of the miner's family was poised.

Miners might have been less reluctant to accept elimination or reduction of the house coal privilege and other customary perquisites had employers offered to compensate them with increased cash wages. But since employers had eliminated house coal in an effort to cut costs, it was not very likely that they would be willing to do this. House coal was a grievance at several mines in the 1905 strike as well as in

1889, but by 1912 many miners may conceivably have been convinced that the right would never be fully restored. This could only have encouraged them to push harder for increased wage rates.

Miners also commonly complained about being mistreated by their supervisors in the pits. In particular they argued that the system of fines used to maintain discipline underground and to penalize miners for sending up impure loads was often employed arbitrarily, sometimes maliciously by the overseers. In the 1905 strike, for instance, the chairman of the Christian Gewerkverein charged that it was especially the "young officials [who] are so quick with the fines."[54] It was also argued by miners that their overseers used verbal and even physical abuse against them; in the 1905 strike miners at a number of local pits demanded more "humane treatment from the overseers."[55]

To some extent, the friction between supervisors and workers *was* the result of individual callousness; the mine overseer who asked the strikers in 1889, "What do you want, you asses?" was one extreme example.[56] But complaints of mistreatment more commonly reflected the problems management confronted in running the new mines rather than individual culpability. As the mines got larger and deeper, and as new, untutored men came to work in them, the overseers at pit level faced the formidable task of maintaining some semblance of discipline and safety among workers spread far apart underground, while at the same time making sure they met production quotas. Since it was logistically impossible to exercise direct and constant supervision of the miners at the pit face, and since overseers themselves seemed to have conceived of labor management primarily in "carrot and stick" terms, it was predictable that they would resort to indirect and seemingly arbitrary means of control: heavy fines, rejection of impure loads, and occasional beatings when tempers wore thin.[57] Labor management in the mines therefore basically amounted to punishment for wrongdoing; a conception of authority that created constant tension between workers and overseers. Fining and mistreatment at the hands of the overseers not only reduced the miner's income and made it quite unpredictable from one pay period to the other, it also injured his pride. Perhaps the new rural recruits to the mines cared only about the money lost, but a sizeable minority of older miners, some of whom provided the leadership for strikes, were equally incensed by the damage to their dignity: "Today," lamented the chairman of the Christian Gewerkverein in 1905, "we are hardly treated as miners at all." Moreover, this was an authority relationship that encouraged extreme animosities. During the 1912 strike, for example, it was reported that miners were trying to maim or kill mine overseers. During the night of March 12/13, at various locations in Bochum and neighboring Hamme, shots were fired at mine officials. The next morning, at the Präsident mine, a crowd of about two hundred stoned a number of mine overseers, who responded by attacking the demonstrators with the butts of their carbines. On the fourteenth, at the Shamrock and von der Heydt mines, mine officials were again stoned and shot at.[58]

Postscript: The Miners and Socialism

It is a paradox of the political history of the Ruhr that this region of mines and factories with a heavily working class population did not prove more hospitable to the "party of the working class," the Social Democrats.[59] An important key to this irony is to be found in the Social Democrats' relationship to the miners. As the largest working class group in the region, miners were obviously the essential base of support for a mass political party. Yet, right down to the war, significant numbers of miners voted for the Zentrum or even the National Liberals, rather than the Socialists, and joined the Christian trade union or remained unorganized rather than supporting the nominally "free" but socialist-oriented Alter Verband.[60]

This is not to say that the socialists had not seemed on their way to considerable success after the anti-socialist law lapsed in 1890. In the 1870s and 1880s the party had been extremely weak in the Bochum electoral district, rarely gaining more than a few percentage points of the vote. But the 1889 miners' strike, in which Social Democrats played an active role, gave the party a significant boost. In 1890 the Social Democratic Reichstag candidate won 14.9 percent of the vote and in 1893 that rose to 29.6 percent. After a setback in the 1898 election in which the party polled only 26.6 percent, it continued to gain strength, winning 35.5 percent of the first-round vote in the 1903 elections and 50.4 percent in the second round, thus for the first time putting a socialist candidate, Otto Hue, leader of the mineworkers' union, into the Reichstag.[61]

During this same period, membership in the Alter Verband grew considerably, especially in the wake of the 1905 strike; the Amtmann in Hordel, northwest of the city, reported, for instance, that after the strike the local branch of the Alter Verband had doubled its membership.[62] In 1902 roughly equal numbers of Ruhr miners had belonged to the Alter Verband and the Christlicher Gewerkverein, but by 1908 the ratio was more than 2 to 1 in the Alter Verband's favor.[63]

Yet, in the years just before the war, both party and union found that it was difficult to expand further; indeed, they were lucky if their support did not actually erode. Although Hue managed to retain his Reichstag seat in 1907 and in 1912 the socialists' share of the first round vote actually rose to 36.8 percent (higher than in any previous year), they gained fewer second-round ballots that year than in 1903 or 1907, and Hue was unseated by an electoral agreement between the National Liberals and the Zentrum. Bochum was now to be represented in the Reichstag by the National Liberal miner, Heckmann.[64] In the immediate pre-war years, socialist activities in the Bochum area were characterized by what the Amtmann in Weitmar termed in 1913 a general "flatness " (Flauheit).[65] Observance of May Day, for example, certainly one of the more important occasions in the socialist calendar, dropped off sharply.[66] In Weitmar, to the southwest, where several hundred workers had stayed off work in 1907, that number had dropped to 160 in 1910. In 1912 it was reported to be "low," and in 1913 only some fifty people stayed away from the pits to go on a walk around the area. A similar picture emerges from other reports; in Hordel, to the northwest, May Day participation went from 310 people in 1907 to none in

1909. In 1912, May Day in Hordel was described as "badly done." Moreover, at the ninth general meeting of the Social Democratic Union for Wahlkreis-Bochum-Gelsenkirchen-Hattingen-Witten in June 1914, Party Secretary Scheibe warned that May Day had degenerated into a mere holiday for the amusement of those who did participate and demanded that its character as a political demonstration be revived.[67]

The Alter Verband experienced even more severe difficulties. From a membership of over 80,000 in the Ruhr as a whole in 1908, it plummeted to less than half that size by 1914.[68] Defections were particularly numerous after the failure of the 1912 strike, which the Alter Verband had promoted and Social Democrats had publicly supported, but which the Christlicher Gewerkverein had resolutely opposed.[69] But though the failure of the 1912 strike certainly did not help the Social Democrats or the Alter Verband, the difficulties they confronted were more fundamental than this. In a recent article, Stephen Hickey suggests that the shape of the labor movement in the Ruhr was very much determined by the nature of the work force it had to deal with and try to organize:

The very speed of industrialization . . . imposed important characteristics on the newly forming working class. It was socially fragmented without any broad historical or cultural experience in common. Many had little experience of industry and had been brought up in an environment profoundly hostile to ideas of class conflict and socialism. Moreover, the various cultural traditions continued to flourish in the new home. The divisions within the working class were nowhere more marked than in the field of religion. The churches continued to exert very considerable social and political influence. The denominational balance tilted from a Catholic ("black") dominance in Essen and the West to largely Protestant Dortmund in the East. Bochum was virtually evenly divided.[70]

These divisions, Hickey argues, were strong enough to constantly undermine the unity that was created by the common experience of work underground. Recognizing that fact and convinced of the necessity of creating a strong, inclusive, disciplined union if concessions were ever to be wrung from the employers, leaders like Hue tried to exclude both religion and politics from trade union affairs. This doctrine of "trade union neutrality" meant that the Alter Verband formally distanced itself from the SPD. But, at the same time, since most of the leaders of the Alter Verband were (and remained) Social Democrats, they were able to use "their considerable authority within the SPD itself to discourage leftist activity which might embarrass them in their attempts to work with the large numbers of miners who were vehemently non-socialist, or were politically apathetic." Reformism, gradualism and a "nonpolitical" trade union movement were all, then (according to Hickey), the results of the need "to meet effectively the challenge of the social and industrial conditions of the Ruhr."[71]

The "nonpolitical" stance of the Alter Verband combined with its emphasis on the need for a solid organization to achieve immediate economic gains certainly helped it to gain ground among miners who had no interest in socialism. In 1906, for example, the Amtmann in Hordel suggested that the Alter Verband's increase in strength locally showed that many workers who "are not the least bit concerned about politics" nevertheless "want . . . an organized fight for wages." Two years later, in Weitmar, the local official reported that only the "convinced Catholics and Protestants" remained true to the Gewerkverein Christlicher Bergarbeiter and, as a result of the present wage situation and the increase in food prices, even some of these had gone over to the Alter Verband.[72]

This new support was extremely volatile. Not only could it be withdrawn when it seemed to miners that their interests were not being properly promoted by the Alter Verband, it could even be transferred to the rival union. In 1912, for example, the Amtmann in Weitmar observed that the Gewerkverein Christlicher Bergarbeiter had recently increased its membership because "a lot of . . . so-called Social Democratic supporters had joined after the failure of the strike."[73]

Indeed, in the years just before the war, it may well have seemed to many miners that the Alter Verband had proved itself incapable of fulfilling even its most basic promises. In a 1901 agitational pamphlet, union spokesmen had blamed the workers for their own suffering:

Who is primarily responsible for the misery we have just described? You yourselves, because you did not respond promptly enough to the call to organize. If ten times as many of the men were in the Bergarbeiterverband as there are now, then the "mine exploiters"

would not be allowed to treat the workers as badly as they do now.
Whoever does not join in the fight with his comrades in the *Verband*
is just an indirect helper of the owners.[74]

Yet, the growing response to the call for organization during
the years that followed had not produced the results claimed
for it. Employers continued to refuse to recognize, let alone to
negotiate with, unions or to make any concessions to strikers.[75] And if, in the years just before the war, they do seem to
have become somewhat more open to the idea of dealing with
unions, they were prepared to do so only with the Christlicher
Gewerkverein and not the Alter Verband.[76] Indeed, the concessions that were made to miners during these years came not
from employers but from the state;[77] and even these, Dieter
Groh suggests, did little (with the exception of the abolition of
the *Wagennullen*) to significantly improve the miner's position.[78] Moreover, during the period after 1905, when membership in the Alter Verband reached peak levels, miners faced
significant reductions in their real wages as the result of both
inflation and wage cuts at the same time that the intensity of
their work was being stepped up.[79] This inability to protect, let
alone to improve the miners' material position, capped by the
fiasco of the 1912 strike, undoubtedly weakened many a
miner's belief in the powers of organization and made it even
more difficult to convince the already "sceptical . . . of the
advantages of trade union membership."[80]

To a certain extent, the local SPD must have felt that it too
was trapped in the same problematic as the Alter Verband. A
good deal of the party's ability to broaden its wedge in the
working class depended on the extent to which it was willing
to support its economic grievances. As Amtmann Hordel
observed in 1905, the strike that year "had given the Social
Democrats the wished-for opportunity to engage in strong,
public agitation"; the reports from several localities in the
next two years suggest that this activity did bring new support
to the party.[81] Yet, as with the union, although not in quite so
immediate a fashion, some of that support would erode as the
miners' grievances remained unredressed and indeed worsened in the period between 1905 and 1912. In that sense, for

the party, as for the union, the 1912 strike must have represented a final setback and not the initial failure.

However, as a political party the SPD obviously confronted separate problems in its relationship with the miners
than those that faced the union, problems that derived from
the very language of local socialism and the social and political vision it conveyed to the miners. It is impossible to piece
together a full picture of the vocabulary and rhetoric
employed by local socialists, for the simple reason that the
SPD press has not been preserved in the archives.[82] Nevertheless, the reports of socialist speeches contained in local police
records do provide some clues.[83] Certainly there were frequent
references to the "fight against capitalism"; but when it came
to illustrating the frequently repeated assertion that Germany
was a *Klassenstaat*, this seldom involved an exploration of the
relationship between capitalists and their workers. On May
Day 1908, for example, the main speaker in Harpen, the book
printer Karl Klotz from Bochum, expounded on the theme of
Prussian *Klassenjustiz* by comparing the cases of two women
charged with theft. If a poor woman, he argued, collected a
few pieces of coal off a tip, she might well be charged with
theft, but Princess Wiede, who had stolen numerous silver
articles, had no charges laid against her (the police reporter
duly noted for his superior's benefit that "the princess suffers
from kleptomania"). Two other cases, both involving aristo-
crats, were also mentioned.[84] Nor was this a particularly idio-
syncratic speech; it meshed well with the particular political
message local socialists seemed to be intent on conveying to
the miners. When socialism finally came there would of
course be a "triumph of true humanity over Mammon, over
the golden calf, over all injustice and oppression . . . [then]
everything would be governed in a brotherly manner, and
world peace would be secured."[85]

However, until that time, the miners' best chances for
improvement lay with the state; "we demand from the state,"
the socialist editor Paul Wolf told his audience in 1908, "that
the eight hour working day be introduced."[86] The problem
was of course that the Wilhelmine state was dominated by
backward Junker forces who supported the employers and

who would block the necessary reform: "It is only the fear felt by the *Junkergesellschaft*," so Frau Nemitz told her audience in Querenburg in 1910, "that prevents the formation of laws which can help the working class."[87] Not surprisingly, then, the major mass political campaign socialists conducted among miners before the war was the Prussian suffrage campaign, an attempt to democratize German politics. In 1910 the Amtmann in Weitmar reported that the local SPD were having mass demonstrations on the issue, and that same year the *Regierung* in Arnsberg warned local officials not to allow May Day processions in the streets because it was feared they would turn into suffrage demonstrations.[88]

Local socialists' emphasis on the role of the state, even if that were a much more democratized state than the Kaiserreich, ran considerable risks. Many miners may have been convinced that improvement of their situation could come only from the state, and that the SPD was the party most likely to force the necessary changes. But some others may have begun to feel that the socialists were hammering on the wrong anvil, since the miners' material situation continued to be undercut, despite the reforms already decreed by the government in 1905. Perhaps, then, the inability of the SPD to become the "party of the working class" in the Ruhr before the war was as much the product of the dynamics of the interrelationship among miners, party, state, and employers as it was the consequence of the static persistence of ethnic and religious divisions that split that class.[89]

Conclusions

"ALL OF US who write on modern German history," Dan White observes in his recent book on National Liberalism,

trace out our investigations under the shadow of the colossal failure of civilized, let alone liberal values in that country during this century. Such a disaster cannot but exercise a sort of magnetic attraction on historical explanation, channeling our lines of reasoning into the boundaries of the national experience, inducing us to attribute more weight to strictly national causes than they should perhaps bear.[1]

For many historians, Germany has been the "exceptional" case—the major deviation from the "normal" path of modern social and political development along which industrialization, on the one hand, and the liberalization and democratization of society, on the other, are presumed to be marching in step together. In Germany, although industrialization went ahead rapidly during the last third of the nineteenth century, social and political modernization was blocked, so it is argued, by entrenched preindustrial elites, who employed various means of political manipulation and social control to maintain their own dominance. It is the "fatal success" of these "imperial power elites" that is regarded as the distinctive national cause of Germany's "misdevelopment."[2]

But if the preindustrial elite were primarily responsible for preserving and encouraging the persistence of traditional attitudes, ideologies and forms of behavior, it is clear (or so much recent work would suggest) that they could count on a good deal of compliance from some of the groups they were trying to manipulate. For example, we have recently been told that the paternalistic behavior of industrialists toward their workers was strongly influenced by "conservative-feudal notions of value" and that the German *Mittelstand* was characterized by a backward-looking psychology and fear of "modernization" that made it a prime candidate for political mobilization by the reactionary elite.[3] Workers are of course somewhat harder to fit into this picture because so many of them gave their support to the SPD, a political party in permanent opposition to the Wilhelmine system. Yet even this fact, so one historian has suggested, may have been a symptom of many workers' inability properly to "adjust" to the new industrial order. As Peter Stearns puts it,

There was a mass of workers, in textiles, mining, machine building and shoe manufacture . . . who . . . were not yet capable of making the basic bargain that industrialization required, to admit new work methods . . . in return for advanced earnings. Here, I think, is the key to the special hold socialism had in Germany at this point. It fit exactly the mood of those workers who hated their work but could not easily find personal compensations.[4]

Obviously it would be misguided to discount the consequences of the political manipulation and social control exercised by the German elites, or to ignore the role played by "pre-industrial attitudes" among other social groups, many of whose members were confronting industrial-urban life for the first time. But by focusing too much attention on the remnants or the memory of the old society, we run the risk of obscuring, even ignoring, the structure and dynamics of the new. In this book I have attempted to redress this analytical imbalance by shifting attention to a consideration of the material circumstances and life situations that actually confronted inhabitants of the new industrial cities like Bochum. Judged by a variety of indicators, Bochum must be considered to have been extremely "modern".[5] "Modern" in terms of the technology involved in industrial production, the division of labor, the size and the scope of enterprise, and the nature of economic organization. "Modern" too in terms of the restless geographic mobility of its inhabitants and, it can also be argued, "modern" in terms of its polarized social structure and limited opportunities for individual social and occupational mobility. And certainly "modern" in terms of its class relations, its industrial and social conflicts. Yet it was precisely the extreme modernity of Bochum in all of these dimensions that made the city inhospitable to the flourishing of that other "modernity" that has so preoccupied Dahrendorf, Wehler, and others—that complex of political, social, and (one might even say) psychological attitudes that, taken together, constitute a "liberal" worldview. If this second "modernity" did not penetrate very deeply into the fabric of local life, that was because it did not offer a very accurate reflection of social reality. Indeed, it explicitly conflicted with most people's actual experience and thus did not provide a compelling prescription for their future behavior.[6] Of course, Bochum was not Germany; nevertheless, Bochum and other industrial towns like it did reflect essential characteristics of the specific stage in the development of capitalist society Germany had reached by the late nineteenth century. In that stage of large-scale, heavy-industry-based, "organized" capitalism the link between liberal ideology and social reality must have seemed far more tenuous, not only in Bochum, but in Germany as a whole, than perhaps it had during the early phases of the English Industrial Revolution.

This may in turn suggest that rather than continuing to "ghettoize" recent German history as an exceptional case, more could be learned by attempting to situate the German experience within the framework of capitalist development in Europe and the world as a whole. Interpretations that argue for the "failed development" and "insufficient modernization" of German society during this period base their case primarily on the absence of a parliamentary regime on the English model. But as Geoff Eley has recently suggested, making liberal democracy into the "unavoidable criterion of successful 'modernization'" runs the risk of confusing form with substance.[7] Not only are the political institutions of a society perhaps the "most unsuitable measure of its 'modernity,'" but it can even be argued that British political development was itself "rather exceptional."[8] An approach that did not concentrate so exclusively on politics but also analyzed the social and economic dimensions in detail might reveal greater parallels between German development and that of other industrial nations than advocates of the German "exceptionalist" argument have been prepared to admit. At the same time, careful comparisons among the industrial nations might demonstrate that, whatever they shared, their different national political structures combined with the necessity each faced of responding in different ways to their relative positions in the European and world economy, meant that the experience of one nation could not really serve as a "model" that could be fully replicated by any other.

This book cannot provide all the answers to these questions, nor was that its original intent. But if it does manage to stimulate other historians to analyze the kinds of problems I have dealt with here in other regions of Germany as well as in other European industrial societies, and, if by doing that, recent German history is able to escape the cul-de-sac into which unreflected notions of German "exceptionalism" threaten to push it, then it will more than have served its purpose.

Notes

Abbreviations Used in the Notes

Jdh   Jahresbericht der Handelskammer zu Bochum

StAB   Stadtarchiv Bochum

STAM   Staatsarchiv Münster

VB   Verwaltungsbericht der Stadt Bochum

WAFKH Werksarchiv Friedrich Krupp Hüttenwerke

Introduction

1. This extremely compressed overview of recent German historical writing owes a good deal to the insightful and much more detailed introduction by Richard Evans to a new collection of essays on German social and political history; see Richard J. Evans "Introduction: Wilhelm II's Germany and the Historians," in *Society and Politics in Wilhelmine Germany* (London: Croom Helm, 1978), pp. 11–39, edited by the same author. For a discussion of the more traditional approach to German history see G. Ritter, "Gegenwartige Lage und Zukunftsausgaben deutscher Geschichtswissenschaft," *Historische Zeitschrift*, 170 (1950).

2. Ralf Dahrendorf, *Society and Democracy in Germany*, p. 14.

3. See Fritz Stern, *The Failure of Illiberalism: Essays on the Political Culture of Modern Germany* (New York: Knopf, 1972).

4. See for example Dahrendorf, *Society and Democracy*, chs. 6, 7, and 8.

5. Dahrendorf, *Society and Democracy*, p. 42.

6. *Ibid.*, pp. 44, 45, 47, 48.

7. *Ibid.*, pp. 43, 44.

8. Evans, "Wilhelm II's Germany and the Historians," p. 14.

9. See Hans-Ulrich Wehler, *Das Deutsche Kaiserreich*, p. 17.

10. On these points see especially the discussion by Geoff Eley, "Capitalism and the Wilhelmine State: Industrial Growth and Political Backwardness in Recent German Historiography, 1890–1918," *Historical Journal* (1978), 21:737–50.

11. Evans, "Wilhelm II's Germany and the Historians," pp. 13–14, and especially the discussion of the German social history journal, *Geschichte und Gesellschaft*, by Geoff Eley, "Memories of Under-Development."

12. Evans, "Wilhelm II's Germany and the Historians," pp. 13–14. It would be unfair here to ignore the earlier work of historians such as Werner Conze, Wolfram

Fischer, Rolf Engelsing, and Wolfgang Köllmann. However, as Eley suggests, most of their work has "proceeded fairly independently of the dramatic public departures of the last decade" and has not necessarily stood as a forerunner to it (Eley, "Memories of Under-Development," p. 785n). See also Heinz-Gerhard Haupt and Hans-Josef Steinberg, "Tendances de l'histoire ouvrière en Republique federale Allemande," *Le Mouvement social*, (July–September 1977), 100:133–142.

13. For an introduction to some of the European work see Robert J. Bezucha, ed., *Modern European Social History*. On America see Tamara K. Hareven, ed., *Anonymous Americans: Explorations in Nineteenth Century Social History* (Englewood Cliffs, N.J.: Prentice-Hall, 1971). For both European and American research see also the *Journal of Social History*.

14. Evans, "Wilhelm II's Germany and the Historians", pp. 14–15.

15. Wehler, *Das Deutsche Kaiserreich*, p. 14.

16. Evans lists four major methods of social control: repression, manipulation, diversion, and negative integration ("Wilhelm II's Germany and the Historians," pp. 17–22).

17. For an interesting critique of one element of Wehler's approach see Geoff Eley, "Social Imperialism: Use and Abuse of an Idea," *Social History*, pp. 265–90.

18. See Eley, "Capitalism and the Wilhelmine State," p. 739.

19. *Ibid.*, p. 741.

20. See especially Stephen Thernstrom and Richard Sennett, eds., *Nineteenth-Century Cities* for a representative sample of work produced in the 1960s.

21. See the articles by William Sewell on Marseilles and Joan Scott on Carmaux in *Le Mouvement social* (July–September 1971), no. 76; William M. Reddy, "The Textile Trade and the Language of the Crowd at Rouen, 1752–1871," *Past and Present* (February 1977), no. 74, pp. 62–89; Robert J. Bezucha, *The Lyon Uprising of 1834* (Cambridge, Mass.: Harvard University Press, 1974); William M. Reddy, "Family and Factory: The Linen Weavers of Armentières," *Journal of Social History* (Winter 1975), 9:102–12. Philip Nord (Columbia University) and Andrew Lincoln (Oxford University) are currently working on doctoral dissertations which examine respectively small shopkeepers in Paris and aspects of the economic and social history of Paris in the second part of the nineteenth century.

22. Evans, "Wilhelm II's Germany and the Historians", p. 24.

23. See Wolfgang Köllmann, *Sozialgeschichte der Stadt Barmen im 19. Jahrhundert*, and W. Köllmann, "Zur Bedeutung der Regionalgeschichte im Rahmen struktur- und sozialgeschichtlicher Konzeption," *Archiv für Sozialgeschichte*, 15 (1975), 45. Among recent exceptions that should be noted: Klaus Tenfelde, *Sozialgeschichte der Bergarbeiterschaft an der Ruhr im 19. Jahrhundert* (Bonn–Bad Godesberg: Neue Gesellschaft, 1977); Stephen Hickey, "The Shaping of the German Labour Movement: Miners in the Ruhr," in Evans, *Society and Politics in Wilhelmine Germany*, pp. 11–39; Lawrence Schofer, *The Formation of a Modern Labor Force*.

24. See John Foster, "Nineteenth-Century Towns." A book which brilliantly explores this interface between "community" and "society" in the eighteenth and early nineteenth centuries is Mack Walker, *German Home Towns: Community, State and General Estate, 1648–1871* (Ithaca, N.Y.: Cornell University Press, 1971).

25. The extreme case in the opposite direction, that is the extreme case of divergence from what seem to be the dominant national social and economic trends, can also be highly illuminating. For a skillful application of this approach see Gareth Stedman Jones, *Outcast London: A Study in the Relationship between the Classes in Victorian London* (Oxford: Clarendon Press, 1971).

26. Norman Pounds, *The Ruhr: A Study in Historical and Economic Geography* (Bloomington: Indiana University Press, 1952), p. 27. See also Wilhelm Brepohl, *Industrievolk im Wandel von der agraren zur industriellen Daseinsform.*

27. Helmuth Croon, "Die Einwirkungen," p. 302; Pounds, *The Ruhr*, pp. 34, 42; *ibid.*, p. 42.

28. Pounds, *The Ruhr*, p. 43.

29. T. C. Banfield, *Industry of the Rhine*, Ser. 1: *Agriculture* (London: C. Knight, 1848), pp. 47–50.

30. Pounds, *The Ruhr*, p. 67, and Croon, "Die Einwirkungen," p. 303; Pounds, *The Ruhr*, pp. 63, 75; Walter Däbritz, *Bochumer Verein für Bergbau und Gusstahlfabrikation in Bochum*, p. 36.

31. Wolfgang Köllmann, "The Process of Urbanization in Germany at the Height of the Industrialization Period," p. 64. The population increase between 1871 and 1910 was 131.9 percent; the urban increase was 601.2 percent. See also Helmuth Croon, "Städtewandlung und Städtebildung im Ruhrgebiet im 19. Jahrhundert."

One: Society and Economy

1. Helmuth Croon, "Studien zur Sozial- und Siedlungsgeschichte der Stadt Bochum," pp. 86, 87.

2. StAB, VB, 1860–61, p. 10, and Franz Darpe, *Geschichte der Stadt Bochum nebst Urkundenbuch*, pp. 530–31. See also W. Fischer, "Rural Industrialization and Population Change."

3. Darpe, *Geschichte der Stadt Bochum nebst Urkundenbuch*, p. 531.

4. *Ibid.*, pp. 526–27, 531.

5. Walter Däbritz, *Bochumer Verein für Bergbau und Gusstahlfabrikation in Bochum*; Helmuth Croon, "Vom Werden des Ruhrgebiets," *Rheinisch-Westfälische Rückblende*, Beiträge zur neueren Landesgeschichte des Rheinlandes und Westfalen, Walter Först, ed. (Cologne and Berlin: 1967), 1:185.

6. Based on figures for seventeen local mines in Mayor Lange, "Die Wohnungsverhältnisse der ärmeren Volksklassen in Bochum," and *Statistik des Deutschen Reiches, Bd. 207.*

7. See p. 19 and also Irmtraud-Dietlinde Wolcke, *Die Entwicklung der Bochumer Innenstadt.*

8. *Statistik des Deutschen Reiches, vol. 117.*

9. In 1907 approximately two-thirds of the work force were employed in 99 percent of the industrial enterprises, while the other third worked in less than 1 percent of the enterprises.

10. StAB, VB, 1860–61, p. 80.

11. StAB, VB, 1900, p. 22.

12. StAB, VB, 1860–61, p. 12; VB, 1871, p. 10; *Adressbuch der Stadt Bochum*, 1874/75. The tax categories were as follows: Class AI (Large Industrialists): total annual profits 50,000 marks or more or fixed capital 1,000,000 marks or more. Class AII (Large Merchants): profits 20,000–50,000 marks or fixed capital 150,000–1,000,-000 marks. Class B (Small Merchants): profits 4,000–20,000 marks or fixed capital 30,000–150,000 marks. Class H (Artisans): profits 1,500–4,000 marks or fixed capital of 3,000–30,000 marks.

13. See pp. 138–42. Hershberg et al., in their work on nineteenth-century Philadelphia, have suggested that the small shop owner "who operated on a thin profit margin and was constantly haunted by the specter of ruin" was actually no better off

financially than many skilled factory workers who were better paid and who also retained considerable direct control over the work process. See Bruce Laurie, Theodore Hershberg, and George Alter, "Immigrants and Industry: The Philadelphia Experience, 1850–1880," *Journal of Social History* (Winter 1975), vol. 9, no. 2.

14. A more exact measurement of income inequality, which the data for Bochum do not permit, is described in Robert R. Schutz, "On the Measurement of Income Inequality," *American Economic Review*, 41 (1951), 107–22.

15. See also Michael Katz, "Social Structure in Hamilton, Ontario" in Stephan Thernstrom and Richard Sennett, eds., *Nineteenth-Century Cities*, p. 211.

16. StAB, VB, 1860–61, p. 78.

17. Max Jürgen Koch, *Die Bergarbeiterbewegung*, Table 1, p. 139; StAB, VB, 1860–61, footnote to pp. 78 and 79.

18. StAB, VB, 1860–61, pp. 78–79. See also H. Rosenberg, "Die Weltwirtschaftskrise von 1857 bis 1859," *Vierteljahrschrift für Sozial und Wirtschafts-Geschichte*, suppl. no. 30 (1934); and E. J. Hobsbawm, *The Age of Capital, 1848–1875* (London: Sphere, 1977), ch. 2.

19. StAB, VB, 1860–61, p. 79 (continuation of footnote to p. 78).

20. On this point see Keith Burgess, *The Origins of British Industrial Relations*, p. 152.

21. Koch, *Die Bergarbeiterbewegung*, Table 3, p. 140: throughout the whole period from 1886 to 1913, the lowest percentage is 46.7 in 1891 and the highest is 60.2 in 1907. See also Burgess, *The Origins of British Industrial Relations*, p. 153.

22. StAB, VB, 1860–61, p. 79 (continuation of footnote to p. 78).

23. See Burgess, *The Origins of British Industrial Relations*, p. 152: "Periods of low or falling prices did not necessarily lead to reductions in output since the coalmasters were more interested in total revenues than the price of a given quantity of production. In fact, the reverse was often the case. The decades 1875–1895 marked a continuous expansion in output although prices were low or declining. This was an attempt to offset unfavourable price movements by increasing output in an effort to maintain total revenues. There was no simple correlation between output, employment and prices in the coal industry"; StAB, VB, 1860–61, footnote to p. 79 continued on p. 80.

24. StAB, VB, 1864, p. 3; StAB, VB, 1874/75, pp. 3–4; StAB, VB, 1875/76, p. 7.

25. StAB, VB, 1878/79, p. 5.

26. Wage reductions and labor intensification are obviously linked here, since miners' wages were based on productivity, not time. Lower piece rates effectively required workers to work harder and/or longer just to keep income at the former level.

27. StAB, VB, 1877/78, p. 4; StAB, VB, 1876/77, p. 4. In 1878/79 the Chamber of Commerce reported that "impoverishment, begging, vagabondage and crime have increased in the most deplorable manner in all regions of the Reich, but especially in the industrial districts." See StAB, VB, 1878/79 p. 5.

28. StAB, VB, 1881/82, p. 14, which refers to "selbstmörderischen Preisschleuderei."

29. StAB, VB, 1878/79, p. 5.

30. StAB, VB, 1879/80, p. 50; StAB, VB, 1888/89 p. 46.

31. On this, see Erich Maschke, "Outline of the History of German Cartels from 1873 to 1914," in F. Crouzet, W. H. Chaloner, and W. M. Stern, eds., *Essays in European Economic History, 1789–1914* (London: St. Martins Press, 1969), pp. 233–34; "The foundations of the modern cartel movement were laid in the long economic stagnation, from 1874 to 1894; the short spells of upswing—1880–82 and 1889–90— merely confirmed businessmen in the consciousness of their dependence on cyclical

fluctuations. The shock of the crisis, the drop in prices, the falling off in sales during the downswing and stagnation which stimulated competition to the point of ruin taught entrepreneurs to meet these evils by voluntary combination. Entrepreneurial reaction to cyclical fluctuations was one of the strongest motives for cartellization."

32. StAB, VB, 1879/80, p. 6; StAB, VB, 1881/82, p. 4, and 1883/84; StAB, VB, 1886/87, p. 15; StAB, VB, 1890/91, p. 16; StAB, VB, 1895/96, p. 15; StAB, VB, 1909, p. 27.

33. StAB, VB, 1860–61, footnote to p. 79 continued on p. 80.

34. StAB, VB, 1876/77, p. 4. The Chamber also suggested that this tactic would not work "unless exports . . . [can find] a steady market at paying prices."

35. StAB, VB, 1885/86, p. 14; StAB, VB, 1890/91, p. 16. Between 1891 and 1893, coke prices dropped some 14 percent and overseas exports in turn rose 172 percent (from 92,000 tons to 250,000 tons; StAB, VB, 1892/93, p. 16).

36. StAB, VB, 1908, p. 24.

37. StAB, VB, 1910, p. 34. Major export areas for Ruhr coal were Holland, Belgium, France, Switzerland, and Italy. The major problem for Ruhr coal producers was transport costs, although, in competing with Belgium, they also had to deal with that country's considerably lower labor costs. The British could deliver coal so much more cheaply because they could transport it by sea, whereas the Ruhr was dependent on more costly rail transport. This meant that at times British coal had a cost advantage over Ruhr coal even within certain parts of the German market (see StAB, VB, 1875/76, p. 7, and 1886/87, p. 16, in which the Chamber of Commerce complained that without a reduction of freight charges to Hamburg it could not compete in the Hamburg market with English coal).

38. StAB, VB, 1910, p. 27.

39. StAB, VB, 1876/77, p. 4.

40. See Burgess, The Origins of British Industrial Relations, p. 152.

41. StAB, VB, 1911, pp. 36–37.

42. Maschke, "Outline of the History of German Cartels," p. 248.

43. A. J. Taylor, "The Coal Industry," in D. H. Aldcroft, ed., The Development of British Industry and Foreign Competition, 1875-1914: Studies in Industrial Enterprise (Toronto: University of Toronto Press, 1968), p. 44.

44. Even though Ruhr coal producers repeatedly petitioned the state for reduction of their other major costs, freight charges, as late as 1911 they continued to complain that they remained disadvantaged by their dependence on railway transport, whereas in Britain, "the proximity of the sea saves heavy industry from expensive land transport"; StAB, VB, 1911, p. 9.

45. By 1914, only 3 percent of German coal production involved the use of the new mining machines, compared to 10 percent in England; Peter N. Stearns, "Adaptation to Industrialization," p. 306.

46. A. J. Taylor, "The Coal Industry," p. 45.

47. Ibid., p. 44.

48. Burgess, The Origins of British Industrial Relations, p. 153, and Taylor, "The Coal Industry," p. 45. For figures see A. J. Taylor, "The Coal Industry," table 4, p. 46. Of course Britain started off from such a high point in the late 1870s that it was able to tolerate this decrease and still retain a significant edge over all other coal producers except Germany.

49. A. J. Taylor, "The Coal Industry," p. 49.

50. On the extension of the working day, see especially Bezirks-Polizei-Kommissar Essen to Regierungspräsident Düsseldorf, February 1, 1904, in Gerhard Adelmann, ed., Quellensammlung zur Geschichte der sozialen Betriebsverfassung, 2:244-45. For

some provocative observations on the intensification of work in the mines see Dieter Groh, "Überlegungen zum Verhältnis von Intensivierung der Arbeit und Arbeitskämpfen im organisierten Kapitalismus in Deutschland (1896–1914)," January 1976. Manuscript. I am indebted to Professor David Montgomery, University of Pittsburgh, for sending me a copy of this paper.

51. Der Klassenkampf im Ruhrrevier (Berlin: n.p., 1905), p. 10.

52. StAB, VB, 1864, p. 3; StAB, VB, 1869, p. 4.

53. StAB, VB, 1874/75, p. 3.

54. StAB, VB, 1874/75, p. 3; StAB, Küppers Nachlass, NI 23a; ibid., p. 49.

55. Ibid., p. 62, 49.

56. Ibid., p. 58.

57. See David Landes, Unbound Prometheus, pp. 89–94, and especially pp. 254–69.

58. Auszug aus dem Generalversammlung. Neuloh breaks up the technological history of Ruhr iron and steel into these three periods: (1) 1858–68, introduction of the Bessemer process for steelmaking alongside puddling; (2) 1867–78, introduction of continuous Siemens-Martin process alongside Bessemer; (3) 1879–1910, introduction of Thomas process alongside Siemens-Martin; see Otto Neuloh, Die Deutsche Betriebsverfassung und ihre sozialformen bis zur Mitbestimmung (Tübingen: Mohr/ Siebeck, 1956), p. 263. The Bochumer Verein completed its first Bessemerwerk in 1865, built a second in 1869 and a third in 1874. Both the Bessemer and the Siemens-Martin processes required nonphosphoric iron ore, which local producers had largely to import (Auszug aus dem Generalversammlung, p. 3), thus putting them in a disadvantageous cost position with regard to England. The discoveries of Gilchrist and Thomas, by allowing the use of phosphoric ores, relieved German and continental producers from this handicap; see Landes, Unbound Prometheus, pp. 258–59.

59. Auszug aus dem Generalversammlung, p. 3.

60. Ibid., p. 2. See also his later comments on the iron district in Scotland. See also StAB, VB, 1880/81, p. 6.

61. StAB, VB, 1881/82, p. 14. reported that not only were many works in the district which had been shut down being put back into operation, but the iron and steel industry was also prepared to introduce the newest technical improvements. It went on to say that there were now in Germany as many converters for the Thomas-Gilchrist process as in England. At the Bochumer Verein production increased by 32 percent over 1880.

62. StAB, VB, 1883/84, p. 15. Earlier, in the 1880/81 report, the Chamber of Commerce pointed to overproduction in Germany and other industrial countries, especially England, and suggested that the Thomas-Gilchrist process, although necessary to Germany's competitive position in world markets, required considerable capital investment and further increased productive capacity "without bringing a profit to them during the long testing period." The question of overproduction still preoccupied the Chamber of Commerce as late as 1900, when it suggested that the real basis of the economic downturn that year was the inner relationships of the German market, especially in the iron industry, where too many works had been founded earlier (StAB, VB, 1900, p. 23).

63. StAB, VB, 1884/85, p. 13.

64. StAB, VB, 1880/81, p. 6; See Auszug aus dem Generalversammlung, p. 3.

65. StAB, VB, 1881/82, p. 14; see also StAB, VB, 1882/83, p. 14, and VB, 1888/89, p. 15: "Without this tariff, England, which possesses much more favorable production conditions, can flood the German market with pig iron as well as iron and steel products."

66. Hermann Levy, *Industrial Germany: A Study of its Monopoly Organisations and their Control by the State* (New York: Cambridge University Press, 1966, reprint of 1935 ed.), p. 58. Levy adds, "The desire to make the utmost out of the protection afforded by the State, instead of losing its benefit by overcompetition, became a very strong stimulus to the formation of industrial combination."

67. Maschke, "Outline of the History of German Cartels", pp. 233, 236. See also Gerald D. Feldman, "The Collapse of the Steel Works Association, 1912–1919. A Case Study in the Operation of German 'Collectivist Capitalism,'" in Hans Ulrich Wehler, ed., *Sozialgeschichte Heute. Festschrift für Hans Rosenberg zum 70. Geburtstag. Kritische Studien zur Geschichtswissenschaft*, (Göttingen: Vandenhoeck and Ruprecht, 1974), 11:576, and also the comments in StAB, VB, 1904, p. 35.

68. StAB, VB, 1907, p. 35.

69. Maschke, "Outline of the History of German Cartels," p. 238.

70. Feldman, "The Collapse of the Steel Works Association," p. 576.

71. StAB, VB, 1891/92, p. 21; StAB, VB, 1892/93, p. 18; StAB, VB, 1893/94, p. 18, and StAB VB, 1911, p. 26.

72. Feldman, "Collapse of the Steel Works Association," p. 567.

73. StAB, VB, 1895/96, p. 17.

74. See for example StAB, VB, 1881/82, p. 19; StAB, VB, 1882/83, p. 14; StAB, VB, 1912, p. 45.

75. *Auszug aus dem Generalversammlung*, p. 2; StAB, VB, 1878/79; StAB, 1877/78. p. 5; *Auszug aus dem Generalversammlung*, p. 3; StAB, VB, 1881/82, p. 14.

76. StAB, VB, 1887/88, pp. 19–20; StAB, VB, 1890/91, p. 21, and VB, 1893/94, p. 18; StAB, VB, 1894/95, p. 19; StAB, VB, 1900, p. 22.

77. StAB, VB, 1890/91, p. 24; StAB, VB, 1898/99, p. 24. The Chamber pointed out, however, that in terms of total volume "foreign business . . . has by no means diminished, but has lost in relative significance . . . Sales are taking place spendidly in the domestic market. Exports may scarcely have exceeded ten percent of the production [of the large local iron and steel works]." Of course, if they were exceptionally fortunate, local industrialists might enjoy both booming domestic and lively foreign markets in the same year. This happened in 1909, for example, so that "the works have jobs for several months ahead and even into the spring of 1910" (StAB, VB, 1909, p. 36). But such combinations were relatively rare and short-lived—the same report went on to observe, early in 1910, that "demand has fallen off and the competition for contracts that are coming on the market is getting sharper" (StAB, VB, 1909, p. 36). On the other hand, local industrialists most feared the possibility that both domestic and foreign markets would become depressed at the same time. Although this was also a comparatively rare phenomenon during this period, it did happen in 1891, when only 17 percent of production could be exported, with the predictable result that considerable numbers of workers were put on short time or laid off (StAB, VB, 1892/93, p. 18) and again in 1901 and in 1908, when the Chamber of Commerce had to report that "the falling off of domestic business cannot be compensated for by extension of foreign trade since the foreign market also does not seem to be particularly receptive and stands at the same time under considerable pressure on prices" (StAB, VB, 1908, p. 29).

78. StAB, VB, 1888/89, p. 19: "We must thank the protective tariff for the fact that we are competitive on the world market."

79. StAB, VB, 1881/82, p. 14.

80. StAB, VB, 1882/83, p. 14.

81. See StAB, Küppers Nachlass, NI 23a; *Auszug aus dem Generalversammlung*, p. 1; StAB, VB, 1882/83, p. 14.

82. StAB, VB, 1886/87, p. 17; StAB, VB, 1891/92, p. 21; see StAB, VB, 1893/94, p. 20, in which the Chamber of Commerce also complained that south German railroad administrations were giving contracts to foreigners and went on to note that, in recent years, foreign and especially Belgian competition had increased because industrialists in these other countries paid their workers less and were not burdened with the obligatory and voluntary *Wohlfahrtseinrichtungen* that German industrialists had set up for their workers.

83. StAB, VB, 1898/99, p. 24.

84. In 1890, freight costs amounted to 12.3 percent of the total value of production at the *Bochumer Verein*, wages 20.6 percent. However, by 1899/1900, freight charges had been reduced to 5.7 percent whereas wages accounted for 17.2 percent. Sources: StAB, VB, 1887/88, and 1899/1900, and Max Seippel, *Bochum Einst und Jetzt*, p. 256.

85. See Levy, *Industrial Germany*, pp. 58 and 59, and StAB, VB, 1886/87, p. 15 and 1911, p. 17.

86. See Levy, *Industrial Germany*, p. 50: "One urgent reason for the acquisition of coal mines and ore properties by iron and steel works was the growing power of the cartels and syndicates in the extractive branches on which furnaces and steel works depended."

87. See Jürgen Kuczynski, *Geschichte der Lage der Arbeiter*, 14:27; Landes, *Unbound Prometheus*, pp. 267–69.

88. Technological advances were also employed to enable German producers to use the phosphor-rich ores that were available to them, i.e. the Thomas-Gilchrist process (see especially StAB, VB, 1880/81, p. 6) and thus free them from dependence on imported ore (see *Auszug aus dem Generalversammlung*, p. 3). However, it is not clear whether this reduced prices compared to British products or simply allowed Ruhr producers to compete in world markets with the British. Later, other economies were made in fuel usage, etc. Nevertheless, the major economies were in labor-saving technology, and since this aspect obviously has the greatest implications for social history, I have examined it in some detail.

89. StAB, Küppers Nachlass, NI 23a, pp. 60 and 62.

90. Landes, *Unbound Prometheus*, pp. 266–67. On American technology see David Brody, *Steelworkers in America*, pp. 27–28: "Labor savings were, in fact, the nub of the American accomplishment. The steelmakers, enterprising as they were, lagged behind Europe in utilizing waste gases and streamlining products. They did attain economies of fuel, transportation and distribution. But their preeminent success came in the area of labor costs. That part of total manufacturing charges shrank almost one-third—from 22.5 to 16.5 percent—in the twenty years after 1890. The proportional reduction of labor cost was the principal achievement of the economizing drive. . . . The goal of economy, as it related to labor, was to multiply the worker's output in relation to his income. Complex enough in its details, the steelmasters' labor policy reduced to that simple objective."

91. Landes, *Unbound Prometheus*, p. 264.

92. W. Däbritz, *Bochumer Verein*, p. 283. See also *Die Schwereisenindustrie*, pp. 74–75.

93. *Reports of the Gainsborough Commission*, p. 25.

94. *Die Schwereisenindustrie*, pp. 70–71.

95. Landes, *Unbound Prometheus*, p. 265; *Die Schwereisenindustrie*, p. 86.

96. *Die Schwereisenindustrie*, p. 88.

97. *Ibid.*, p. 477.

Output per Worker (tons/man at the blast furnace)
1890	187.49
1895	227.12
1900	245.24
1905	282.77
1909	299.44

However, this should be compared to the American situation, in which output per workman in blast furnaces and in steel plants nearly tripled in the twenty years after 1890 (Brody, *Steelworkers in America*, p. 40).

98. *Die Schwereisenindustrie*, pp. 477, 482. In his 1875 report, Baare had suggested that piece work was more widespread in Germany than in England.

99. *Ibid.*, p. 486.

100. See for example Georg Wiebe, *Die Handelskammer zu Bochum von 1856– 1906*, p. 34. In the 1860s the working day at the Bochumer Verein was twelve hours except that "in the smelter, time depends on production needs" (WAFKH, Gusstahlwerk Bochumer Verein, 2100, Nr. 1. Bestimmungen zur Aufrechterhaltung der Ordnung für Meister and Arbeiter auf der Gusstahlfabrik des Bochumer Vereins für Bergbau und Gusstahlfabrikation, 1865, Article 5). By 1901 the working day had only been reduced to eleven hours (StAB. Z.S. Nr. 127 I. *An Alle Metallarbeiter von Bochum und Umgegend*). When the Gainsborough Commission visited Bochum it discovered that the average weekly hours worked were sixty in iron and steel works, forty-eight underground in coal mines (six-day week) (*Reports of the Gainsborough Commission*, p. 23-29). American steel mills initially reduced the working day when new machinery was applied but then reestablished it at twelve hours (see Brody, *Steelworkers in America*, p. 37). On the Flottmann incident see Karl Brinkmann, *Die Geschichte der Flottmannwerke*, p. 95.

101. On this see Ernst Barth, *Entwicklungslinien der deutschen Maschinenindustrie von 1870–1914* (Berlin: Akademie, 1973), p. 75, who notes that by the early twentieth century, even old established south German engineering firms such as Maschinenfabrik Augsburg-Nürnberg AG were setting up new branches in the Ruhr to be closer to raw materials and to develop the regional market for industrial machinery–thus MAN constructed a foundry and a machine works for building large gas machines and cranes in Duisburg between 1910 and 1912. Similarly, Arthur Köppel (Berlin) had already set up a branch in Bochum in 1872 and the Bochumer Verein itself produced not only basic iron and steel products but used a considerable amount of its own raw materials to make locomotives, axles, and other railroad equipment.

102. *Statistik des Deutschen Reiches*, 217/1, p. 159.

103. On the importance of this for industrial relations and social history in Britain see John Foster, *Class Struggle and the Industrial Revolution: Early Industrial Capitalism in Three English Towns* (London: Weidenfeld and Nicolson, 1974), pp. 224–29, and Burgess, *Origins of British Industrial Relations*, pp. 25–34. See also S. B. Saul, "The Engineering Industry," in Derek H. Aldcroft, ed., *The Development of British Industry and Foreign Competition, 1875–1914: Studies in Industrial Enterprise* (Toronto: University of Toronto Press, 1968), pp. 227–37. One exception to this characterization of Bochum's metalworking trades was the wire and wire-rope industry, which, the Chamber reported in 1887, could only sell one-third of its production in the domestic market and therefore relied heavily on exports (StAB, VB, 1887/88, p. 18).

104. StAB, VB, 1911, p. 40.

105. StAB, VB, 1877/78, p. 7; StAB, VB, 1911, p. 40. Among the major local companies in metalworking and machine building, Eickhoff produced mostly mining equipment as did Flottmann, Heintzmann and Dreyer; Mummenhoff and Stegemann produced files, Venneman and Company, wire rope, and Seippel, safety lamps and equipment, all products used in the mining industry, iron and steel production, or metalfinishing. See StAB, VB, 1877/78, pp. 6–7.

106. See Maschke, "Outline of the History of German Cartels," p. 328: "Cartelization encountered the greatest difficulty in the mechanical engineering industry," and the recent unpublished paper by Gerald D. Feldman and Ulrich Nocken, "Trade Associations and Economic Power: A Comparison of Interest Group Development in the German Iron and Steel and Machine Building Industries, 1900–1933."

107. StAB, VB, 1908, p. 22. See also StAB, VB, 1898/99, p. 23, and VB, 1895/96, p. 17.

108. StAB, VB, 1907, p. 36. For similar complaints see VB, 1906, p. 24, and 1911, p. 40.

109. A survey of local enterprises reported in StAB, VB, 1877/78, showed that the Eickhoff Brothers Foundry and Machine Works already had four banks of lathes, one shaping machine, two drilling machines, and one Roots-Blower, and that Flottmann's Metal Foundry and Machine Shop had five banks of lathes, one planing machine, one drilling machine, one milling machine, and one emery polishing machine, whereas Mummenhoff and Stegemann's file cutting shop and Seippel's safety lamp works seem to have produced primarily by hand (StAB, VB, 1877/78, pp. 6 and 7).

110. StAB, VB, 1906, p. 24.

111. In 1911, for example, even though the market was busy, the Chamber of Commerce reported that "the high prices of raw materials and the increasing sharpness of competition . . . mean that not as much profit is being made as could be" (StAB, VB, 1911, p. 40).

112. A 1908 British survey revealed that skilled engineering workers' wages in Bochum were, on average, somewhat higher than skilled men in the iron and steel industry; see Board of Trade. Accounts and Papers, vol. 108. Cost of Living in German Towns (London: 1908), pp. 84 and 85. For comments on industrial relations in the machine building industry see also Feldman and Nocken, "Trade Associations and Economic Power,"

113. StAB, VB, 1907, p. 30. See also Heinrich August Winkler, ed., Organisierter Kapitalismus. Voraussetzungen und Anfänge (Göttingen: Vandenhoeck and Ruprecht, 1974).

114. StAB, 1909, p. 19.

115. See StAB, VB, 1909, p. 29.

116. StAB, VB, 1882, pp. 12–18.

117. Däbritz, Bochumer Verein, Statistischer Anhang; StAB, JdH, 1895, p. 32.

118. StAB, VB, 1907, p. 29; Däbritz, Bochumer Verein, Statistischer Anhang; StAB, VB, 1907, pp. 29, 32.

119. For analyses of family structure and family economy in these other types of industrial contexts see Michael Anderson, Family Structure in Nineteenth Century Lancashire; Tamara K. Hareven, "Family Time and Industrial Time: Family and Work in a Planned Corporation Town, 1900–1924," in Tamara K. Hareven, ed., Family and Kin in Urban Communities, 1700–1930 (New York: New Viewpoints, 1977), pp. 187–206; Virginia McLaughlin, "Patterns of Work and Family Organization: Buffalo's Italians," Journal of Interdisciplinary History (1970), 2:299–314. Lynn H. Lees, "Migration and the Irish Family Economy," Manuscript.

120. W. Köllmann, *Sozialgeschichte der Stadt Barmen*, p. 99, and *Statistik des Deutschen Reiches*, vol 210/2.

121. Lady Florence Bell, *At the Works*, p. 178. See also Board of Trade, *Accounts and Papers*, p. 84: "Few women or girls are employed in the staple industries of Bochum, in any capacity, whatever, and in general female labour plays there a very insignificant part in industrial organization." This is not, of course, to ignore the fact that women made other nonwage economic contributions to the family budget; in particular, tending small garden patches, raising animals, doing laundry and taking in lodgers. See Tenfelde, *Sozialgeschichte der Bergarbeiterschaft*, pp. 323–24, and K. Schmidthaus, "Essen und Trinken. Der Tageslauf im Haushalt," *Rheinisch-Westfälische Zeitschrift für Volkskunde* (1964), vol. 11.

122. *Statistik des Deutschen Reiches*, vol. 210/2.

123. Louise Tilly and Joan Scott, "Women's Work and the Family in Nineteenth-Century Europe," in Charles E. Rosenberg, ed., *The Family in History*, (Philadelphia: University of Pennsylvania Press, 1975), pp. 149–50; *Statistik des Deutschen Reiches*, vol. 210/2.

124. Tilly and Scott, "Women's Work and the Family," p. 152f. For a discussion of family budget surveys and methods of analyzing them see John Modell, "The Fruits of Their Toil: The Family Economy of American Working Men in the Late Nineteenth Century," in T. K. Hareven and M. Vinovskis, eds., *Nineteenth Century Family Behavior* (in press), and also Michael Haines, "Industrial Work and the Family Life Cycle, 1889–1890," Department of Economics Working Paper no. 111, Cornell University, 1976.

125. *Statistik des Deutschen Reiches*, vol. 210/2.

126. *Ibid.*

127. StAB, VB, 1907, pp. 41–42; *Statistik des Deutschen Reiches*, vol. 210/2.

128. WAFKH, Gusstahlwerk Bochumer Verein, 2100, Nr. 7, 14. February 1887; StAB, VB, 1911, p. 38.

129. See Lutz Niethammer with the assistance of Franz Brüggemeier, "Wie Wohnten Arbeiter im Kaiserreich?" *Archiv für Sozialgeschichte*, 16 (1976), 61–134, and also John Modell and Tamara K. Hareven, "Urbanization and the Malleable Household: An Examination of Boarding and Lodging in American Families," in Tamara K. Hareven, ed., *Family and Kin in Urban Communities*, pp. 164–86.

130. The following are some comparative figures on the percentages of households listed as containing *Schlafgänger*, *Zimmerabmieter* and *Chambregarnisten* in 1910: Berlin, 19.6 percent; Bochum, 13.8 percent; Dortmund, 14.6 percent; Düsseldorf, 14.1 percent; Duisburg, 13.3 percent; Cologne, 11.4 percent; Barmen, 5.9 percent; Aachen, 6.6 percent; Krefeld, 5.5 percent (source: *Statistik des Deutschen Reiches*, vol. 240/2).

131. Niethammer and Brüggemeier, "Wie Wohnten Arbeiter im Kaiserreich?" p. 118.

132. Bell, *At the Works*, p. 50; Koch, *Die Bergarbeiterbewegung im Ruhrgebiet*, Table 11, p. 145, StAB, VB, 1875/76, p. 32.

133. On contributions by young girls to the family economy even when no longer living at home see Tilly and Scott, "Women's Work and the Family," p. 166.

134. In 1900, mean age at marriage was 27.7 for miners, 27.6 for unskilled factory workers, and 25.7 for skilled metalworkers (Rathaus Bochum, Familienbuch, 1900).

135. On this see also E. J. Hobsbawm, *Age of Capital*, p. 219: "If any single factor dominated the lives of nineteenth-century workers it was insecurity. They did not know at the beginning of the week how much they would bring home at the end. They

did not know how long their present work would last or, if they lost it, when they would get another job or under what conditions. They did not know when accident or sickness would hit them, and though they knew that some time in middle age—perhaps in the forties for unskilled labourers, perhaps in the fifties for the more skilled—they would become incapable of doing a full measure of adult physical labour, they did not know what would happen to them between then and death. Theirs was not the insecurity of peasants, at the mercy of periodic . . . catastrophes such as drought and famine, but capable of predicting with some accuracy how a poor man or woman would spend most days of their lives . . . It was more a profound unpredictability. . . ."

136. See for example StAB, Acta des königl. Landrathsamtes des Landkreises Bochum betreffend die sozialdemokratische und anarchistische Bewegung, 480, 1900–1905. Amtmann Hofstede to Landrat, July 31, 1901: "In the past year, no [socialist] agitational activity has been observed. The industrial recession has put the employers in the position of being able to get rid of the less reliable elements among their workers."

137. For some interesting speculations on this point see Josephine Klein, *Samples from English Culture* (London: Routledge and Kegan Paul, 1965), 1:89.

Two: Geographic Mobility

1. Carl Lange, "Die Wohnungsverhältnisse der ärmeren Volksklassen in Bochum," p. 73.

2. Helmuth Croon, "Studien zur Sozial- und Siedlungsgeschichte der Stadt Bochum"; *Statistik des Deutschen Reiches*, vol. 210/2, pp. 191–92; StAB, VB, 1871, p. 12, and *Statistik des Deutschen Reichs*, Bd. 210,2, p. 192. See also Wolfgang Köllmann, "Binnenwanderung und Bevölkerungsstrukturen."

3. Migrants from the eastern provinces were sometimes recruited directly by mine agents; see Dieter Fricke, *Der Ruhrbergarbeiterstreik von 1905*. But in general this movement seems to have been stimulated by word of mouth. Co-villagers, friends, and relatives who already lived in the Ruhr would write or return home telling others about the possibilities for work there. See Wilhelm Brepohl, *Der Aufbau des Ruhrvolkes*.

4. The increasing importance of the northeastern Germans in the far migrant group can be seen from the following table:

Composition of the Far Migrant Group, 1885 and 1907

	1885	1907
Hessen/Waldeck	35.3	11.1
N.E. Germany:	20.4	50.2
(E. Prussia		29.7)
(W. Prussia		7.6)
(Posen		12.9)
Rest of Prussia	23.7	21.0
Rest of Germany	17.8	11.5
Foreign Countries	2.8	6.2
	100.0	100.0

(SOURCE: *Preussische Statistik. Die Endgültigen Ergebnisse der Volkszählung im preussischen Staate vom 1. Dez. 1885*, 90:446, and *Statistik des Deutschen Reiches*, vol. 210/2, pp. 194–94.)

5. *Statistik des Deutschen Reichs,* vol. 210/2, p. 192.

6. Calculated from the reports of the *Standesamt* in StAB, VB, 1880–1900.

7. With the exception of the research conducted by Rudolf Heberle and Fritz Meyer in the 1930s (*Die Grosstädte im Strome der Binnenwanderung*), few scholars have analyzed urban migration in terms of annual population turnover. The most common approach has been to examine the origins of urban inhabitants at different points in time on the basis of data from the periodic census. See, for example, Wolfgang Köllman, "Industrialisierung, Binnenwanderung und 'Soziale Frage.' Zur Entstehungsgeschichte der deutschen Industriegrosstädte im 19. Jahrhundert," *Vierteljahrschrift für Sozial- und Wirtschaftsgeschichte,* vol. 46 (1959). However, a census provides a rather static picture of the process of urban migration and seriously underestimates the actual fluidity of urban populations. As Thernstrom and Knights observe in their pioneering article on nineteenth-century American cities, "Men in Motion": "The first step in a complex process—the initial move from country to city—was taken for the whole and the fluidity of urban population was grossly underestimated . . . Net population changes from census to census were thus taken to be an adequate measure of the volume of in-migration. But this assumes that migration was a one-way, one-step process . . . . This was far from the case. Migration out of nineteenth century cities took place on a massive scale." See also the article by Gordon W. Kirk, Jr., and Carolyn Tyirin Kirk, "Migration, Mobility and the Transformation of the Occupational Structure."

8. For example, 71 percent of a random sample of adult males listed in the 1880 city directory were still in Bochum in 1882. Applying this persistence rate to the total 1880 population, we would expect to find that about 9,511 people would have left the city during this two-year period. However, registration records reveal that at least 14,754 people actually left, indicating that more than 5,000 came into the city after the census for the directory was taken in 1880 and then left before the next census in 1882.

9. See *Statistisches Jahrbuch deutscher Städte,* vols. 7–11, 1898–1902; William H. Hubbard, "A Social History of Graz, Austria, 1861–1914" (Ph.D. dissertation, Columbia University, 1973), p. 86.

10. Data on American cities from Thernstrom and Knights, "Men in Motion," pp. 20–21; StAB, VB, 1913–24, p. 15.

11. Seasonal migration between agriculture and minework also continued to play some role into the 1880s and 1890s, although it was more common in the 1860s and 1870s. Local registration statistics do not permit a monthly breakdown of arrivals and departures, which might help to indicate the dimensions of these seasonal migrations more precisely; however, the two-year persistence rate quoted above in n. 8 suggests that by the 1880s the proportions of seasonal migrants cannot have been particularly large. For a discussion of the earlier period see Tenfelde, *Sozialgeschichte der Bergarbeiterschaft,* pp. 232–33.

12. StAB, JdH, 1899, p. 65. See also StAB, JdH, 1879, p. 23, and *Reports of the Gainsborough Commission,* p. 26; *Preussische Statistik,* 96:100; in 1900, the mean age at marriage for miners was 27.7, for unskilled factory hands, 27.6, for skilled metalworkers 25.7; calculated from Rathaus Bochum, Familienbuch, 1900. What follows deals rather exclusively with male workers; their experience was most readily accessible through the sources available for this study. However, this is not to say that the experience of the working class in Bochum can be fully understood without investigating the experience of women. For some indications see also above pp. 53-54 and below, footnote 24.

13. StAB, Acta des Landratsamtes, 479, III, July 31, 1900; Amtmann Hofstede to

Landrat and StAB, Z.S. 105, *Verhandlungen der Kreissynode Bochum* (Hofstede, June 12, 1899).

14. StAB, Küppers Nachlass, NI 23a, p. 62; StAB, JdH, 1899, p. 65; StAB, VB, 1913–24, p. 15.

15. Theodor Cassau, *Die Gewerkschaftsbewegung. Ihre Soziologie und ihr Kampf* (Halberstadt: H. Meyer, 1925), p. 194. See also R. J., "Erlebnisse eines Metalldrehers."

16. On the effects of heavy industry on the family life cycle and family economy, see pp. 54–55. For a comparative reference see Bell, *At the Works*, p. 49.

17. In 1899, for example, the Chamber of Commerce reported that, in response to high rates of job changing in the local iron and steel industry, "almost all the firms are making an effort, at considerable cost to themselves, to build up a strong, loyal work force" (StAB, JdH, 1899, p. 65). See also WAFKH, Gusstahlwerk Bochumer Verein, 25200, Nr. 1 (1863, 1896), Nr. 2 (1896), Nr. 4a (1871/72), and 25201, Nr. 1.

18. STAM, Regierung Arnsberg, Polizeiabteilung I.29. Arbeitseinstellungen in anderen Betrieben als Kohlenbergwerken: Report on "Streik der Drahtzieher auf den Westfälischen Drahtwerken in Werne," January 15, 1904.

19. StAB, Küppers Nachlass, NI 23a, p. 62.

20. StAB, VB, 1880/81; StAB, VB, 1879; StAB, VB, 1878.

21. StAB, JdH, 1907, pp. 36–37.

22. *Ibid.* Similar comments were made in 1902: "There is an overflow of workers, but not of the responsible, skilled men"; and in 1913; "Several large and middle sized plants are complaining about the lack of skilled and specialized workers"; StAB, JdH, 1902, p. 6, and 1913, p. 23. Unskilled and skilled men thus worked in fundamentally different labor markets, which seriously influenced their life chances. As E. J. Hobsbawm observes with regard to early nineteenth century England, "the first group lived in what amounted to a permanently glutted labour market, the second in one of permanent relative labour scarcity, except during bad slumps"; see E. J. Hobsbawm, "The British Standard of Living, 1790–1850," in *Labouring Men: Studies in the History of Labour* (New York, Basic Books, 1964), p. 70. In general terms, I think this observation also applies to German industrial workers during the second half of the nineteenth century. See also WAFKH, Gusstahlwerk Bochumer Verein, 15100, Nr. 1 and Nr. 2.

23. Similarly, in his study of Poughkeepsie, New York, Clyde Griffen argues that "for skilled workers, departure from the city even during business depressions seems more often to be a deliberate move to a known opportunity elsewhere" (Clyde Griffen, "Workers Divided: The Effect of Craft and Ethnic Differences in Poughkeepsie, New York, 1850–1880," in Stephan Thernstrom and Richard Sennett, eds., *Nineteenth-Century Cities*, p. 68).

24. The actual percentages of in-migrants receiving aid were:

Year	%	Year	%
1884	18.8	1893	16.3
1885	14.0	1894	18.1
1886	13.0	1895	12.3
1887	8.8	1896	7.6
1888	16.3	1897	9.2
1889	11.3	1898	8.2
1890	16.4	1899	8.4
1891	21.6	1900	9.4
1892	52.1		

25. StAB, VB, 1913–24, p. 15.

26. "Persisters" refers to those people in the sample still remaining by 1890; "out-migrants" means all those who had left the city before 1890 for whom changes in occupational status could be observed. Unfortunately this excludes the large number of out-migrants who left the city between 1880 and 1882, since obviously their occupations were listed only in 1880. The data presented in Table 2.4 are derived from the mobility study.

27. In his work on Newburyport, Massachusetts, Stephan Thernstrom suggests that "to find sufficiently stable employment to maintain a settled residence was itself success of a kind" (Stephan Thernstrom, Poverty and Progress, p. 90).

28. Helmuth Croon, "Die Einwirkungen der Industrialisierung," p. 309; StAB, Märkischer Sprecher, January 20, 1905; StAB, Z.S. Nr. 127 I, "An Alle Metallarbeiter vom Bochum und Umgegend" (1901).

29. Thernstrom, Poverty and Progress, p. 31.

30. Wolfram Fischer, "Soziale Unterschichtung im Zeitalter der Frühindustriali-sierung," International Review of Social History, 8 (1963), p. 417. See also Mack Walker, German Home Towns: Community, State, and General Estate, 1648–1871 (Ithaca, N.Y.: Cornell University Press, 1971) p. 105.

31. Fischer "Soziale Unterschichtung," p. 423.

32. Rudolf Braun, Sozialer und Kultureller Wandel in einem ländlichen Indus-triegebiet (Zürcher Oberland) unter Einwirkung des Maschinen- und Fabrikwesens im 19. und 20. Jahrhundert (Zurich/Stuttgart: E. Rentsch, 1965), p. 39.

33. Wolfram Fischer, Herz des Reviers. 125 Jahre Wirtschaftsgeschichte des Industrie- und Handelskammerbezirks Essen. Mühlheim. Oberhausen (Essen: R. Bacht, 1965), pp. 289–90. For similar statements in Bochum see StAB, JdH, 1881, p. 11, and StAB, Küppers Nachlass, NI 23a, p. 63.

34. Stanley Buder, Pullman: An Experiment in Industrial Order and Community Planning, 1880–1930 (New York: Oxford University Press, 1967), p. 229.

35. See Thernstrom, Poverty and Progress, pp. 84–90, and Thernstrom and Knights, "Men in Motion," pp. 34–37.

36. For a discussion of these issues in the contemporary Ruhr see Helmuth Croon, "Die Grosstadt als Heimat," Rheinische Heimatpflege (1964), n.s. 4:7-8.

Three: Social Mobility

1. The main exceptions being the highly interesting but somewhat limited series of investigations carried out in various branches of German industry under the guidance of Max Weber and subsequently published in the Schriften des Vereins für Sozialpolitik. Among the most interesting and detailed are Marie Bernays, "Auslese und Anpassung der Arbeiterschaft der geschlossenen Grossindustrie"; Clemens Heiss, "Auslese und Anpassung der Arbeiter in der Berliner Feinmechanik"; Elise Hermann, "Auslese und Anpassung der Arbeiterschaft in der Wollhutindustrie," Schriften des Vereins für Sozialpolitik, 135, No. 4 (Leipzig, 1912). A sociological analysis of a small German industrial town (Euskirchen) that plots intergenerational mobility in the nineteenth and twentieth centuries seems to have passed unnoticed by most historians; Renate Mayntz, Soziale Schichtung und Sozialer Wandel. Received just as this book was going to press, an important new contribution to the historical analysis of social mobility in Germany is that of Hartmut Kaelble, ed., Geschichte der sozialen Mobilitat seit der Industriellen Revolution.

2. Most recently this argument has been discussed by Stephen Thernstrom in Poverty and Progress. See also David M. Potter, People of Plenty: Economic Abundance and the American Character (Chicago: University of Chicago Press, 1966), ch.

4. Among nineteenth century observers, both Tocqueville and Bryce commented on the differences between the prospects of the lower classes in America and in Europe.

3. Seymour Martin Lipset and Reinhard Bendix, *Social Mobility in Industrial Society*. The literature on European mobility referred to by these authors is reported in more detail in the earlier work of Pitirim Sorokin, *Social Mobility*.

4. As Thernstrom points out, most of the materials on European social mobility deal with the period after 1900 and are concerned only with occupational mobility and intra-generational movement.

5. Among the numerous works in this vein: Fritz Stern, *The Politics of Cultural Despair: A Study in the Rise of the Germanic Ideology* (Garden City, N.Y.: Doubleday, 1965) and especially David Schoenbaum, *Hitler's Social Revolution: Class and Status in Nazi Germany, 1933–1939* (Garden City, N.Y.: Doubleday, 1966), in particular ch. 8. Others include Herman Lebovics, "'Agrarians' versus 'Industrializers,'" and Kenneth Barkin, *The Controversy over German Industrialization, 1890–1902* (Chicago: University of Chicago Press, 1970).

6. For example: Fritz K. Ringer, *The Decline of the German Mandarins: The German Academic Community, 1890–1933* (Cambridge, Mass: Harvard University Press, 1969).

7. This time period was chosen because (1) it covers years in which significant economic growth and social change occurred in the town; (2) 1880 was the first year in which adequate information on occupation, homeownership, and residence was presented in the city directories; (3) after 1901 the city directories were no longer compiled by city authorities and were considerably less reliable; and (4) after twenty-one years the remaining sample members were judged too small a group for further analysis.

8. Rathaus Bochum, Standesamt Bochum Mitte, Familienbuch, 1900.

9. WAFKH, Gusstahlwerk Bochumer Verein, 25000, Nr. 1, Nr. 4. Lehrlinge 1878–88, 1889–95; StAB, Akten der Schulverwaltung der Stadt Bochum, Schulgeldhebelisten, Gymnasium, Gewerbeschule, Oberrealschule (1870–1901).

10. Dahrendorf presents a similar image of contemporary German society; Ralf Dahrendorf, *Society and Democracy in Germany*, p. 109.

11. Paul B. Worthman, "Working Class Mobility in Birmingham, Alabama, 1880–1914," in Tamara K. Hareven, ed. *Anonymous Americans; Explorations in Nineteenth Century Social History* (Englewood Cliffs, N.J.: Prentice-Hall, 1971), p. 196.

12. Richard J. Hopkins, "Status, Mobility and the Dimensions of Change in a Southern City: Atlanta, 1880–1890," in Kenneth T. Jackson and Stanley K. Schutz, ed., *Cities in American History* (New York: Knopf, 1972), pp. 216–31.

13. Stephan Thernstrom, "Immigrants and Wasps: Ethnic Differences in Occupational Mobility in Boston, 1890–1940," in Stephan Thernstrom and Richard Sennett, eds., *Nineteenth Century Cities*, p. 129.

14. Hopkins, "Status, Mobility and the Dimensions of Change," p. 223.

15. On this point see also Thernstrom, *Poverty and Progress*, pp. 31, 134.

16. This is also reflected in *Bericht über die Jübelfeier des Bochumer Vereins*. For an analysis of the relationship between stability and advancement at the Krupp works see Richard Ehrenberg, "Krupp'sche Arbeiterfamilien. Entwicklung und Entwicklungsfaktoren," *Thunen-Archiv* (Jena 1911), 3:394.

17. There were three main divisions of work in the mine. The beginner, whether young or old, started as a *Schlepper*, the man who moved wagons about in the mine. After two years he began, as a *Lehrhauer*, to dig coal under the supervision of the *Hauer*. When he was deemed capable of working coal independently, he too became a *Hauer*. The *Schlepper* was generally paid a set daily wage; the others according to

how much coal they produced. But wage differentials were not all that great; at most perhaps they stood in the ratio of 1: 1.50; see Aurel von Jüchen, "Beim Bergarbeiter," in G. Koepper, *In Schacht und Hütte: Die Industrie des Ruhr-Kohlenbezirks und benachbarten Gebiete* (Reutlingen, n.d.), p. 74.

18. Gerhard Adelmann, ed., *Quellensammlung zur Geschichte der sozialen Betriebsverfassung*, vol. 1, no. 335. Oberbergamt Dortmund to Minister für Handel und Gewerbe Freiherr von Berlepsch, July 3, 1890, p. 522.

19. Helmuth Croon notes that local artisans preferred local boys to those from the east as apprentices (H. Croon, "Vom Werden des Ruhrgebietes," p. 213). For a description of the attitudes of the inhabitants of a small industrial town toward these outsiders see H. Croon and K. Utermann, *Zeche und Gemeinde*.

20. As David Blackbourn has recently observed, some of these miners may have moved into the small-retail sector to support themselves after having been blacklisted for trade union or political activity; moreover, it should be pointed out that many of the miners, and for that matter other industrial workers, who escaped into small shopkeeping probably remained culturally close to the working class; see David Blackbourn, "The Mittelstand in German Society and Politics, 1871–1914," *Social History* (January 1977) no. 4, p. 430.

21. The impact of downward mobility on the skilled worker in psychological terms considered apart from any economic consequences is difficult to grasp unless one is familiar with the social distance that separated skilled and unskilled workers in most nineteenth century industries. Workers noted, often with some anger, that the skilled held themselves more aloof from the unskilled than did the managers. Certain rituals pointed up distinctions of status; in some factories, for example, the unskilled could not be paid before the skilled. See Leo Uhen, *Gruppenbewusstsein und informelle Gruppenbildungen bei deutschen Arbeitern* (Berlin: Duncker and Humboldt, 1964), pp. 27–28. For an analysis of all the varied factors that determined prestige and status within the early German factory see Wolfram Fischer, "Innerbetrieblicher und sozialer Status der frühen Fabrikarbeiterschaft," in Friedrich Lütge, ed., *Die Wirtschaftliche Situation in Deutschland und Osterreich um die Wende vom 18. zum 19. Jahrhundert. Berichte über die erste Arbeitstagung der Gesellschaft für Sozial- und Wirtschaftsgeschichte in Mainz. 4.–6. März, 1963* (Stuttgart: G. Fischer, 1964).

22. Although R. J.'s father did not want him to become a "dependent" factory worker and sought to apprentice the boy to a craft, he did not seem to have regarded his son's later apprenticeship as a metal turner in a factory as a step down (R. J., "Erlebnisse eines Metalldrehers," p. 730; see also Fischer, "Innerbetrieblicher und sozialer Status," p. 199). Information on conditions of apprenticeship at Bochumer Verein is contained in WAFKH, Gusstahlwerk Bochumer Verein, 25000, Lehrvertrag, Nr. 1, 3, and 5.

23. See StAB, JdH, 1898, p. 56, and also 1899, p. 65.

24. During the period under consideration, 261 apprentices received the *Lehrbrief* in various skilled metal occupations: *Dreher, Former, Schlosser, Walzer*, etc. Of these, 204 could be identified as definitely coming from families resident in Bochum; the rest were outsiders who came to the city to learn a trade. Slightly less than 8 percent of parents resident in the city could not be positively identified. In almost 15 percent of the cases, the parent listed was the mother; often simply as a widow, otherwise as a working woman, usually in a low status job such as seamstress or maid. In these cases, it was impossible to compare the occupations of fathers and sons.

25. StAB, VB, 1864, p. 22; StAB, VB, 1913–24, p. 237; StAB, VB, 1913–24, pp. 234 and 237. From contemporary accounts, these schools often served a very necessary function, since apprentices, especially those in factories where only a limited variety of work was performed, were not well instructed in certain aspects of their

trades. For example, see Clemens Heiss, "Auslese und Anpassung der Arbeiter in der Berliner Feinmechanik," p. 190, and R. J., "Erlebnisse eines Metalldrehers," p. 753.

26. StAB, VB, 1864, p. 7.

27. StAB, VB, 1880–81, p. 45, and WAFKH, Gusstahlwerk Bochumer Verein, 25000, Nr. 1. Lehrvertrag, Nr. 5; StAB, VB, 1880–81, pp. 45, 49; StAB, Z.S. "Orts-Statut betr. die gewerbliche Fortbildungsschule in der Stadt Bochum" (1892), in *Lokalverordnungen der Stadt Bochum* (Bochum, 1895), p. 391; StAB, VB, 1900, p. 94; StAB, *Märkischer Sprecher,* March 8, 1912, p. 3.

28. StAB, VB, 1913–24, p. 237; Aurel von Juchen, "Beim Bergarbeiter," p. 74.

29. StAB, VB, 1913–24, p. 238. The instruction itself was free (Aurel von Juchen, "Beim Bergarbeiter," p. 74). See also Elaine Glovka Spencer, "Between Capital and Labor: Supervisory Personnel in Ruhr Heavy Industry before 1914," *Journal of Social History* (Winter 1975), no. 2, p. 183: "the two grueling years at the *Bergschule,* often requiring changes of residence for that period, appeared as a major hurdle for most young miners, especially since several years of mining experience, preparatory classes and currying favor with company bosses were necessary just to gain admission."

30. StAB. Z.S., *Festschrift zur 75-Jährigen Jubelfeier der Oberrealschule Bochum* (Bochum, n.d.), p. 14.

31. As the following table, calculated from StAB, Städt. Hauptkasse, Schulgeld-liste-Gewerbeschule, Ostern, 1880, reveals:

Fathers of Gewerbeschule Students (1880)

Unskilled workers	0
Skilled and artisanal workers	7
Merchants and tradesmen	9
Innkeepers	3
Lower white collar workers	4
Lower civil servants	6
Higher white collar workers	5
Higher civil servants	1
Factory owners and other proprietors	6
Landwirte	3
Rentier	1

32. See Ringer, *The Decline of the German Mandarins,* pp. 31–32.

33. StAB, Städt. Hauptkasse, Schulgeldliste-Gymnasium: January-March 1882, Pfändungs-Protokoll. For a modern example see the interview with Clemens K. in Erika Runge, *Bottroper Protokolle* (Frankfurt: Suhrkamp, 1968), p. 11. Clemens K., the son of a miner, was singled out by his teacher as being especially bright, and the family was advised to send him to a *Klosterschule.* His mother wanted him to start working but allowed him to continue his education "since then we'll all go to Heaven later."

34. The 1906 class had to be excluded because most students were still in school by 1910. The two sources for this analysis are StAB, Schulgeldlisten Gymnasium, 1876, 1886, 1896, and the list of graduates in StAB, Z.S. *Festschrift zur funfzigjähri-gen Jubelfeier des königlichen Gymnasiums zu Bochum* (Bochum, 1910), pp. 71–72. For a contemporary comparison see Renate Mayntz, *Soziale Schichtung und Sozialer Wandel,* p. 187: Mayntz concludes that as late as the 1950s, at least, these schools "served . . . quite definite groups in the population and specifically as vehicles for occupational and status continuity."

35. On the attitudes of Bochum's industrialists and the local *Mittelstand* regarding the functions of working class savings see pp. 123–24.

36. In the first years of the bank's operation, it seemed doubtful whether the institution would survive at all. The city fathers complained that whereas in England the average size of a savings account in 1859 was 183 thaler (549 marks), in Prussia it was only 80 thaler (240 marks). In Bochum itself, the picture was brighter; there the average account was 159 thaler (577 marks), and every sixth inhabitant, compared to every seventeenth in England and every thirty first in Prussia, possessed a savings book. Yet Bochum still remained far behind other and younger savings banks in the rest of Westphalia. After 1860, however, deposits increased considerably and observers were careful to point out that it was primarily workers who were saving more. Nevertheless, as the following table suggests, the total proportions of working-class depositors was never particularly high, with the possible exception of miners. The rate for miners may be too high since those living outside Bochum no doubt also made deposits at the Sparkasse, whereas I could only use the census figures for miners actually living within the administrative confines of the town as a base for the rate.

Depositors among Occupational Groups

Year	Occupation	Depositors per 100 Workers
1867	Miners	42
	Journeymen and factory workers	8
1871	Miners	70
	Journeymen and factory workers	8
1895	Miners	
	Journeymen and factory workers	11

37. The following table indicates the average size of worker accounts (in marks):

Average Size of Worker Accounts (in Marks)

Year	Journeymen	Master Craftsmen	Factory Workers	Miners
1856	294	435	358	285
1860	445	442	427	397
1864	294	573	477	405
1867	300	759	405	486
1870	392	961	536	616
1873	486	1,308	684	807
1880	674	2,182	785	947
1885	564	2,368	699	840
1890	472	2,289	798	1,031
1895	548	2,205	884	1,190

38. Comments on the moral value of homeownership can be found, among other places, in StAB. Z.S., *Verhandlungen der Kreissynode Bochum* (Hofstede, June 12, 1899), p. 105. See also H. Croon, "Studien zur Sozial- und Siedlungsgeschichte der Stadt Bochum," p. 107. See also on this question W. Fischer, "Soziale Unterschichten," p. 423, and Croon and Utermann, *Zeche und Gemeinde*, pp. 20–21. Homeowners certainly were more settled than renters; by 1890, for instance, among members of the mobility sample, no fewer than 78.4 percent of those who owned their own homes in 1880 were still resident in Bochum compared to only 41.2 percent of renters. By 1901, 47.4 percent of the 1880 homeowners remained compared to only 25.0 percent of those renting their dwellings.

39. StAB, VB, 1877–78, p. 28.

40. In the Bochum area, workers at the Hannover and Hannibal mines, owned by Krupp, could get mortgage loans at 3 percent (see Bergassessor Hundt's report on worker housing in *Mittheilungen über den Niederrheinischen Westfälischen Steinkohlen Bergbau* (Dortmund, 1901), p. 208). On Krupp company welfare programs in Essen see *Wohlfahrtseinrichtungen der Fried. Krupp'schen Gusstahlfabrik zu Essen zum Besten ihrer Arbeiter und Beamten* (n.p., 1883), and Gerhard Adelmann, ed., *Quellensammlung zur Geschichte der Sozialen Betriebsverfassung*, vol. 2. A description of Bochumer Verein housing policy can be found in WAFKH, Gusstahlwerk Bochumer Verein, 25200, Nr. 1.

41. On the cooperative housing movement in Bochum, see Paul Küppers, *Bochumer Heimstätten-Gesellschaft, G.m.b.H. 1917–1927* (Bochum, 1929), *25 Jahre Gemeinnütziger Wohnungsverein*, and *Eigenheim Bochum. Eine Darstellung zu der an den Magistrat der Stadt gerichteten Bitte um Unterstützung des Eigenheim-Wohnungsbaues* (Bochum, 1912). The role of the city government in public housing is considered in StAB, VB, 1913–24, pp. 107–8, and in a *Denkschrift* by Baumeister Diefenbach prepared in 1921. The formation of a Spar- und Bauverein in 1900 indicates the close connection between savings and homeownership (Heinrich Hoffmann, *Die Gründung und die Werdegang des Spar- und Bauvereins Bochum*, and Paul Küppers, *Spar- und Bauverein 25-Jährigen Bestehens . . . 1925* (StAB, Z.S. Nr. 77), but a report in the local paper in 1912 indicated that the Verein was in serious financial troubles and had to look to "one of the larger local companies" for help (StAB, *Märkischer Sprecher*, March 9, 1912).

42. This practice is reminiscent of the formal agreement described in Lutz Berkner, "The Stem Family and the Developmental Cycle of the Peasant Household; An Eighteenth Century Austrian Example," *American Historical Review*, vol. 77, no. 2 (1972). Dr. Croon informed me that in many cases a family acquired a home, then if possible, set about building houses for each of the children.

43. Data derived from mobility study. Lisa Peattie provides an interesting discussion of the idea that homeownership may provide a toehold in the urban economy, at least in developing cities in Latin America. She regards it as a way "in which people at the bottom can acquire capital and a social base", see L. Peattie, "Social Issues in Housing," in Frieden et al., eds., *Shaping an Urban Future* (Cambridge, Mass.: Harvard University Press, 1969), p. 27. Engels, on the other hand, saw homeownership as a trap that forced the worker to submit to employers; see Friedrich Engels, *The Housing Problem* (Moscow: Foreign Languages Publishing House, 1955), p. 75.

44. Thernstrom examines this problem in Newburyport (*Poverty and Progress*, pp. 155–56).

45. Adolf Weber, *Die Grosstadt und ihre sozialen Probleme* (Leipzig: Quelle and Meyer, 1918), p. 99.

46. Ralf Dahrendorf, *Society and Democracy in Germany*, p. 111.

47. *Ibid.*, pp. 111, 114.

48. Moreover, Dahrendorf argues that it has important implications for contemporary politics (see *ibid.*, p. 106): "There may be societies that are formally developed in the sense that they promise equal rights to their citizens, but that remain substantively traditional because the citizens, chained to ascribed social positions, are unable to exercise their rights. The social universe is modern, but its inhabitants have remained unmodern, and the road to liberalism is barred. These are extreme and obviously abstract statements; yet they describe a noteworthy feature of German society, which documents once again those explosive faults left behind by Imperial Germany and the industrial revolution" (see also pp. 115–19).

49. *Ibid.*, pp. 112 and 112–13.

50. *Bericht über die Jubelfeier des Bochumer Vereins*, p. 6.

51. Peter N. Stearns, *Lives of Labour: Work in a Maturing Industrial Society* (London: Croon Helm, 1975), p. 338.

52. The phrase is John Foster's. See John Foster, "Nineteenth-Century Towns—a Class Dimension," p. 283.

53. See Stearns, *Lives of Labour*, p. 337, and also the discussion by H. F. Moorhouse, "The Marxist theory of the Labour Aristocracy", *Social History*, Vol. 3 (January 1978), pp. 61–82.

Four: Industrialists, "Mittelstand," and Workers

1. John Friedmann, "Cities in Social Transformation," *Comparative Studies in Society and History* (November 1961), 4:89.

2. As Köllmann notes, the Ruhr heavy industry towns were in general characterized by relatively smaller elites than were the textile towns in the Rhineland, a reflection of their differing social and economic structures (W. Köllmann, *Sozialgeschichte der Stadt Barmen*, p. 123). See also the comparison between Bochum and Krefeld in H. Croon, "Die Städtevertretung in Krefeld und Bochum im 19. Jh.," p. 35.

3. On this point see H. Croon, "Studien zur Sozial-und Siedlungsgeschichte der Stadt Bochum," p. 90.

4. Walter Bertram, "Jacob Mayer," in *Rheinisch-Westfälische Wirtschaftsbiographien* (Münster: Aschendorff, 1954), 5:36–59.

5. The only readily available local fuel, charcoal, was too expensive for industrial use.

6. Bertram, "Jacob Mayer," pp. 37, 38, 40.

7. The favorable comments of the Solingen Chamber of Commerce to the Regierung in Düsseldorf (March 7, 1847) regarding Bochum steel are reproduced in *Aus der Geschichte der Industrie und Handelskammer zu Bochum*, p. 10.

8. Mayer and Kuhne had already applied to the Prussian Finance Minister for financial aid in 1845. Their request was rejected.

9. The most prominent participants in this venture were two Cologne banking houses: A. Schaffhausen'sche Bankverein and Bankhaus Sal. Oppenheim. The others were Rhineland and Westphalian merchants.

10. Wilhelm Endemann, "Darstellung seines Werdegangs," in Franz Mariaux, *Gedenkwort zum hundertjährigen Bestehen der Industrie und Handelskammer zu Bochum* (Bochum: Industrie and Handelskammer Bochum, 1965), pp. 500–502, 503.

11. Karl-Heinz Hemeyer, "Der Bochumer Wirtschaftstraum," pp. 158 and 159. Grimberg was also involved in opening up several undeveloped coal fields that were later sold to the Lothringische Eisengesellschaft de Wendel & Cie (Paris) and to the Stumm Concern. In addition to this, he owned a cement factory and a factory manufacturing miners' safety lamps.

12. See Wilhelm Schulte, *Westfälische Köpfe* (Münster: Aschendorff, 1963), p. 12; *Neue Deutsche Biographie* (Berlin: International Publications Service, 1953), 2:477 and Walter Bacmeister, *Louis Baare*, p. 93. The company's reputation for *Sozialpolitik* spread at least as far as Italy, as witnessed by a letter asking on behalf of an Italian manufacturer for details of the company's housing program (WAFKH, Gusstahlwerk Bochumer Verein, 25200, Nr. I).

13. Ivo N. Lambi, *Free Trade and Protection in Germany*, p. 98. See also Bacmeister, *Louis Baare*, p. 189, and StAB, Küppers Nachlass, NI 23a.

14. StAB, Küppers Nachlass, NI 23a, and W. Vogel, *Bismarcks Arbeiterversicherung* (Braunschweig: G. Westermann, 1951), pp. 39–40.

15. H. Jaeger, *Unternehmer in der Deutschen Politik*. Baare's two sons, Fritz and Wilhelm, held seats from 1905 to 1917 and from 1917 to 1919 respectively.

16. *Neue Deutsche Biographie*, p. 478.

17. Hemeyer, *Der Bochumer Wirtschaftsraum*, p. 55.

18. Hans Dieter Krampe, *Der Staatseinfluss auf den Ruhrkohlenbergbau in der Zeit von 1800–1865* (Cologne: Rheinisch-Westfälischen Wirtschaftsarchiv zu Koln, 1961) p. 55.

19. Friedrich Zunkel, "Beamtenschaft und Unternehmertum," p. 273. Many also invested in industry or were given shares.

20. Mariaux, *Gedenkwort*, p. 549.

21. Schulte, *Westfälische Köpfe*, p. 230; Zunkel, "Beamtenschaft und Unternehmertum," p. 274; and Mariaux, *Gedenkwort*, p. 545. Heintzmann was also a co-partner in the Bochumer Eisenhütte and a member of the Bochumer Verein board.

22. StAB, Küppers Nachlass, NI, 4, IV, p. 83.

23. StAB, Küppers Nachlass, NI, 4, IV, p. 67.

24. K. Brinkmann, *Geschichte der Flottmannwerke*, pp. 7–13.

25. In this respect, Bochum's industrial leaders were not particularly exceptional in the Rhineland-Westfalen area, nor for that matter in Prussia as a whole; see Friedrich Zunkel, *Der Rheinisch-Westfälische Unternehmer*, pp. 23–24; Heintz Wutzmer, "Die Herkunft der industriellen Bourgeoisie in Preussen in den vierziger Jahren des 19. Jahrunderts," in Hans Mottek et al., *Studien zur Geschichte der industriellen Revolution in Deutschland* (East Berlin: Akademie, 1960); Hartmut Kaelble, *Berliner Unternehmer*. See also Franz Decker, *Die Betriebliche Sozialordnung der Dürener Industrie*; W. Köllmann, *Sozialgeschichte der Stadt Barmen*; W. Zorn, "Typen und Entwicklungskräfte deutschen Unternehmertums"; and Heinz Sachtler, "Wandlungen des industriellen Unternehmers in Deutschland seit Beginn des 19. Jahrhunderts. Ein Versuch der Typologie des Unternehmers" (Rechts u. Staatswiss. Dissertation, Berlin, 1937).

26. John Foster, "Nineteenth-Century Towns," pp. 281–99; Asa Briggs, *Victorian Cities*; W. Köllmann, *Sozialgeschichte der Stadt Barmen*.

27. Schulte, *Westfälische Köpfe*, p. 12, and Hemeyer, *Der Bochumer Wirtschaftsraum*, p. 54.

28. Herbert G. Gutman, "Class, Status, and Community Power in Nineteenth-Century American Industrial Cities," pp. 236-37.

29. *Ibid.*, pp. 237, 243, 242–54.

30. *Ibid.*, p. 256.

31. Geoffrey Crossick, "The Emergence of the Lower Middle Class in Britain: A Discussion," in Geoffrey Crossick, ed., *The Lower Middle Class in Britain* (London: Croom Helm, 1977), p. 44.

32. Croon, "Vom Werden des Ruhrgebietes," p. 189.

33. Darpe, *Geschichte der Stadt Bochum*, pp. 526–27.

34. StAB, VB, 1860–61, pp. 83–84.

35. Darpe, *Geschichte der Stadt Bochum*, pp. 526–27.

36. StAB, VB, 1860–61, p. 28.

37. StAB, VB, 1860–61, p. 28. Köllmann notes that in Barmen under pressure from local industrialists, the city government similarly reduced the Einzugsgeld in 1861 and abolished it in 1867 (*Sozialgeschichte der Stadt Barmen*, p. 82).

38. StAB, VB, 1864, p. 3.

39. StAB, VB, 1860–61, p. 87.

40. StAB, VB, 1860–61, p. 86 and p. 12. However, this was lower than the ratio in the commercial city of Cologne, where in the same year some 28 percent were assessed. See Pierre Ayçoberry, "Probleme der Sozialschichtung in Köln im Zeitalter der frühen Industrialisierung," in W. Fischer, ed., *Wirtschafts- und Sozialgeschichtliche Probleme der frühen Industrialisierung*, p. 521.

41. StAB, VB, 1860–61, p. 89, and VB, 1866, p. 33. See also Gutman, "Class, Status, and Community Power," p. 240: "Rapid growth in the 1850s and 1860s illustrated in Paterson all the severe dislocations incident to quick industrialization and urbanization everywhere, but it also opened new opportunities for small retail businesses. Between 1859 and 1870, for example, the number of grocers rose from 105 to 230 and the number of saloonkeepers from 46 to 270."

42. StAB, VB, 1864, p. 78; StAB, VB, 1860–61, p. 56; StAB, VB, 1864, p. 4 and VB, 1871, p. 11.

43. Sources for the trace were the lists of assessed businesses in StAB, *Adressbuch der Stadt Bochum*, 1874/75 and 1884.

44. StAB, *Märkischer Sprecher*, January 11, 1889.

45. StAB, VB, 1877/78, p. 16; StAB, Städt. Hauptkasse, Schulgeldliste, Gymnasium, Pfändungs-Protokoll, January-March 1882.

46. StAB, VB, 1877/78, p. 4.

47. StAB, VB, 1885/86, p. 15.

48. StAB, JdH, 1878, p. 18.

49. StAB, VB, 1883/84, p. 49.

50. StAB, VB, 1882/83, p. 46; StAB, VB, 1883/84, p. 49.

51. StAB, VB, 1886/87, p. 53.

52. StAB, JdH, 1878, p. 19.

53. StAB, JdH, 1878, p. 17.

54. *Ibid.*, p. 17.

55. *Ibid.*, p. 17.

56. The *Arbeitsbuch* was similar in conception to the *Dienstbuch* required of domestic servants. Local industrialists, like those elsewhere in Germany, did not abandon their efforts to control workers in this fashion when legal requirements were not instituted. Blacklists were compiled and circulated among employers, and workers often had to have a certificate of good conduct from their former employer in order to get work; see Karl Erich Born, *Staat und Sozialpolitik seit Bismarcks Sturz. Ein Beitrag zur Geschichte der Innenpolitischen Entwicklung des Deutschen Reiches, 1890–1914* (Wiesbaden: Steiner, 1957), p. 82; see also WAFKH, Gusstahlwerk Bochumer Verein, 15100, Nr. 7. Akten betr. Arbeiter. Legal restrictions on young workers were a fairly frequently proposed and utilized means of social control although they affected only a fraction of all workers. See, for example, the Chamber of Commerce's proposal for compulsory savings for young workers (StAB, JdH, 1897, p. 28).

57. StAB, VB, 1880/81, p. 29.

58. StAB, VB, 1860/61, p. 42.

59. StAB, VB, 1877/78, p. 37.

60. StAB, VB, 1880/81, p. 30.

61. The Armenverwaltung was run on an unpaid, voluntary basis by civic-minded small property owners; as late as 1879, of the twelve *Armenvorsteher* for the various districts of the city, only one could properly be identified as an industrial manufacturer, while no fewer than three were master artisans, one a small shopkeeper, one an innkeeper, and four were merchants (StAB, *Adressbuch der Stadt Bochum*, 1879, p. 11).

62. StAB, VB, 1880/81, p. 29.

63. Carl Lange, "Die Wohnungsverhältnisse der ärmeren Volksklassen in Bochum," p. 99. The mayor of Essen envisioned a similar function for the city's new theater (see Eugene McCreary, "Essen, 1860-1914").

64. StAB, VB, 1860–61, pp. 45, 30.

65. StAB, JdH, 1881, p. 13. For comments on the intended role of the savings bank in America see Thernstrom, *Poverty and Progress*, pp. 122–23. Thernstrom argues that when savings banks were transplanted from Europe to America, "they were quickly given a different rationale. They were no longer viewed primarily as instruments providing security for men destined to remain in the working class, but rather as vehicles for upward mobility" (p. 125). On the development of savings banks in England as a response to "dissatisfactions" with the new economic position of the worker which resulted from industrialization, see Neil Smelser, *Social Change in the Industrial Revolution*.

66. StAB, VB, 1860–61, p. 46.

67. Local workers could deposit weekly amounts in one of the various *Sterbelade* that provided a sort of funeral insurance. See, for example, StAB, Z.S. Nr. 125, I, "Statut der Unterstützungskasse zu Bochum" (1909). The city government regarded these organizations as ineffective utilization of worker savings: "The effectiveness of these clubs is very limited. The *Sterbegeld* is usually totally used up for the burial of the member concerned without helping out the survivors any more than this" (StAB, VB, 1860–61, p. 56).

68. StAB, JdH, 1889, p. 34.

69. StAB, Küppers Nachlass, NI, 22, 3, p. 199. Transcript of the original letter, which has not been preserved in the Stadtarchiv.

70. StAB, Küppers Nachlass, NI, 23a, p. 150.

71. StAB, JdH, 1879, p. 18.

72. StAB, Küppers Nachlass, NI, 23a, p. 150.

73. *Ibid.*, p. 150.

74. *Ibid.*, p. 149. The Armenverwaltung presented another side to the argument (and some sympathy for workers) when it suggested that the real problem was that workers feared or could not afford to go to court, and therefore settled for too little (see StAB, VB, 1875/76, p. 32).

75. StAB. Küppers Nachlass, NI, 23a, p. 149.

76. The *Bochumer Verein* sickness and accident fund was compulsory and the worker lost all the money he had paid in if he left the company (WAFKH, Gusstahlwerk Bochumer Verein, 2100, Nr. 2. "Statuten der Kranken und Unterstützungskasse für die Meister und Arbeiter," 1881, Nr. 7, p. 5).

77. StAB, Küppers Nachlass, NI, 23a, p. 175.

78. StAB, *Märkischer Sprecher*, January 28, 1889.

79. StAB, Küppers Nachlass, NI 23a, p. 191.

80. StAB, *Märkischer Sprecher*, November 27, 1878.

81. StAB, *Märkischer Sprecher*, November 23, 1888.

82. Koch, *Die Bergarbeiterbewegung*, p. 31.

83. StAB, VB, 1871, and Küppers Nachlass, NI, 5, V, p. 361.

84. StAB, *Märkischer Sprecher*, January 8, 1889, p. 3.

85. StAB, Küppers Nachlass, NI, 5, V, p. 327.

86. *Der Bochumer Steuerprozess. Verhandlungen der Strafkammer des königlichen Landgerichts zu Essen* (Hagen/Westfalen, 1891), p. 6.

87. StAB, *Märkischer Sprecher*, January 18 and February 20 and 21, 1889; StAB, Küppers, NI, 5, V, p. 361.

88. Since these issues of the *Westfälische Volkszeitung* have not been preserved in the Stadtarchiv, the following discussion is drawn largely from the testimony given at the *Steuerprozess*.

89. *Steuerprozess*, p. 8.

90. *Ibid.*, p. 11.

91. *Ibid.*, p. 14.

92. *Ibid.*, p. 25.

93. *Ibid.*, p. 74.

94. *Ibid.*, p. 15.

95. *Ibid.*, pp. 43, 15.

96. *Ibid.*, p. 86.

97. *Ibid.*, p. 57.

98. *Ibid.*, pp. 34–35.

99. *Ibid.*, pp. 54, 40.

100. Fusangel's lawyer actually argued that his client's criticisms were intended to reform German industrial society, the better to preserve it (*Steuerprozess*, p. 74). Certainly, from his statements in the 1889 miners' strike, Fusangel had already shown himself to be distinctly unsympathetic to more radical perspectives: "Fusangel repeatedly argued that Schroder [one of the strike leaders] and his friends were Social Democrats in disguise who wanted to deprive the miners of their religious and patriotic ideals and who had robbed them of public sympathy by their immoderate claims" (Koch, *Die Bergarbeiterbewegung*, p. 53).

101. Koch, *Die Bergarbeiterbewegung*, p. 31.

102. StAB, Küppers NI, 22, 3, pp. 185, 183.

103. *Ibid.*, p. 183.

104. StAB, Acta des Königlichen Landrathsamtes des Landkreises Bochum betreffend Christlich-Soziale Agitation unter den Berg-und Fabrikarbeiter des Landkreises Bochum, 475, 1881–93; StAB, *Märkischer Sprecher*, May 9, 1889.

105. StAB, *Märkischer Sprecher*, February 14 and 15, 1889, and November 17, 1890.

106. *Monatshefte zur Statistik des Deutschen Reichs*, Jg. 1887 (IV31) and *Vierteljahrshefte zur Statistik des Deutschen Reichs* Jg. 1893 (SIV/1).

107. *Steuerprozess*, p. 70. For similar comments see StAB, JdH, 1889/90, p. 15, and STAM Oberpräsidium B, Nr. 2693, vol. I, fol. 88–89, reproduced in Karl Alexander Hellfaier, "Probleme und Quellen zur Frühgeschichte der Sozialdemokratie in Westfalen," p. 198.

108. StAB, JdH, 1889/90, p. 15. This is part of a detailed assessment of the reemergence of organized socialism in the Bochum area published by the Chamber of Commerce.

109. *Ibid.*, p. 15; Walter Bacmeister, *Hugo Schultz*, p. 129.

110. Fusangel moved to Hagen to run another newspaper. He eventually came into opposition with the *Zentrum*; when, after leaving Bochum, he was elected to the Reichstag he was not accepted into the Zentrum *Fraktion* (StAB, Küppers Nachlass, NI, 5, V, p. 365).

111. StAB, Küppers Nachlass, NI, 1, I, p. 249; see also *Märkischer Sprecher*, November 20, 1892.

112. StAB, *Märkischer Sprecher*, November 10, 1902.

113. The paper talks about Social Democratic voters "streaming in from the *Vororten*"—mining villages, which had recently (1904) been incorporated into the town (StAB, *Märkischer Sprecher*, November 8, 1906).

114. StAB, *Märkischer Sprecher*, November 3, 8, 1908; November 9, 1912.

115. StAB, VB, 1902, p. 18; StAB, VB, 1909, p. 46.

116. StAB, VB, 1902, p. 18; StAB, *Märkischer Sprecher*, March 5, 1901.

117. StAB, VB, 1902, p. 18.

118. *Ibid.*

119. StAB, VB, 1908, p. 35. See also StAB, Acta des Kgl. Landrathsamtes, 480, 1905, in which it was reported that during and after the 1905 miners' strike, the members of the Social Democratic Konsumvereine in the area increased considerably, "since during this period members have been granted the widest reaching credit." (see also StAB, Acta des Kgl. Landrathsamtes, 481). Amt Bochum Sud to Landrat, August 28, 1907, which described a Social Democratic Konsumverein in Laer: "The customers receive percentages. The small shopkeepers are thereby quite injured." With regard to "Werkskonsumanstalten" see Lange, "Wohnungsverhältnisse," p. 79.

120. Calculated from StAB, Staatssteurrolle, 1901.

121. StAB, Städt. Hauptkasse, Schulgeldisten.

122. StAB, *Märkischer Sprecher*, Monday, November 26, 1883; StAB, Küppers Nachlass, NI, 5, V, p. 355, and NI, 25, p. 86 (for evidence on support for the local anti-Semitic movement see StAB, Vereinswesen, Anti-Semitische Bewegung); Shulamit Angel-Volkov, "The Social and Political Function of Late Nineteenth-Century Anti-Semitism: The Case of the Small Handicraft Masters" in Hans-Ulrich Wehler, ed., *Sozialgeschichte Heute. Festschrift für Hans Rosenberg zum 70 Gebürtstag* (Kritische Studien zur Geschichtswissenschaft, Bd. 11) (Göttingen, 1974), p. 426.

123. StAB, *Märkischer Sprecher*, January 25, 1905, March 14, 1912, November 9, 1906; StAB, Acta des Kgl. Landrathsamtes, 481. Amt Bochum Sud to Landrat, November 30, 1906. See also John Foster, *Class Struggle and the Industrial Revolution*, pp. 52–53.

124. StAB, Vereinswesen, 1876; StAB, Acta des Kgl. Landrathsamtes, 479, 480, 481; 1895–1909, STAM, I, Nr. 159–62. See also StAB, 480, 1900–1905, report of Amtmann Weitmar to Landrat, August 31, 1905, which argued that some of the miners' leaders who had been fired from the mines went to Bochum, received political training in courses given by the Arbeitersekretariat in Bochum, and returned to spread social democratic ideas among the workers; "at the same time," the report continued, "they do a little trade in foodstuffs etc. as a cover for their agitational activities."

125. Gutman, "Class, Status and Community Power," pp. 255, 256, 258, On p. 256 Gutman discusses the use of state troops in industrial disputes: "Such action may have resulted from the low status and power the industrialist had in his local community. Unable to gain support from locally elected officials and law enforcement groups and unable to exercise coercive power in the community, he reached upward to the state level, where direct local pressures were felt less strongly."

126. *Ibid.*, p. 259.

127. See for example David Blackbourn, "The Mittelstand in German Society and Politics, 1871–1914," *Social History*, No. 4 (January 1977), p. 430, and also the interesting discussion in John Foster, *Class Struggle and the Industrial Revolution*, pp. 166–177.

128. See especially Elaine Glovka Spencer, who argues that "an analysis of actual policy decisions made by Ruhr industrial leaders reveals that by 1914 the proponents of confrontation at any price were balanced, indeed outnumbered, by those who did not rule out the possibility of cautious accomodation with organized labor" ("Employer Response to Unionism: Ruhr Coal Industrialists before 1914," p. 398) but whose evidence does not strongly support that argument. For comparative

information on Upper Silesia see Lawrence Schofer, *The Formation of a Modern Labor Force*, pp. 137–64. Certainly it is true that local heavy industrialists were, by the immediate prewar years, prepared to support "yellow" company unions as well as to make some, albeit ambivalent, gestures toward the Catholic miners' union (Glovka Spencer, pp. 406–7). However, whether or not this actually meant that "the coal industrialists were moving toward more stable and rational relations with their workers" (Spencer, p. 412) just before the war seems to be still an open question.

129. See, for example, the various reports in *Die Schwereisenindustrie*, pp. 492 and 634. On blacklisting in the coal industry see Spencer, "Employer Response to Unionism," p. 405. See also StAB, *Märkischer Sprecher*, January 17, 1905. See also Klaus J. Mattheier, "Werkvereine und wirtschaftsfriedlich-nationale (gelbe) Arbeiterbewegung im Ruhrgebiet" in Jürgen Reulecke, ed., *Arbeiterbewegung an Rhein und Ruhr*, pp. 173–204; and Klaus Saul, *Staat, Industrie, und Arbeiterbewegung* (Düsseldorf: 1974).

130. StAB, VB, 1878, 47.

131. StAB, *Märkischer Sprecher*, May 13, 1889, and January 26 and 31, 1905.

132. StAB, JdH, 1902, p. 6, and also WAFKH, Gusstahlwerk Bochumer Verein, 15100, Nr. 1.

133. StAB, VB, 1878.

134. StAB, Küppers Nachlass, NI, 23a, pp. 63–64.

135. WAFKH, Gusstahlwerk Bochumer Verein, 2100, Nr. 2 and 6; WAFKH, Gusstahlwerk Bochumer Verein, 25200, Nr. 1, and 25201, Nr. 1.

136. WAFKH, Gusstahlwerk Bochum Verein, 25200, Nr. 1, 1892: This document, in describing the company's *Kolonie*, remarked that "all 'foreign' elements are absolutely kept away." On the important role played by industrial firms in the actual building of Ruhr cities see H. Croon, "Der Strukturwandel des Ruhrgebietes," pp. 422–23.

137. Company housing, originally intended mainly to stabilize skilled workers, was at least as early as the 1880s being conceived of primarily in terms of "social control." In his 1885 report, Mayor Lange noted that the main requirement for getting a company house was not the skills the worker had to offer but rather his loyalty and good behavior: "The *Bochumer Verein* as a rule gives these houses only to orderly, reliable workers who have already worked for the company for some time and against whose conduct no complaints have been raised" (Lange, "Die Wohnungsverhältnisse," p. 79).

138. StAB, VB, 1864, p. 5; StAB, *Bericht des Bürgermeisters Lange betreffend die Unterbringung der Obdachlosen in der Stadt Bochum* (Bochum, 1884), p. 8; quoted in Brinkmann, *Die Geschichte der Flottmannwerke*, p. 54. For an excellent introduction to the question of working-class housing in late nineteenth-century Germany see Lutz Niethammer, with the assistance of Franz Brüggemeier, "Wie wohnten Arbeiter im Kaiserreich?" *Archiv für Sozialgeschichte* (1976) 16:61–134.

139. StAB, VB, 1864, p. 4.

140. Lange noted that families that did not enjoy the advantage of living in company homes had to pay out a much higher rent although he did not specify local rent prices (Lange, "Die Wohnungsverhältnisse," p. 98). See also his comments on the generally more healthy and convenient environment provided by company homes (*ibid.*, p. 79). In 1892 a family dwelling at the Bochumer Verein rented for from 88 to 185 marks per year, roughly 7–17 percent of that year's average wage for workers in the steel mill (WAFKH, Gusstahlwerk Bochumer Verein, 25200, Nr. 1). In addition to having a cheaper rent to begin with, company dwellings offered other financial advantages. The Bochumer Verein took the rent out of the worker's pay directly as he

received it every two weeks, thus, according to the company at least, eliminating "the disadvantages associated with the normal procedure of paying a quarter and even a half-year's rent in advance, which often leads to pawning to meet the installments and the interest on them" (WAFKH, Gusstahlwerk Bochumer Verein, 25200, Nr. 1).

141. Lange, "Die Wohnungsverhältnisse," p. 79.

142. In particular, overcrowding caused by taking in single, young men as boarders. On this problem and middle class reactions to it see Lange, "Die Wohnungs-verhältnisse," pp. 92–93. For the housing regulations see StAB, "Polizei-Verordnung betr. das Kost und Quartiergangerwesen," in Bürgerbuch der Stadt Bochum (Bochum, 1909), p. 782.

143. StAB, Bericht des Bürgermeisters Lange, p. 8.

144. StAB, VB, 1900, p. 70.

145. WAFKH, Gusstahlwerk Bochumer Verein, 25200, Nr. 1. Rent Contract, 1865. In one case, Baare did refrain from evicting a group of strike leaders at a company mine but only until the strike had ended so as not to inflame their followers (WAFKH, Gusstahlwerk Bochum Verein, 21700, Nr. 1, April 20, 1891).

146. Evidence suggests that the companies were successful to a certain extent in achieving at least the first of these goals. Workers in the mobility sample who lived in company housing were over 10 percent more stable than those who rented on the open market.

147. Adolph Gunther and Rene Prévôt, "Die Wohlfahrtseinrichtungen in Deutschland und Frankreich," p. 106.

148. Lange, "Die Wohnungsverhältnisse," p. 80.

149. Ibid., pp. 83–85; Articles 3, 4, 6 of the General Regulations and Articles 4 and 9 of the Stubenordnung.

150. WAFKH, Gusstahlwerk Bochumer Verein, 25200, Nr. 1. For an interesting non-European comparison, see Charles van Onselen, Chibaro, African Mine Labour in Southern Rhodesia, 1900–1933 (London: Pluto Press, 1976), especially pp. 128–97.

151. See Ludwig Puppke, Sozialpolitik und Soziale Anschauungen, p. 184.

152. Bacmeister, Louis Baare, p. 210, and Brinkmann, Die Geschichte der Flott-mannwerke, p. 54.

153. Bericht über die Jubelfeier, p. 1.

154. Ibid., p. 5. Rittershaus lived in Barmen, where he was known as a Heimatdi-chter. He acted as general agent for several insurance companies and in 1874 founded the "Verein für Ferienkolonien" (Köllmann, Sozialgeschichte der Stadt Barmen, p. 214–15).

155. Bericht über die Jubelfeier, p. 5.

156. Ibid.

157. Ibid., p. 6.

158. Ibid., p. 8.

159. Bericht über die Jubelfeier, passim.

160. See for example Dahrendorf, Society and Democracy in Germany, pp. 49–50, Glovka Spencer, "Employer Response to Unionism," p. 412, and Schofer, The Formation of a Modern Labor Force, pp. 157 and 163. Schofer postulates a "moderniza-tion" of paternalism among Upper Silesian employers from the 1870s to the early twentieth century: "Though records on the 1870s are sparse, enough information exists to show that the group of Upper Silesian industrialists and top managers made an obvious attempt in this decade to direct the daily lives of the workers" but, thereafter, as the labor force expanded, "it proved quite difficult to maintain close supervision over the home lives of the members of a rapidly changing labor force regardless of employer intent" and thus "welfare projects became simply tools in

attracting and keeping employees and perhaps were useful in limiting the latter's occupational and geographic mobility." (pp. 100, 101). However, earlier, citing two cases that date from the relatively late years 1893 and 1894, Schofer suggests that "this remarkable close watch over the details of everyday living emerged quite often, for paternal care also included paternal strictures" (p. 94).

161. Schofer, The Formation of a Modern Labor Force, p. 157. For a fuller discussion of these issues see my review of Schofer's book in International Working Class and Labor History Newsletter, 1977, pp. 44–46.

162. On the notion of "rule-learning" see Schofer, The Formation of a Modern Labor Force, pp. 162–63. On closely related notions of "adjustment" see Peter N. Stearns, "Adaptation to Industrialization," pp. 303–31.

163. See especially the recent unpublished paper by Gerald D. Feldman and Ulrich Nocken, "Trade Associations and Economic Power: A Comparison of Interest Group Development in the German Iron and Steel and Machine Building Industries, 1900–1933."

164. For stimulating comments on this see the review article by Geoff Eley, "Capitalism and the Wilhelmine State: Industrial Growth and Political Backwardness in Recent German Historiography, 1890–1918," Historical Journal (1978), 21(3):737–50.

165. For some stimulating but conflicting viewpoints on historians' use of the sociological concept of "social control," see A. P. Donajgrodzki, Introduction to Social Control in Nineteenth Century Britain (London: Croom Helm, 1977), edited by the same author, and Gareth Stedman Jones, "Class Expression versus Social Control?" History Workshop (Autumn 1977), 4:163–70.

Five: The Foundations of Worker Protest: Miners and Metalworkers

1. StAB, Märkischer Sprecher, March 13, 1912.

2. StAB, Märkischer Sprecher, March 14, 1912. Some of the strike leaders labeled members of the crowd who engaged in these attacks on police as "Moabiter," a reference to the violent neighborhood war between police and workers that had raged in the Berlin district of Moabit two years earlier (see StAB, Märkischer Sprecher, March 15, 1912, and also Helmut Bleiber, "Die Moabiter Unruhen, 1910," Zeitschrift für Geschichtswissenschaft (1954), pp. 370–400.

3. StAB, Märkischer Sprecher, March 14 and 15, 1912.

4. StAB, Märkischer Sprecher, March 14, 1912.

5. StAB, Märkischer Sprecher, March 14 and 16, 1912.

6. For an interesting analysis of these smaller strikes see Stephen Hickey, "The Shaping of the German Labour Movement: Miners in the Ruhr."

7. Based on a search of Bochumer Verein company records for this period (WAFKH, Gusstahlwerk Bochum, 21700, Nr. 1, and also STAM, P.A. Reg. Arnsberg, I, I; I.1463; and I.24–I.34). See also Board of Trade. Accounts and Papers. Vol. 108. Cost of Living in German Towns (London, 1908), p. 79: "It is the boast of the largest industrial company in the Bochum district that during a period of several decades there has been no strike amongst its workmen. Even to-day, when labor organisation is so general and so vigorous, the misunderstandings which inevitably arise from time to time are still found capable of amical adjustment."

8. StAB, Märkischer Sprecher, July 11, 1872; StAB, Z.S. Nr. 127 I, "An Alle Metallarbeiter"; Statistik des Deutschen Reichs, II, 74. Bd. 178, 1905. A 1900 police report also indicated that there had been an earlier strike that year involving 27 of the 81 strikers, all of them working in the Handfeilenhauerei (STAM, I.28. Stadt. Bochum, June 6, 1900). For detailed reports on the 1901 strike see STAM, I.28. Report of the

Kgl. Gewerbeinspektor zu Bochum, November 12, 1901; clipping from Rh. Westf. Arbeiterzeitung in Dortmund, October 1, 1901; clipping from Volksblatt, October 10, 1901.

9. Statistisches Jahrbuch deutscher Städte, V, 13, Bd. 178, 1905; Statistik des Deutschen Reiches, II, 74, Bd. 178, 1905; StAB, Acta des Landratsamtes, Amt. Weitmar, July 1911.

10. StAB, Festschrift zum Gewerkschafts-Fest der christlichen-nationalen Arbeiterschaft auf dem Schutzenhöfe Bochum. Am 1. Sept., 1912; StAB, Acta des Landratsamtes des Landkreises Bochum, 481. During the 1905 strike, Reichstagsabgeordneter Sachse (Alter Verband) suggested that the miners were 40 percent organized (StAB, Märkischer Sprecher, January 17, 1905).

11. Information derived from a portion of an unpublished manuscript on the Social Democrats in Bochum by Phillip Sommerlad, printed in Bochum. Stadt der Zukunft. Sommerlad suggests that a Fachgruppe of filemakers was formed somewhat earlier. See also STAM, P.A.I, 24, Report of Mayor Lange, July 12, 1889, which lists a Kranken-Unterstützungs Bund der Schmiede with 32 members and an Orts-Verein der Machinenbauer und Metallarbeiter Bochums und Kranken und Sterbekasse (Hirsch Duncker) with 25 members.

12. Two possible figures are given here as the sources do not fully agree; Neumann argues that there were only 436 organized metalworkers in 1907 in Bochum whereas Hirschfeld suggests that there were a total of 750 in 1906. Of course membership could have declined by the difference between these two figures in the intervening year (Walter Neumann, Die Gewerkschaften im Ruhrgebiet, Voraussetzung, Entwicklung und Wirksamkeit (Cologne: Bund, 1951), p. 132, and Dr. Paul Hirschfeld, Die Freien Gewerkschaften in Deutschland. Ihre Verbreitung und Entwicklung, 1896–1906 (Jena: Fischer, 1908). See also Gerhard A. Ritter, Die Arbeiterbewegung im Wilhelminischen Reich. Die Sozialdemokratische Partei und die Freien Gewerschaften, 1890–1900 (Berlin: Colloquium, 1959), p. 111; Gerhard A. Ritter and Klaus Ten Felde, "Der Durchbruch der Freien Gewerkschaften Deutschlands zur Massenbewegung im letzten Viertel des 19. Jahrhunderts," in Heinz Oskar Vetter, ed., Vom Sozialistengesetz zur Mitbestimmung (Cologne: Bund, 1975), pp. 61–120; also Dieter Groh, "Überlegung zum Verhältniss von Intensivierung der Arbeit und Arbeitskämpfen im organisierten Kapitalismus in Deutschland (1896–1914)." Manuscript. For the village of Weitmar: StAB, Acta des Landratsamtes, 479.

13. Clark Kerr et al., Industrialism and Industrial Man, p. 172.

14. Louis Chevalier, La Formation de la population parisienne au XIXe siecle (Paris: Presses Universitaires de France, 1950), and Laboring Classes and Dangerous Classes.

15. Chevalier, Laboring Classes and Dangerous Classes, pp. 71, 265, 469, and 553.

16. M. Girard, "Études comparées des mouvements révolutionnaires en France en 1830, 1840 et 1870–71," Cours de Sorbonne (Paris, n.d.), p. 46, cited in G. Rudé, Debate on Europe, 1815–1850 (London: Harper and Row, 1972), p. 81.

17. David Pinkney, "A New Look at the French Revolution of 1830," Review of Politics, 23:490–501.

18. M. D. George, London Life in the Eighteenth Century (New York: Putnam, 1965) and A. J. P. Taylor, The Hapsburg Monarchy, 1809–1918 (Chicago: University of Chicago Press, 1965), p. 58.

19. Val Lorwin, "Working Class Politics and Economic Development in Western Europe," American Historical Review (January 1958), 63(2), 338–51.

20. Wolfgang Köllmann, "The Process of Urbanization in Germany at the Height of the Industrialization Period," Journal of Contemporary History (July 1969), 4(3):72.

21. Wolfgang Köllmann, "Industrialisierung, Binnenwanderung und 'Soziale Frage.' Zur Entstehungsgeschichte der deutschen Industriegrosstädte im 19. Jahrhundert," *Vierteljahrschrift für Sozial- und Wirtschaftsgeschichte,* (1959), 46:60.

22. Charles Tilly, "Urbanization and Political Disturbances in Nineteenth Century France," paper presented to the Annual Meeting of the Society for French Historical Studies, Ann Arbor, cited in Rudé, *Debate,* p. 86. See also Charles Tilley et al., *The Rebellious Century.*

23. Richard Tilly, "Popular Disturbances in Nineteenth-Century Germany, p. 30. For indications of the directions recent work in Germany has followed see Richard H. Tilly, ed., "Sozialer Protest." Special issue of *Geschichte und Gesellschaft,*Jg. 3, 1977/ Heft. 2.

24. Louise A. Tilly, "I Fatti di Maggio," p. 148.

25. StAB, Rathaus Bochum, Familienbuch, 1900.

26. StAB, VB, 1913–24, p. 15.

27. StAB, JdH, 1892, p. 24.

28. Seidl argues that job changing was an early form of class struggle. While in some measure at least, it is correct to see job changing as an expression of grievances, it was at most an individual protest and often provided an alternative to collective action; as one trade union leader observed during the 1905 miners' strike, without strong organizations "the men do not have the courage to speak out freely, so they choose a back door and move around from mine to mine" (StAB, *Märkischer Sprecher,* January 17, 1905). Yet it is difficult to agree with Stephan Thernstrom, who argues that high rates of transience worked to defuse social conflict because they meant that exactly those workers who were most potentially radical were not in one place long enough to organize and make their protest felt. Though it is true that transience posed serious hindrances to the maintenance of permanent labor organizations, there was no particular reason why geographic mobility, in and of itself, should prevent workers from engaging in strikes (H. Seidl, "Der Arbeitsplatzwechsel als eine frühe Form des Klassenkampfes"; Stephan Thermstrom, "Urbanization, Migration and Social Mobility," p. 168). See also Schofer, *The Formation of a Modern Labor Force,* pp. 121–30, and my earlier article, "Regionale Mobilität und Arbeiterklasse. Das Beispiel Bochum 1880–1901," *Geschichte und Gesellschaft* (1975) 1:99–120.

29. Wilhelm Brepohl, *Industrievolk im Wandel,* p. 109.

30. For a brilliant exposition of the functioning of kinship networks among the working class inhabitants of a nineteenth century industrial city see Michael Anderson, *Family Structure in Nineteenth Century Lancashire.*

31. StAB, Z.S. 105, Verhandlungen der Kreissynode Bochum (Hofstede, June 12, 1899).

32. Max Jürgen Koch, *Die Bergarbeiterbewegung,* p. 15.

33. StAB, VB, 1873/74, p. 2.

34. StAB Adressbuch der Stadt Bochum, 1876. See also Koch, *Die Bergarbeiterbewegung,* p. 21; O. Taeglichsbeck, *Die Belegschaft der Bergwerke und Salinen,* vol. 2, table 1.

35. Wolfgang Köllmann, ed., *Der Bergarbeiter Streik von 1889.*

36. For an interesting analysis of the relationship between economic conditions and working class militancy see John Foster, *Class Struggle and the Industrial Revolution: Early Industrial Capitalism in Three English Towns* (London: Weidenfeld and Nicolson, 1974), pp. 73–99. See also the discussion in Jon Amsden and Stephen Brier, "Coal Miners on Strike," pp. 583–86.

37. Koch, *Die Bergarbeiterbewegung,* p. 18; StAB, *Märkischer Sprecher,* March 9, 1912.

38. Smelser, *Social Change in the Industrial Revolution,* p. 398.

39. Neil Smelser, "Mechanisms of Change and Adjustment to Change," in Hoselitz and Moore, eds., Industrialization and Society pp. 35, 32, 37.

40. Smelser, Social Change in the Industrial Revolution, p. 398.

41. Conrad Arensberg, "Industry and Community," in C. Arensberg and S. T. Kimball, Culture and Community (New York: Peter Smith, 1965), p. 294.

42. Gerhard Adelmann, Die Soziale Betriebsverfassung des Ruhrbergbaues.

43. Koch, Die Bergarbeiterbewegung, p. 135.

44. Miners did not experience the same disruption of their family lives that cotton workers underwent, since their work and their home had not been as intimately associated before industrialization. "Structural change" in mining affected other aspects of the miners' experience more profoundly, in particular their social, economic, and legal roles in German society.

45. "Knappschaft Ordnung für die Bergleute in den Bezirken des Märkischen Essen-Werdenschen Bergamts," in Die Entwicklung, p. 144.

46. Adelmann, Die Soziale Betriebsverfassung, pp. 44–45. See also reprint of "General Privilegium der Bergleute den 16. May, 1767," in Der Anschnitt. Zeitschrift für Kunst und Kultur im Bergbau (1955), 7(5):7–8.

47. See Mack Walker, German Home Towns: Community, State and General Estate (Ithaca, N. Y.: Cornell University Press, 1971), p. 98.

48. See Klaus Tenfelde, Sozialgeschichte der Bergarbeiterschaft an der Ruhr im 19. Jahrhundert (Bonn-Bad Godesberg: Verlag Neue Gesellschaft, 1977), pp. 87–131.

49. Gerhard Adelmann, ed., Quellensammlung zur Geschichte der sozialen Betriebsverfassung 1(96):140–41: "Oberbergamt Dortmund an Minister der öffentlichen Arbeiten, 23 November, 1889."

50. StAB, VB, 1860–61, p. 54, and Koch, Die Bergarbeiterbewegung, p. 31.

51. Koch, Die Bergarbeiterbewegung, p. 28.

52. Die Entwicklung 4, 4:70; Peter Stearns, "Adaptation to Industrialization: German Workers as a Test Case," Central European History (1970), 3:306.

53. See David Landes, The Unbound Prometheus, and N. J. G. Pounds and W. N. Parker, Coal and Steel in Western Europe (Bloomington: Indiana University Press, 1957).

54. See for example J. P. Courthéoux, "Privilèges et misères d'un métier sidérurgique au XIXe siècle; le puddleur," Revue d'Histoire économique et sociale (1959), 37:161–84.

55. Bacmeister, Louis Baare, pp. 143, 166–67. Mayer usually drank a toast with the men each time a casting was made.

56. Däbritz, Bochumer Verein, p. 340.

57. WAFKH, Gusstahlwerk Bochumer Verein, 21000, Nr. 1. For instance, masters were no longer permitted to board their apprentices.

58. Hans Mauersberg, Deutsche Industrien im Zeitgeschehen Eines Jahrhunderts p. 277.

59. StAB, JdH, 1902.

60. Die Schwereisenindustrie, p. 489. One significant difference between Britain and Germany may well be that whereas in England technological innovations were introduced to a labor force with a deeply imbedded craft tradition and strong craft union organizations which allowed them to offer considerable resistance, in Germany this new technology was much more rapidly superimposed on a largely new work force and at a time when the capacities of craft workers to resist had been seriously undercut by the political repression of the post-1848 period. See for example Dick Geary, "The German Labour Movement, 1848–1919," European Studies Review (1976), 6:297–330.

61. See Landes, The Unbound Prometheus, pp. 257–269, and also Reports of the

Gainsborough Commission, p. 20, which describes the Krupp operation: "Watching the way the ore was brought to the furnace from the barges in the private harbor adjoining the Rhine by the most elaborate machinery, we had a most excellent object-lesson of how human labour is ousted by machinery." For American developments see David Brody, *Steelworkers in America,* chs. 1 and 2.

62. On this point see especially Keith Burgess, "Technological Change and the 1852 Lock-Out in the British Engineering Industry," *International Review of Social History,* part 2 (1969), 14:215–36.

63. See Peter Stearns, "Adaptation to Industrialization," pp. 317–18.

64. Franz Schulze, *Die polnische Zuwanderung im Ruhrrevier und ihre Wirkung* (Munich, 1909).

65. Koch, *Die Bergarbeiterbewegung,* p. 20.

66. Richard Tilly, "Popular Disturbances in Nineteenth-Century Germany," p. 33.

67. Rudé, *Debate,* pp. 83–84.

68. E. J. Hobsawm. "The Machine Breakers," *Past and Present,* vol. 1 (1952).

69. Aurel von Jüchen, "Beim Bergarbeiter," in G. Koeppers, *In Schacht und Hütte,* p. 74.

70. Adelmann, *Die Soziale Betriebsverfassung,* pp. 29–30.

71. Jüchen, "Beim Bergarbeiter," p. 74.

72. *Die Entwicklung,* p. 79, and StAB, Staatssteuerrolle, 1901. In saying this I am not ignoring the very real elements of differentiation and division created by the wage and work structure in mining. As Stephen Hickey correctly points out, the spread of individual earnings underground could be quite considerable as a result both of differences in the physical conditions of the work site and differences in the skills and strength of teams (see Stephen Hickey, forthcoming Oxford University dissertation on miners in the eastern Ruhr, chap. 4). Added to this were the effects of a competitive system of bidding among work teams for the right to work a given place (*Der Klassenkampf im Ruhrrevier,* pp. 16–17). Nevertheless, the point to be made is that, compared to the iron and steel industry, the wage and work structure in mining had much greater potential to promote solidarity among mineworkers.

73. J. Hoffmann, *Die Ewige Bergmann,* old miner's saying, p. 82.

74. See Brody, *Steelworkers in America,* pp. 86–87, Uhen, *Gruppenbewusstsein,* pp. 27–28, and *Die Schwereisenindustrie,* p. 333.

75. The piece rate system, common in the metal industry, contributed to the fragmentation of the work process; See Louis Baare, *Auszug aus dem Generalversammlung des Bochumer Vereins für Bergbau und Gusstahlfabrikation* (Bochum, 1875).

76. *Die Schwereisenindustrie,* p. 331. For that matter, the compilers of this survey did not think that some skilled jobs rated the special status that was given them: "The title *Walzmeister* can give the unitiated the impression of a quite special position, but . . . in most cases the *Walzmeister* are simply workers who, through one circumstance or another, have been put into the group of *Walzmeister.* The responsibility . . . of the first men is in no way that much greater that the considerable difference in size of their wages can thereby be justified" (p. 333).

77. *Die Schwereisenindustrie,* p. 333, and StAB, Staatssteurrolle, 1901.

78. *Die Schwereisenindustrie,* p. 333.

79. *Ibid.* Moreover, the report observed that "the companies have a lively interest in maintaining this system and think more about extending it than restricting it" (p. 333). See also the discussion in Katherine Stone, "The Origin of Job Structures in the Steel Industry," and David Montgomery, "Workers' Control of Machine Production in the Nineteenth Century," *Labor History* (Fall 1976), pp. 485–509.

80. Disagreement over the effects of transience on worker militance seem to stem

from a confusion of terms. If by militance, trade union or political party organization and involvement is meant, then it must be conceded that transience did hinder or restrict worker participation in collective expressions of grievances. In the Bochum area, transience does certainly seem to have been one important factor hindering the maintenance of permanent trade union organizations; indeed, the great preponderance of leaders and agitators were drawn from the ranks of the older, married, and more geographically settled workers (StAB, Acta des königlichen Landrathsamtes des Landkreises Bochum betreffend Nachweisung der als Sozialdemokratische Führer, Agitatoren und Anarchisten hervorgetretenen Persönlichkeiten, 483, 1902–7, and STAM, I, Nr. 159–62). But high rates of turnover certainly do not seem to have prevented miners at least from engaging in strikes. The crucial factors involved seem to have been the extent of solidarity among workers in an occupation, not simply in a locality, and the continuity of their experience from one area to another. For the "transience hinders protest" hypothesis see Stephan Thernstrom, "Working Class Social Mobility in Industrial America." See also my earlier article, "Regionale Mobilität und Arbeiterklasse."

81. StAB, VB, 1880; Croon, "Studien zur Sozial- und Siedlungsgeschichte der Stadt Bochum," pp. 111–12.

82. R. J., "Erlebnisse eines Metalldrehers," p. 743 (although the commentator on this piece disputes this claim).

83. On this point see in particular Clark Kerr and Abraham Siegel, "The Interindustry Propensity to Strike."

84. On Capellestrasse, for example, 26 of the 35 small homes were owned by the company and inhabited by unskilled metalworkers in 1880 (StAB, Adressbuch der Stadt Bochum, 1880).

85. F. Schoeningh, Die Geschichte und wirtschaftliche Bedeutung der Kleinbahnen, p. 176. Schoeningh noted that many workers did travel fairly long distances to work but that there were not enough of them in concentrated masses going to the same area to make special workers' cars profitable. Aside from these few commuters, most of the traffic was for shopping or pleasure (p. 176). Workers also stayed in their neighborhoods for less tangible reasons, including the difficulty of maintaining accepted cultural patterns in the suburbs. Tremohlen notes, for example, that a common objection by workers to the new garden cities was that the distance to work made it difficult to continue the practice of having the wife or children bring a hot meal to the father at noon; see Ernst Tremohlen, Wohnungsfürsorge für Industriearbeiter in der Provinz Westphalen unter besonderer Berücksichtigung des Kleinwohnungsbaues (Jena, 1911), p. 70. Moreover, where miners were predominantly migrants from the east, residential segregation often resulted from discrimination on the part of native and west German inhabitants (see for example H. Croon and K. Utermann, Zeche und Gemeinde.

86. Charles Tilly used the Intermarriage Index (the term is his) in The Vendée (Cambridge, Mass.: Harvard University Press, 1964), p. 94. See also T. Geiger, "Soziale Umschichtungen," Acta Jutlandica (1951); J. Berent, "Social Mobility and Marriage: A Study of Trends in England and Wales" in D. V. Glass, ed., Social Mobility in Britain, London: Routledge and Kegan Paul, (1954), p. 321–22; and John Foster, "Nineteenth-Century Towns," p. 297, for information on the formula and its use.

87. Rathaus Bochum, Standesamt Familienbuch, 1900. For an interesting general discussion of "occupational communities" see John Alt, "Beyond Class: The Decline of Industrial Labor and Leisure," Telos (Summer 1976), no. 28, pp. 58–68.

88. The organization of work in the iron and steel industry seems constantly to have hindered the emergence of a strong sense of solidarity among the great majority

of iron and steel workers during the years before World War I. Indeed, it seems to have been only in response to the effects of the war and the new political impetus provided by the German Revolution and the immediate postwar mass workers' movements that iron and steel workers developed any greater ability to engage in collective protest than they had displayed in the prewar years. For some indications of the changes in consciousness and militance among iron and steelworkers after the war see the discussion in Larry Peterson's forthcoming Columbia University Ph.D. dissertation: "The Policies and Work of the KPD in the Free Labor Unions of Rhineland-Westphalia, 1920–24." The history of the Ruhr iron and steel workers, both before and after the war, still remains largely unexplored Brockhaus suggests that they are a "proletariat without a history"; Eckhard Brockhaus, Zusammensetzung und Neustrukturierung der Arbeiterklasse vor dem Ersten Weltkrieg. Zur Krise der professionellen Arbeiterbewegung (München: Trikont, 1975), p. 131. In my future research, I intend to explore the history of the Ruhr iron and steel workers in greater detail as well as to compare them with their counterparts in France and England. For another preliminary approach to the problem, see Barrington Moore, Jr., Injustice: The Social Bases of Obedience and Revolt (White Plains, New York: Sharpe, 1978), pp. 227–74.

Six: Miners' Strikes in 1889, 1905, and 1912

1. Peter Stearns, "The European Labor Movement and the Working Classes, 1890–1914," in Harvey Mitchell and Peter Stearns, Workers and Protest (Itasca, Ill.: 1971), p. 164.

2. The 1872 strike did not involve miners in the Bochum area; on June 25, 1872, the local newspaper reported that the strike had spread from Essen to the Oberbergamtsbezirk Dortmund but that local miners were still working. On June 27 it reported that, despite rumors to the contrary, no one had struck in the area. On June 29 it observed that, despite "outside agitation" there was still no strike (StAB, Märkischer Sprecher, June 25–29, 1872). For descriptions of the 1872 strike see Max Jürgen Koch, Die Bergarbeiterbewegung, pp. 25–26, and Gerhard Adelmann, Quellensammlung zur Geschichte der sozialen Betriebsverfassung, vol. 1, p. 203.

3. Koch, Die Bergarbeiterbewegung, pp. 53–54. See also the documents in W. Köllmann, ed., Der Bergarbeiterstreik von 1889.

4. On the Rechtsschutzvereine see StAB, Küppers Nachlass, NI, 1, and Koch, Die Bergarbeiterbewegung, p. 31. On the other organizations see StAB, Acta des Landrathsamtes, 475, 1881–93, especially clipping from the Emscher Zeitung, Wattenscheid, April 17, 1882; also StAB, Acta des Landrathsamtes betr. die ev. Arbeiterverein, christl. social Arbeiterverein und katholischen Arbeiterverein, 477, 1883–1907, Amt Bochum Sud to Landrat, April 22, 1885.

5. For a discussion of the "structural differentiation" of trade unions from the early worker clubs see Neil Smelser, Social Change in the Industrial Revolution, pp. 313–14.

6. StAB, Acta des Landrathsamtes, 477, 1883–1907; Amt Bochum Sud to Landrat, April 22, 1885. In 1882 the confessional workers' newspaper, Der Christliche Arbeiter, described the goals of these clubs in the following manner: "Who can be of use to a club that calls itself Christian? . . . He who, as man and Christian, in word and deed, in bearing and manner, does the club honor . . . However, the one who damages his name as a Christian by drinking too much, running after amusement, getting himself easily into debt, being addicted to slander, arguments . . . being work shy, he is not suitable for membership in the Verein. He who, as husband and father, tries to live an exemplary life, who cares for his wife and children in holy Christian love, who

is parsimonious, who raises his children with Christian discipline, who works hand in hand with teacher and priest, who diligently sends his children to church and school—and who teaches them to be religious ... obedient, truthful and to adopt a simplicity in clothing suitable to their estate—and who keeps even his grown sons and daughters in a holy discipline, he belongs in the *Verein*. ... but he who spends all his spare time in the bar, instead of spending some part of it with his family, he does not belong in the *Verein*" (StAB, Acta des Landrathsamtes, January 8, 1882, Nr. 2).

7. The Gewerkverein christlicher Bergarbeiter, with its seat in Essen, was not formed, for example, until 1894 (StAB, Z.S. *Festschrift zum Gewerkschafts-Fest der christlich-nationalen Arbeiterschaft auf dem Schutzenhöfe in Bochum am 1. Sept. 1912*, p. 11).

8. Leaders and agitators in the Alter Verband do seem to have been primarily miners; in the confessional unions the leadership also included priests and members of the local Catholic *Mittelstand*; see StAB, Acta des Landrathsamtes, 475, 1881–1893.

9. StAB, *Märkischer Sprecher*, May 17, 1889.

10. StAB, *Märkischer Sprecher*, May 17, 1889.

11. StAB, *Märkischer Sprecher*, January 9, 12, and 27, 1905.

12. See Koch, *Die Bergarbeiterbewegung*, pp. 121–22.

13. StAB, *Märkischer Sprecher*, March 14 and 18, 1912.

14. StAB, *Märkischer Sprecher*, January 25, 1905.

15. StAB, *Märkischer Sprecher*, March 16, 1912.

16. StAB, *Märkischer Sprecher*, May 13, 1889, January 25, 1905, and March 16, 1912.

17. StAB, *Märkischer Sprecher*, January 10 and 19, 1905.

18. StAB, *Märkischer Sprecher*, January 25, 1905.

19. StAB, *Märkischer Sprecher*, March 9, 1912. This would in effect have meant that miners over forty could no longer risk working in the mines since they would receive no compensation if injured.

20. StAB, *Märkischer Sprecher*, May 7, 8, and 9, 1889.

21. StAB, *Märkischer Sprecher*, May 13, 1889. The miners also demanded that no strikers be disciplined or fired, especially not the strike delegation.

22. StAB, *Märkischer Sprecher*, May 15 and 24, 1889.

23. StAB, *Märkischer Sprecher*, January 7 and 11, 1905.

24. StAB, *Märkischer Sprecher*, January 11, 1905. For detailed comments on the relationship between miners and overseers see Gerhard Adelmann, ed., *Die soziale Betriebsverfassung des Ruhrbergbaus*, pp. 89–91 and 183–84, and also *Die Entwicklung des Niederrheinischen-Westfälischen Steinkohlen Bergbaues in der zweiten Hälfte des 19. Jahrhunderts* (Berlin, 1903), 12:3.

25. StAB, *Märkischer Sprecher*, January 11, 1905.

26. *Ibid.*, January 13, 1905.

27. *Ibid.*, January 19, 1905.

28. *Ibid.*, January 13, 1905.

29. *Ibid.*, January 20, 1905. Kuhne also demanded that the miners' organizations be recognized and that the "bosses must accept the modern idea that the workers are equal."

30. Koch, *Die Bergarbeiterbewegung*, pp. 121–22. See also H. Imbusch, *Ist eine Verschmelzung der Bergarbeiterorganisationen möglich?*

31. StAB, *Märkischer Sprecher*, March 8, 9, 12, and 13, 1912.

32. *Ibid.*, March 14 and 18, 1912.

33. *Ibid.*, March 19, 1912.

34. StAB, *Märkischer Sprecher*, May 8, 1889; see *Die Entwicklung*, vol. 4.

35. *Der Klassenkampf im Ruhrrevier* (Berlin, 1905), p. 9.

36. *Ibid.*, pp. 9 and 10.

37. See *Die Entwicklung*, vol. 4, and also Adelmann, *Die soziale Betriebsverfassung*, p. 83.

38. *Der Klassenkampf im Ruhrrevier*, p. 10.

39. StAB, *Markischer Sprecher*, May 9, 1889, January 7 and 20, 1905, StAB, Acta des Landrathsamtes, 481, Weitmar *Polizeiverwaltung* to Landrat, May 3, 1908.

40. "Prevailing conditions," as the agitational pamphlet, *Der Klassenkampf im Ruhrrevier*, pointed out, included a highly competitive system of bidding for the right to work a particular seam. Team leaders submitted bids from which the overseer usually chose the lowest one. The pamphlet complained that whenever a *Kameradschaft* (team of workers) began to earn "too much" on a seam it was switched by the overseer to another, or the contract price for that seam was reduced. It then went on to suggest that "these conditions explain, at least in part, the unanimous demand of the workers for a minimum wage." (pp. 16–17).

41. Peter N. Stearns, "Measuring the Evolution of Strike Movements," *International Review of Social History*, 19 (1974), 17–25. See also the same author's "Adaptation to Industrialization," pp. 309–10. This analysis is based on income figures and food prices presented in the following: Klaus Tenfelde, *Sozialgeschichte der Bergarbeiterschaft*, pp. 292–320; Koch, *Die Bergarbeiterbewegung*, p. 80 and pp. 148–50; *Die Entwicklung des Niederrheinisch-Westfälischen Steinkohlen-Bergbaues*, pp. 80–81; StAB, VB, 1886–1912.

42. See for example, StAB, VB, 1882/83, p. 13; 1886/87, p. 15; 1888/89, p. 16; 1900, p. 26; 1901, p. 23.

43. StAB, VB, 1898/99, p. 19.

44. *Board of Trade, Accounts and Papers.* Vol. 108. *Cost of Living in German Towns* (London: 1908), p. 79.

45. StAB, VB, 1888/89, p. 16.

46. StAB, VB, 1878/89, p. 5, reported that in 1874 wages were still on average 4.05–3.90 marks per man/shift.

47. Calculated from data presented in Koch, *Die Bergarbeiterbewegung*, Table 14, pp. 149–50. See also Dieter Groh, "Überlegungen zum Verhältnis von Intensivierung der Arbeit und Arbeitskämpfen im organisierten Kapitalismus in Deutschland (1896–1914)," pp. 26–30 and pp. 42–44. Manuscript.

48. See also Kurt Bergmann, "Die Stellungnahme der organisierten Arbeiter zum Stücklohn," Inaugural-Dissertation. Friedrich-Alexanders Universität Erlangen (Berlin, 1909), pp. 33–34.

49. Edward Shorter and Charles Tilly, *Strikes in France*, p. 67. On a similar shift in strike demands among Upper Silesian miners see Lawrence Schofer, *The Formation of a Modern Labor Force*, pp. 145–58.

50. Keith Burgess, *The Origins of British Industrial Relations*, p. 187.

51. Albin Gladen, "Die Streiks der Bergarbeiter im Ruhrgebiet," p. 126, and Hickey, ch. 5. On the union leadership's conception of its role see especially Otto Hue, *Neutrale oder parteische Gewerkschaften* (Bochum, 1900), pp. 130–57.

52. It is significant that the combined demand for reduced hours and increased wages reappeared during the German Revolution: according to von Oertzen, "in the forefront" of the miners movement in November "stood wishes for wage increases, reduction of hours . . . The unions were negative towards this spontaneous movement; they were anxious about the fact that coal production was already declining and urged the miners to be still" (Peter von Oertzen, *Betriebsräte in der Novemberrevolution* (Düsseldorf: Droste, 1963). p. 111).

53. See Karl Schmidthaus, "Essen und Trinken," for an interesting description of the miner's "domestic economy" in the Bochum area as late as the 1930s; on livestock see StAB, VB, 1907.

54. StAB, *Märkischer Sprecher*, May 7, 1889, January 11 and 20, 1905.

55. StAB, *Märkischer Sprecher*, January 11, 1905, at Dannenbaum II and III, Hercules, Dorstfeld, Borussia, Margarethe, Prinz Regent, and Friederika.

56. StAB, *Märkischer Sprecher*, May 28, 1889.

57. See also Schofer, *The Formation of a Modern Labor Force*, p. 146.

58. StAB, *Märkischer Sprecher*, January 20, 1905, and March 14, 1912.

59. A paradox of which the Social Democrats were themselves quite well aware; see, for example, the remarks of local SPD leaders in the *Arbeiter-Zeitung*, just before the war, quoted in Stephen Hickey's forthcoming dissertation (Oxford University), ch. 6.

60. For figures on union membership see Christoph Klessmann, "Klassensolidarität und nationales Bewusstsein. Das Verhältnis zwischen der Polnischen Berufsvereinigung (ZZP) und den deutschen Bergarbeitergewerkschaften im Ruhrgebiet, 1902–1923," *Internationale Wissenschaftliche Korrespondenz zur Geschichte der deutschen Arbeiterbewegung*, Jg. 10 (June 1974), book 2, p. 154.

61. StAB, 479, "Stand der sozialdemokratsiche Bewegung, 1898"; Küppers Nachlass, NI, 25; *Statistik des Deutschen Reiches*, 1st ser. vols 8, 14, 37, and 53; *Monatshefte zur Statistik des Deutschen Reichs*, Jg. 1885, 1887, and 1890; *Vierteljahrshefte zur Statistik des Deutschen Reichs*, 1893, 1898, 1899, 1900, 1903, 1904, 1905, and 1907.

62. StAB, 480, Amtmann Hordel to Landrat, August 1, 1905. See also StAB, 481, Amt Bochum II Sud to Landrat, August 27, 1906, and Amt Weitmar to Landrat, August 31, 1906.

63. See Klessmann, "Klassensolidarität und nationales Bewusstsein," p. 154.

64. StAB, Küppers Nachlass, NI, 25; *Statistik des Deutschen Reiches*, vol. 250.

65. StAB, 482, Amt Weitmar to Landrat, August 22, 1913.

66. The editor Witt from Bochum speaking at a May Day meeting in Harpen in 1907 described it as a day on which socialists demonstrated for "the 8-hour day, for world peace, for another order of society and for the *Bergarbeiterschutz*" (StAB, 481, Amt Harpen to Landrat, May 2, 1907).

67. StAB, 481, Amt Weitmar to Landrat, August 7, 1907; 482, Amt Weitmar to Landrat, August 8, 1910; Amt Weitmar to Landrat, August 20, 1912; Amt Weitmar to Landrat, August 22, 1913; 481, Amt Harpen to Landrat, May 2, 1907; Amt Harpen to Landrat, August 17, 1909; 482, Amt Harpen, August 26, 1909; Königliche Polizei Präsident in Bochum to Regierungs Präsident Arnsberg, July 6, 1914.

68. Christoph Klessmann, "Klassensolidarität und nationales Bewusstsein," p. 154.

69. See StAB, 482, Amt Bochum II Sud to Landrat, August 12, 1912, and Amt Weitmar to Landrat, August 20, 1912.

70. Stephen Hickey, "The Shaping of the German Labour Movement," p. 218.

71. *Ibid.*, pp. 235–36.

72. StAB, 481, Amt Hordel to Landrat, August 31, 1906, Amt Weitmar to Landrat, August 9, 1908.

73. StAB, 482, Amt Weitmar to Landrat, August 20, 1912.

74. StAB, 480, Amt Hofstede to Landrat, May 14, 1901; "Flugblatt an die Bergleute und deren Frauen. Ein Wort zur Ernsten Zeit."

75. Hickey, "The Shaping of the German Labour Movement," p. 232.

76. Glovka Spencer, "Employer Response to Unionism," pp. 406–7.

77. See Hickey, "The Shaping of the German Labour Movement," pp. 234–35.

78. Dieter Groh, "Überlegungen zum Verhältnis von Intensivierung der Arbeit und Arbeitskämpfen im organisierten Kapitalismus in Deutschland (1896–1914)." Manuscript.

79. On this see *ibid.* and also this book, pp. 204–7.

80. Hickey, "The Shaping of the German Labour Movement," p. 236.

81. StAB, 480, Amtmann Hordel to Landrat, August 1, 1905; StAB, 481, Amtmann Hordel to Landrat, August 31, 1906; StAB, 481, Amtmann Weitmar to Landrat, August 7, 1907.

82. The Mikrofilmarchiv der deutschsprachigen Presse e.V possesses only the following issues of the Bochum *Volksblatt:* 1899 (January–June), 1900–1901 (July), 1902 (July–September), 1914 (August)–1919.

83. For the most part these involve May Day speeches but also include other speeches and talks presented by socialist leaders.

84. StAB, 481, Amtmann Harpen to Landrat, May 2, 1908.

85. StAB, 479, Amtmann Weitmar to Landrat, January 8, 1897; from a handbill circulated in the area; the second part of the quotation is from a May Day speech given by Frau Nemitz in 1910 (StAB, 482, Polizeiverwaltung Altenbochum to Landrat, May 1, 1910).

86. StAB, 481, Polizeiverwaltung Weitmar to Landrat, May 3, 1908.

87. StAB, 482, Polizeiverwaltung Altenbochum to Landrat, May 1, 1910.

88. StAB, 482, Amtmann Weitmar to Landrat, August 8, 1910, and Reg. Präsident to Landrat, I, 1, Nr. 475, Arnsberg, April 19, 1910.

89. For a stimulating discussion of this question in a much broader context see the conclusion to Dieter Groh, "Überlegungen zum Verhältnis von Intensivierung der Arbeit und Arbeitskämpfen im organisierten Kapitalismus in Deutschland (1896–1914.)" Manuscript.

Conclusion

1. Dan S. White, *The Splintered Party: National Liberalism in Hessen and the Reich, 1867–1918* (Cambridge, Mass.: Harvard University Press, 1976), p. 200.

2. Hans-Ulrich Wehler, *Das Deutsche Kaiserreich, 1871–1918* (Göttingen: Vandenhoeck and Ruprecht, 1975), p. 238.

3. On these points see the discussion in Geoff Eley, "Capitalism and the Wilhelmine State: Industrial Growth and Political Backwardness in Recent German Historiography, 1890–1918," *Historical Journal* (1978), 21(3):737–50; Geoff Eley, "Memories of under-development," p. 787. For some important criticisms of the standard approach to the *Mittelstand,* David Blackbourn, "The Mittelstand in German Society and Politics, 1871–1914," *Social History* (January 1977), no. 4, 409–33.

4. Peter N. Stearns, "Adaptation to Industrialization," pp. 323–24.

5. My use of the term "modern" in this connection clearly conflicts with the distinctions made between "modernization" and "industrialization" by E. A. Wrigley ("The Process of Modernization and the Industrial Revolution in England"). However, it seems to me that what Wrigley here takes to be "modernity" can better be understood as one stage in the development of capitalism; if towns like Bochum do not conform to the model developed from that stage, I would argue that is because they reflect another, later stage in capitalist development. For a stimulating discussion of the difficulties with "modernization" theory in general see Dean C. Tipps, "Modernization Theory and the Study of National Societies."

6. For an interesting discussion of the ways in which liberal ideology may have

been more or less convincing, depending on the differences in the nature of local social structures in a variety of towns within the same national context see John Foster, *Class Struggle and the Industrial Revolution: Early Industrial Capitalism in Three English Towns* (London: Weidenfeld and Nicolson, 1974). See also the discussion of the disjunction between middle class liberal worldviews and the social reality of the casual poor in London in Gareth Stedman Jones, *Outcast London*.

7. Geoff Eley, "Die 'Kehrites' und das Kaiserreich: Bemerkungen zu einer aktuellen Kontroverse," *Geschichte und Gesellschaft*, (1978), 1, p. 102.

8. *Ibid.*

Bibliography

Archival Sources

Unpublished Materials

STAM.   Staatsarchiv Münster. Polizeiabteilung, Regierung Arnsberg.

I. I. Arbeiter Streiks, 1874–89. Vol. 2.

I.1463. Streiks, Aussperrungen. Vol. 2. 1908–1910.

I.24. Streike in anderen Betrieben als Kohlenbergwerken, 1889–1891.

I.25. desgl. 1892–1895.

I.26. Arbeitseinstellungen in anderen Betrieben als Kohlenbergwerken. Statistik des Streiks u. Aussperrungen, 1895–1898.

I.27. desgl. 1898–1900.

I.28. desgl. 1900–1902.

I.29. desgl. 1902–1904.

I.30. desgl. 1904–1905.

I.31. desgl. 1905.

I.32. desgl. 1905–1906.

I.33. desgl. 1906.

I.34. desgl. 1907–1908.

I.59–162. Veränderungen unter den Führer und Agitatoren der sozialdemokratischen Partei in hiesigen Stadt (1894–1898).

StAB.   Stadtarchiv, Bochum/Nordrhein-Westfalen.

475. Acta des Königlichen Landrathsamtes des Landkreises Bochum betreffend Christlich-Soziale Agitation unter den Berg- und Fabrikarbeiter des Landkreises Bochum, 1881–1893.

477. Acta des Königlichen Landrathsamtes des Landkreises Bochum betreffend die evangelischen Arbeiterverein, christlich socialverein und katholischen Arbeiterverein, 1883–1907.

479, 480, 481, 482. Acta des Königlichen Landrathsamtes des Landkreises Bochum betreffend Sozialdemokratische und

Anarchistische Bewegung, 1895–1901, 1900–1906, 1906–1909, 1909–1918.

483. Acta des Königlichen Landrathsamtes des Landkreises Bochum betreffend Nachweisung der als Sozialdemokratische Führer, Agitatoren und Anarchisten hervorgetretenen Persönlichkeiten, 1902–1907.

1000. Acta des Königlichen Landrathsamtes des Landkreises Bochum betreffend die Wahlen für die Reichstag, 1890–95.

Nachlass Küppers, vols. 1, 4, 5, 6, 11, 14, 15, 16, 17, 18, 22(3), 23a, 25, 34.

Akten der Schulverwaltung der Stadt Bochum, Städtische Hauptkasse, Buchhälterei II, Schulgeldhebelisten: Gymnasium, 1870–1880, 1881–1889, 1890–1896, 1897–1898, 1898–1899, 1906. Gewerbeschule, 1877–1885. Oberrealschule, 1895–1896, 1897–1898, 1898–1899, 1900, 1901.

Staatssteuerrolle, 1901.

Acta/Vereinswesen, 1875–90.

RB.   Rathaus Bochum. Standesamt Bochum (Mitte), Familienbuch, 1900. Vols. 1 to 3.

WAFKH   Werksarchiv Friedrich Krupp Hüttenwerke AG. Gusstahlwerk Bochumer Verein

15100, Nr. 1. Correspondenzen betreffend Differenzen wegen Übertritts von Arbeitern pp. anderer Werke in unsere Dienst und Umgekehrt, 1872–1880.

15100, Nr. 2. Correspondenzen betreffend Arbeiter, 1896.

21000, Nr. 1, 2, 3, 4, 6. Tarifverträge, Arbeitsordnungen beziehungsweise Fabrikordnung, 1855–1896, ab 1897.

21000, Nr. 7. Fabrikreglement.

21200, Nr. 1. Lohn- und Gehaltsfragen.

21700, Nr. 1. Streiks, 1865.

21700, Nr. 2. Presse und Streiks, 1905.

25000, Nr. 1. Lehrlinge, 1878–1888.

25000, Nr. 2. Lehrlingswerkstätten, Werkschulen, 1879.

25000, Nr. 4. Lehrlinge, 1889–1895.

25000, Nr. 5. Lehrlinge, 1894–1904.

25200, Nr. 1. Stahlhausen, 1863, 1896.

25200, Nr. 2. Stahlhausen, 1896.

25200, Nr. 4. Wohnungswesen, Allgemein.

25200, Nr. 4a. Arbeiter-Genossenschaft für Wohnungsbau, 1871/72.

25201, Nr. 1. Wohnungswesen, Siedlung, Allgemein.

Published Materials

StAB   Stadtarchiv. Bochum/Nordrhein-Westfalen.

Adressbuch der Stadt Bochum. Bochum, 1874, 1876, 1880, 1882, 1884, 1886, 1888, 1890, 1892, 1894, 1897, 1899, 1901.

Adressbuch des Amtes Bochum I (Nord) herausgegeben nach amtlichen Materials von einem Beamten des Amtes. Bochum: Fasbender, 1889.

An alle Metallarbeiter von Bochum und Umgegend. Essen: Wilhelm Duwell, 1901.

Baupolizeiverordnung für den Stadtbezirk Bochum. Bochum: Stumpf, 1911.

Bericht des Bürgermeisters Lange betreffend die Unterbringung der Obdachlosen in der Stadt Bochum. Bochum: Stumpf, 1884.

Der Bochumer Steuerprozess. Verhandlungen der Strafkammer des Königlichen Landgerichts zu Essen. Hagen i. Westfalen: L. Wrietzner, 1891.

Bürgerbuch der Stadt Bochum. Auf Grund amtlichen Materials zusammengestellt von Stadtrentmeister Sottuth, Stadtsekretär Claas, Rendant Josephs und Revisor Jungst in Bochum. Bochum: Stumpf, 1909.

Festschrift zum Gewerkschaftsfest der christlichen-nationalen Arbeiterschaft auf dem Schutzenhofe in Bochum am 1. Sept., 1912. Bochum, 1912.

Jahresbericht der Handelskammer zu Bochum. Bochum, 1873, 1875, 1878, 1879, 1881, 1885, 1886, 1887, 1888, 1889, 1890, 1891, 1892, 1893, 1894, 1895, 1896, 1897, 1898, 1899, 1900, 1901, 1902, 1903, 1904, 1905, 1913.

Lokalverordnungen der Stadt Bochum von W. Akmann (Polizei-Commissar, Bochum). Mühlheim/Ruhr: Jul. Bagel, 1895.

Märkischer Sprecher. Bochum, 1872–1912.

Statistik des Landkreises Bochum, 1876–1880. Bochum, 1881.

Satzungen der Neustadter Sterbelade zu Bochum. Bochum: Freiloh, 1909.

Statut der Unterstützungs-Kasse "Zum Fliegenden Rad" (Eingeschriebene Hulfskasse im Bochum). Bochum: Fasbender, 1878.

Sterbe- und Unterstützungskasse der Krieger- Bürger- und Knappenverein im Amt Bochum Sud, 1874–1900. N.p., n.d.

Telegraphische Depesche an Herrn Direktor Koehler, Bochum, 1890.

Verwaltungsbericht des Kreis-Ausschusses des Landkreises Bochum, 1911/12. Bochum, n.d.

Verwaltungsbericht der Stadt Bochum. Bochum, 1860, 1864, 1866, 1868, 1869, 1871, 1873/74–1898/99, 1900–1912, 1913–1924.

Verhandlungen der Kreissynode Bochum. Witten, 1899; Dortmund, 1908. Die Westfälische Volkszeitung und die Thätigkeit des Herrn Fusangel in Reichstagswahlkreise Bochum. Essen, n.d.

Secondary Works: Local and Regional History and Statistical Sources

Articles

Adelmann, Gerhard. "Die Beziehungen zwischen Arbeitgeber und Arbeitnehmer in der Ruhrindustrie vor 1914." *Jahrbücher für Nationalökonomie und Statistik* (1963), p. 175.

——"Führende Unternehmer im Rheinland und in Westfalen, 1850–1914." *Rheinische Vierteljahrsblätter* (1971), 35:335–52.

Bork, Kunibert K. "Die sozialen Wandlungen in der Stadt Duisburg in den ersten Jahrzehnten der Industrialisierung." *Duisburger Forschungen. Schriftenreihe für Geschichte und Heimatkunde Duisburgs in Verbindung mit der Mercator Gesellschaft* (1965), 8:54–129.

Croon, Helmuth. "Bürgertum und Verwaltung in den Städten des Ruhrgebiets im 19. Jahrhundert." *Tradition: Zeitschrift für Firmen Geschichte und Unternehmer Biographie* (1964), 9:23–41.

——"Die Einwirkungen der Industrialisierung auf die gesellschaftliche Schichtung der Bevölkerung im rheinisch-westfälischen Industriegebiet." *Rheinische Vierteljahrsblätter* (1955), 20:301–16.

——"Die gesellschaftliche Auswirkungen des Gemeindewahlrechtes in den Gemeinden und Kreisen des Rheinlandes und Westfalen im 19. Jh." *Forschungsberichte des Landes Nordrhein-Westfalen, Nr. 564.* Cologne and Opladen: Westdeutscher, 1960.

——"Die Grosstadt als Heimat." *Rheinische Heimatpflege* (1964), n.f. 4:3–15.

——"Methoden zur Erforschung der Gemeindlichen Sozialgeschichte des 19. und 20. Jahrhunderts. Erfahrungen aus sozialgeschichtlichen Forschungen im Ruhrgebiet." *Westfälische Forschungen. Mitteilungen des Provinzialinstituts für westfälische Landes- und Volkskunde* (1955), 8:139–49.

——"Städtewandlung und Städtebildung im Ruhrgebiet im 19. Jahrhundert." *Aus Geschichte und Landeskunde. Forschungen und Darstellungen Franz Steinbach zum 65. Geburtstag gewidmet von seinen Freunden und Schülern,* pp. 484–501. Bonn: Ludwig Rohrscheid, 1960.

——"Die Städtevertretung in Krefeld und Bochum im 19. Jahrhundert. Ein Beitrag zur Geschichte der Selbstverwaltung der rheinischen und westfälischen Städte." In Richard Dietrich and Gerhard Oestreich, eds., *Forschungen zu Staat und Verfassung: Festgabe für Fritz Hartung,* pp. 289–306. Berlin: Duncker & Humblot, 1958.

——"Der Strukturwandel des Ruhrgebietes und seine Auswirkungen auf die Archive." *Der Archivar. Mitteilungsblatt für deutsche Archivwesen* (1960), 13(4):419–36.

——"Studien zur Sozial- und Siedlungsgeschichte der Stadt Bochum." *Bochum und das Mittlere Ruhrgebiet. Festschrift zum 35. Deutschen*

Geographentag vom 8. Juni bis 11. Juni 1965 in Bochum. Paderborn, 1965, pp. 85–114.

Fischer, Wolfram. "Die Bedeutung der preussischen Bergrechtsreform für die industrieller Ausbau des Ruhrgebietes." *Vortragsreihe der Gesselschaft für Westfälische Wirtschaftsgeschichte e.V.* (1961), vol. 9.

"Gesetz betreffend die Erweiterung des Stadtkreises Bochum vom 1. Juni, 1904." *Gesetz Sammlung für die Königliche preussische Staaten* (1904), 13:87–103.

Gilsing, A. "Die Kommunalpolitischen Verhältnisse in den Landtagswahlkreisen Bochum-Herne und Witten-Hattingen." *Kommunalpolitische Blatter* (1913), 4:243–44.

Gladin, Alben. "Die Streiks der Bergarbeiter im Ruhrgebiet in den Jahren 1889, 1905 und 1912." In Hans Jürgen Reulecke, ed., *Arbeiterbewegung an Rhein und Ruhr* (Wuppertal: Peter Hammer, 1975).

Hellfaier, Karl Alexander. "Probleme und Quellen zur Frühgeschichte der Sozialdemokratie in Westfalen." *Archiv für Sozialgeschichte* (1963), 3:157–222.

Hickey, S. H. F. "The Shaping of the German Labour Movement: Miners in the Ruhr," R. J. Evans, ed., *Society and Politics in Wilhelmine Germany*, pp. 215–40. London: Croom Helm, 1978.

Köllmann, Wolfgang, "Die Bevölkerung Rheinland-Westfalens in der Hochindustrialisierungsperiode" in Wolfgang Köllmann, *Bevölkerung in der industriellen Revolution. Studien zur Bevölkerungsgeschichte Deutschlands*, pp. 229–49. (Göttingen: Vandenhoeck and Ruprecht, 1974).

——"Binnenwanderung und Bevölkerungsstrukturen der Ruhrgebiets–Grosstädte im Jahre 1907." In Wolfgang Köllmann, *Bevölkerung in der industriellen Revolution. Studien zur Bevölkerungsgeschichte Deutschlands* (Göttingen: Vandenhoeck and Ruprecht, 1974), pp. 171–85.

Lange, Carl. "Die Wohnungsverhältnisse der ärmeren Volksklassen in Bochum." *Schriften des Vereins für Sozialpolitik* (1886), 30:73–105.

Lehmkuhler, Marlis. "Streik als Soziale Krise des Grossbetriebs: eine historische-soziologische Studie über den Ruhrbergbau." *Soziale Welt* (1952), 3(2), 143–55.

Schmidt, H. "Belegschaftsbildung im Ruhrgebiet im Zeichen der Industrialisierung Erläutert am Beispiel der Zechen Prosper I–III der Arenberg Bergbau GmbH in Bottrop (Westfalen)." *Tradition. Zeitschrift für Firmen Geschichte und Unternehmer Biographie* (1957), 1:265–72.

Schmidthaus, Karl. "Essen und Trinken. Der Tageslauf im Haushalt." *Rheinisch-westfälische Zeitschrift für Volkskunde* (1964), vol. 11.

Spencer, Elaine Glovka. "Employer Response to Unionism: Ruhr Coal Industrialists before 1914." *Journal of Modern History*, 48 (September 1976), 48:397–412.

Tremohlen, Ernst. "Wohnungsfürsorge für Industriearbeiter in der Provinz Westfalen." *Abhandlungen des Staatswiss. Seminars zu Jena* (1921), vol. 11.

Wetzker, Heinrich, "Die Grosstadt Bochum." *Kommunale Praxis* (1907), 7:893–96.

Zunkel, Friedrich. "Beamtenschaft und Unternehmertum beim Aufbau der Ruhrindustrie, 1849 bis 1880." *Tradition. Zeitschrift für Firmen Geschichte und Unternehmer Biographie* (1964), 9:261–77.

Books

1817–1967. Gesellschaft Harmonie Bochum: Festschrift zum 150. Gründungsfest der Harmonie. Bochum: n.p., 1967.

Adelmann, Gerhard. *Die Soziale Betriebsverfassung des Ruhrbergbaus vom Anfang des 19. Jahrhunderts bis zum Ersten Weltkrieg.* Bonn: Ludwig Rohrscheid, 1962.

Adelmann, Gerhard, ed. *Quellensammlung zur Geschichte der sozialen Betriebsverfassung. Ruhrindustrie unter besonder- Berücksichtigung des Industrie und Handelskammerbezirks Essen. Bd. i. Überbetriebliche Einwirkungen auf die soziale Betriebsverfassung der Ruhrindustrie. Bd. ii. Soziale Betriebsverfassung einzelner Unternehmen der Ruhrindustrie.* Bonn: Peter Hanstein, 1965.

Albrecht, Heinrich. *Handbuch der sozialen Wohlfahrtspflege in Deutschland auf Grund des Materials der Zentralstelle für Arbeiterwohlfahrts-Einrichtungen bearbeitet.* Berlin: Heymann, 1902.

Die Arbeiterwohnungen des Bochumer Vereins für Bergbau und Gusstahlfabrikation zu Bochum in Westfalen. Berlin: Kerskes and Hohman, 1883.

Aus der Geschichte der Industrie und Handelskammer zu Bochum zu ihrem 73 jährigen Bestehen. Prepared by the Geschaftsausführung der Industrie und Handelskammer zu Bochum. Hattingen/Ruhr: C. Hundt, 1932.

Der Ausstand der niederrheinisch-westfälischen Bergleute. May, 1889. Styrum/Rhineland and Leipzig: Spaarmann, 1889.

Auszug aus dem Generalversammlung des Bochumer Vereins für Bergbau und Gusstahlfabrikation von dem General-Director des Vereins Herrn Commerzienrath Baare am 28. Sept. 1875 erstatteten Bericht soweit derselbe die Überproduktion die wirtschaftliche Krisis und die Eisenzollfrage betrifft. Bochum: Stumpf, 1875.

Bacmeister, Walter. *Hugo Schulz. Das Lebensbild eines grossen Ruhrbergmanns.* Essen: Bacmeister, 1938.

——*Louis Baare. Ein Westfälischer Wirtschaftsführer aus der Bismarkzeit.* Essen: Bacmeister, 1937.

Benedict, Walter. *Aus der Geschichte unseres Werkes, 1820–1920. Von der Alleestrasse zur Grossenvöde.* Bochum. n.d.

Bericht über die Jubelfeier des Bochumer Vereins für Bergbau und Gusstahlfabrikation und von 298 seiner Beamten, Meister und Arbeiter am 14. Oktober 1894 nebst einem alphabetischen Namensverzeichniss der Jubilare. Den Jubilaren gewidmet. Bochum: Hoppstaedter, 1894.

Bochum. Geschichte und Entwicklung der Stadt. Leipzig: Verkehrsverein Bochum, 1918.

Bochum. Stadt der Zukunft. 100 Jahre Demokratischer Sozialismus. Festwoche vom 21–27 April, 1963. Bochum: n.p., 1963.

Der Bochumer Krieger- und Landwehr Verein seit seiner Gründung am 10. Marz 1844. Herausgegeben zum 90. jährigen Bestehen am 10. Marz 1934. Bochum: n.p., 1934.

Bochumer Verein für Bergbau und Gusstahlfabrikation. Entgegnung auf die jüngste dem deutschen Reichstag von den Vorstehern der Kaufmannschaft zu Stettin überreichte Denkschrift zur Eisenzollfrage. Berlin: Eisner, 1876.

Bochumer Verein für Bergbau und Gusstahlfabrikation. Steel Works (St. Louis Exposition). Berlin: Ringer, 1904.

Brepohl, Wilhelm. Der Aufbau des Ruhrvolkes im Zuge der Ost-Westwanderung. Beiträge zur deutschen Sozialgeschichte des 19. und 20. Jhs. Recklinghausen: Bitter, 1948.

——Industrievolk im Wandel von der agraren zur industriellen Daseinsform, dargestellt am Ruhrgebiet. Tübingen: Mohr/Siebeck, 1957.

Brinkmann, Karl. Bochum. Aus der Geschichte einer Grosstadt des Reviers. Bochum: Schurmann and Klagges, 1968.

——Die Geschichte der Flottmanwerke G.m.b.H. Bochum: n.p., 1955.

——100 Jahre Chemische Fabrik J. Chr. Leye. Bochum: Stumpf, 1956.

Busch, Paul, ed. Bochum und das mittlere Ruhrgebiet. Festschrift zum 35. Deutschen Geographentag vom 8. Juni bis 11. Juni 1965 in Bochum. Paderborn: Gesellschaft für Geographie und Geologie Bochum e.V., 1965.

Croon, Helmuth and Kurt Utermann. Zeche und Gemeinde. Untersuchungen über den Strukturwandel einer Zechengemeinde im nördlichen Ruhrgebiet. Tübingen: Mohr, 1958.

Däbritz, W. Bochumer Verein für Bergbau und Gusstahlfabrikation in Bochum. Neun Jahrzehnte seiner Geschichte im Rahmen der Wirtschaft des Ruhrbezirkes. Düsseldorf: Stahleisen, 1934.

Darpe, Franz. Geschichte der Stadt Bochum nebst Urkundenbuch, einer Siegeltafel und einer Ansicht der Stadt aus dem Anfang des 18. Jhs. Bochum: Stumpf, 1894.

Decker, Franz. Die betriebliche Sozialordnung der Dürener Industrie im 19. Jahrhundert. Schriften zur Rheinisch-Westfälischen Wirtschafts-Geschichte, vol. 12. Cologne: Rheinisch-Westfälischen Wirtschafts-Archiv zu Köln, 1965.

Ehrenberg, Richard and Hugo Racine. Krupp'sche Arbeiter-Familien. Entwicklung und Entwicklungs Faktoren von drei Generationen Deutscher Arbeiter. Archiv für Exakte Wirtschaftsforschung. Thünen-Archiv. Ergänzungsheft 4–6. Jena: Gustav Fischer, 1912.

Faber, Carl. Streifzüge durch Alt-Bochum und Umgebung. Bochum: n.p., 1895.

Festschrift zur Feier des Fünfzigjährigen Bestehens des Vereins für die Bergbaulichen Interessen im Oberbergamtsbezirk Dortmund in Essen,

1855–1908. Edited by Dr. Ernst Jüngst. Essen: Berg- und Hüttenmannischen Zeitschrift "Glückauf," 1908.

Festschrift zur 75-jährigen Jubelfeier der Oberrealschule Bochum. Bochum: Schurmann and Klagges, 1926.

Festschrift zur fünfzigjährigen Jubelfeier des Königlichen Gymnasiums zu Bochum. Bochum: Stumpf, 1910.

Fischer, Wolfram. *Herz des Reviers. 125 Jahre Wirtschafts-Geschichte des Industrie und Handelskammerbezirks Essen, Mühlheim, Oberhausen.* Essen: Bacht, 1965.

Först, Walter, ed. *Ruhrgebiet und Neues Land. Beiträge zur Neueren Landesgeschichte des Rheinlandes und Westfalens.* Bd. 2. Cologne and Berlin: Grote, 1968.

Fricke, Dieter. *Der Ruhrbergarbeiterstreik von 1905.* Berlin; Rütten and Loening, 1955.

Frings, Joseph. *Die Einkommens- und Vermögensverhältnisse im Regierungsbezirk Arnsberg unter besonderer Berücksichtigung der zur ehemaligen Grafschaft Mark gehörigen Kreise.* Berlin: Puttkammer and Muhlbrecht, 1913.

Fritz, Rolf, ed. *Das Ruhrgebiet vor Hundert Jahren. Gesicht einer Landschaft.* Dortmund: Ardey, 1956.

25 Jahre Gemeinnütziger Wohnungsverein zu Bochum e.G.m.b.H. Denkschrift zur Feier des 25 jährigen Bestehens am 7. Mai, 1927. Bochum: Selbstverlag, 1927.

Gebhardt, Gerhard. *Ruhrbergbau. Geschichte. Aufbau und Verflechtung seiner Gesellschaften und Organisationen.* Essen: Glückauf, 1957.

Heinrichsbauer, August. *Industrielle Siedlung im Ruhrgebiet in Vergangenheit, Gegenwart und Zukunft.* Essen: Glückauf, 1936.

Hellgrewe, Henny. *Dortmund als Industrie und Arbeiterstadt. Eine Untersuchung der wirtschaftlichen und sozialen Entwicklung der Stadt.* Dortmund: Ardey, 1951.

Hemeyer, Karl-Heinz. "Der Bochumer Wirtschaftsraum von 1840 bis zur Jahrhundertwende." Unpublished Diplomarbeit, Wirtschafts-Hochschule Mannheim, 1959/60.

Hempel, G. *Bochumer Eisenhütte. Heintzmann & Compagnie. G.m.b.H. 100 Jahre Bochumer Eisenhütte.* Bochum: 1951.

Hoffman, Heinrich. *Die Gründung und der Werdegang des Spar-und Bauvereins Bochum e.G.m.b.H. in Bochum.* Düsseldorf: Rhenania, 1928.

Hofmann, Wolfgang. *Die Bielefelder Stadtverordneten. Ein Beitrag zu bürgerlicher Selbstverwaltung und sozialem Wandel, 1850 bis 1914.* Historische Studien. no. 390. Lübeck and Hamburg: Matthiesen, 1964.

Jacobi, Ludwig. *Das Berg-Hütten- und Gewerbewesen des Regierungsbezirks Arnsberg.* Iserlohn, 1857.

Jantke, Carl. *Bergmann und Zeche. Die sozialen Arbeitsverhältnisse einer Schachtanlage des nördlichen Ruhrgebiets in der Sicht der Bergleute.* Tübingen: Mohr/Siebeck, 1953.

Jeidels, Otto. *Die Methoden der Arbeiterentlohnung in der Rheinisch-West-fälischen Eisenindustrie.* Berlin: Simion, 1907.

Kirchhoff, Hans Georg. *Die Staatliche Sozialpolitik im Ruhrbergbau, 1871–1914.* Wissenschaftliche Abhandlungen der Arbeitsgemeinschaft für Forschung des Landes Nordrhein-Westfalen, vol. 4, Cologne and Opladen: Westdeutscher, 1958.

Koch, Max Jurgen. *Die Bergarbeiterbewegung im Ruhrgebiet zur Zeit Wilhelms II (1889–1914).* Beiträge zur Geschichte des Parlamentarismus und der Politischen Parteien, no. 5. Düsseldorf: Droste, 1954.

Köllman, Wolfgang. *Sozialgeschichte der Stadt Barmen im 19. Jahrhundert.* Tübingen: Mohr/Siebeck, 1960.

Köllmann, Wolfgang, ed. *Der Bergarbeiter Streik von 1889 und die Gründung des "Alten Verbandes" in ausgewählten Dokumenten der Zeit.* Presented on behalf of the Industriegewerkschaft Bergbau und Energie. Bochum: Berg, 1969.

Koeppers, G. *In Schacht und Hütte. Die Industrie des Ruhrkohlenbezirks und benachbarten Gebiete.* Reutlingen: n.p., 1912.

McCreary, Eugene C. "Essen, 1860–1914. A Case Study of the Impact of Industrialization on German Community Life." Ph.D. dissertation, Yale University, 1963.

Mariaux, Franz. *Gedenkwort zum Hundertjährigen Bestehen der Industrie und Handelskammer zu Bochum.* Bochum: Industrie und Handelskammer Bochum, 1965.

Mette, Alexander. *Geschichte der Stadt Bochum.* Festschrift 24. Dortmund: Hauptversammlung Verein deutscher Ingenieure, 1883.

Mitteilungen über den Niederrheinisch-Westfälischen Steinkohlenbergbau. Den Theilnehmern am VIII Allgemeinen Deutschen Bergmannstag zu Dortmund Sept. 1901 gewidmet vom Verein für die bergbaulichen Interessen im Oberbergamtsbezirk Dortmund zu Essen. (Berlin, 1901).

Palseur, R. *Bochum: Geographische Betrachtung einer Grosstadt im Ruhrgebiet.* Würzburg: Aumuhle, 1938.

Pieper, L. *Die Lage der Bergarbeiter im Ruhrrevier.* Stuttgart: Cott'sche, 1903.

Pounds, Norman J. G. *The Ruhr: A Study in Historical and Economic Geography.* Bloomington: Indiana University Press, 1952.

Pounds, Norman J. G., and William N. Parker. *Coal and Steel in Western Europe: The Influence of Resources and Techniques on Production.* Bloomington: Indiana University Press, 1957.

Preussische Statistik. Vols 39, 96, 148, 177, 206, 234. Berlin: 1877, 1888, 1898, 1900, 1908, 1913.

Puppke, Ludwig. *Sozialpolitik und Soziale Anschauungen Frühindustrieller Unternehmer in Rheinland-Westfalen.* Schriften zur Rheinisch-Westfälischen Wirtschaftsgeschichte, vol. 13. Cologne: Rheinisch-Westfälischen Wirtschaftsarchiv zu Köln, 1966.

Reekers, Stephanie. *Westfalens Bevölkerung, 1818–1955.* Münster: Aschendorff, 1957.

Reulecke, Hans-Jürgen, ed. *Arbeiterbewegung an Rhein und Ruhr.* Wuppertal: Peter Hammer, 1975.

Rheinisch-Westfälische Wirtschafts Biographien, vols. 1–6. Münster: Aschendorff, 1932–54.

Rinne, Will. *Eisenkraftfeld Ruhr. Werden und Wandlungen der Eisenschaffenden Industrie an Ruhr und Rhein.* Kevelaer: Butzon and Bercker, 1949.

Schnadt, Theodor. *Bochum. Wirtschaftsstruktur und Verflechtung einer Grosstadt des Ruhrgebietes.* Bochum/Langendreer: Heinrich Poppinghaus, 1936.

Schoeningh, F. *Die Geschichte und wirtschaftliche Bedeutung der Kleinbahnen (Überlandstrassenbahnen) im Rheinisch-Westfälischen Kohlenrevier unter besonderer Berücksichtigung der Stellung der Staatseisenbahnverwaltung und der Kommunen zum Strassenbahnbau.* Paderborn: Schoeningh, 1911.

Schuhmacher, Wilma. *Das Stadtbild von Bochum.* Bochum/Langendreer: Heinrich Poppinghaus, 1937.

Schulte, Wilhelm. *Volk und Staat. Westfalen in Vormärz und in der Revolution 1848/9.* Munster: Regensburg, 1954.

——*Westfälische Köpfe. 300 Lebensbilder bedeutender Westfalen.* Münster: Aschendorff, 1963.

Seippel, Max. *Bochum Einst und Jetzt. Ein Rück- und Rundblick bei der Wende des Jahrhunderts.* Bochum: Rheinisch-Westfälische Verlags-Anstalt, 1901.

Silbergleit, H. *Preussens Städte. Denkschrift zum 100 Jährigen Jubiläum der Städteordnung vom 19. Nov. 1808.* Presented on behalf of the Vorstandes des preussischen Städtetages. Berlin: Carl Heymanns, 1908.

Statistisches Jahrbuch deutscher Städte, vols. 1–21. Jena: G. Fischer, 1890–1916.

Statistik des Deutschen Reiches. N.S., vol. 2/2 *Die Bevölkerung der kleineren Verwaltungsbezirke am 5. Juni 1882 nach Berufsgruppen.* Berlin: Puttkammer and Muhlbrecht.

——*Vol. 109. Berufs- und Gewerbezählung vom 14. Juni 1895. Berufsstatistik der kleineren Verwaltungsbezirke.* Berlin: Puttkammer and Muhlbrecht, 1897.

——*N.S., vol. 117. Berufs- und Gewerbezählung vom 14. Juni 1895. Erster Theil. Kleinere Verwaltungsbezirke Preussens.* Berlin: Puttkammer and Muhlbrecht, 1898.

——*N.S., vol. 207. Berufs- und Betriebszählung vom 12. Juni 1907.* Berlin: Puttkammer and Muhlbrecht, 1910.

——*N.S., vol. 219/2. Die Bevölkerung nach Hauptberuf und Gebürtigkeit. Teil 2. Grosstädte.* Berlin: Puttkammer and Muhlbrecht, 1910.

——*N.S., vol. 217/1. Berufs- und Betriebszählung vom 12. Juni 1907. Gewerbliche Betriebsstatistik.* Berlin: Puttkammer and Mulbrecht, 1909.

Stephan, Enno. *Das Reviere der Pioniere. Werden und Wachsen des Ruhrge-biets.* Hamburg: Mosaik, 1966.

Taeglichsbeck, O. *Die Belegschaft der Bergwerke und Salinen im Oberber-gamtsbezirk Dortmund nach der Zählung vom 16.12.1893.* Dortmund, 1896.

Tenfelde, Klaus. *Sozialgeschichte der Bergarbeiterschaft an der Ruhr im 19. Jahrhundert.* Bonn-Bad Godesberg: Neue Gesellschaft, 1977.

Verein für die bergbaulichen Interessen, Essen. *Die Entwickelung des Nei-derrheinisch-Westfälischen Steinkohlen Bergbaues in der zweiten Hälfte des 19. Jahrhunderts,* vols 4, 5, 12. Berlin: Springer, 1902.

Vier Generationen. Vier Epochen. Herausgegeben aus Anlass des 100 Jähri-gen Bestehens von Gebr. Eickhoff Maschinenfabrik und Eisengiesserei m.b.H. Bochum. Bochum: n.p., n.d.

Wehrmann, Karl. *Zur Geschichte der Gesellschaft Harmonie in Bochum.* n.p., n.d.

Wiebe, Georg. *Die Handelskammer zu Bochum von 1856–1906. Festschrift aus Anlass der Feier des 50 jährigen Bestehens der Handelskammer.* Bochum: Friedrich Jahn, 1906.

Wilhelmi, Friedrich. "Die Finanzentwicklung der Städte Bonn und Bochum als Typen einer Rentner- und Industriearbeiterstadt, von 1870–1913." Dissertation, University of Freiburg/Breisgau, 1921.

Wolcke, Irmtraud-Dietlinde. *Die Entwicklung der Bochumer Innenstadt.* Schriften des Geographischen Instituts der Universität Kiel, vol. 28, no. 1. Kiel: Geographischen Instituts der Universität Kiel, 1968.

Wrigley, E. A. *Industrial Growth and Population Change. A Regional Study of the Coalfield Areas of North-West Europe in the Later Nineteenth Century.* Cambridge, Eng: At the University Press, 1961.

Zunkel, Friedrich. *Der Rheinisch-Westfälische Unternehmer, 1834–1879. Ein Beitrag zur Geschichte des deutschen Bürgertums im 19. Jahrhun-dert.* Dortmunder Schriften zur Sozialforschung, Bd. 19. Cologne and Opladen: Westdeutscher, 1962.

200 Jahre Tabakfabrik F. D. Cramer. Bochum, n.p., 1925.

Other Secondary Works

A. Articles

Amsden, Jon and Stephen Brier. "Coal Miners on Strike: The Transforma-tion of Strike Demands and the Formation of a National Union." *Journal of Interdisciplinary History* (Spring 1977), 7: 583–616.

Bernays, Marie. "Auslese und Anpassung der Arbeiterschaft der geschlosse-nen Grossindustrie dargestellt an den Verhältnissen der 'Gladbacher Spinnerei und Weberei A-G' zu München-Gladbach im Rheinland." *Schriften des Vereins für Sozialpolitik* (1910), 133(1).

Born, Karl Erich. "Der soziale und wirtschaftliche Strukturwandel Deutschlands am Ende des 19. Jahrhunderts." *Vierteljahrschrift für Sozial- und Wirtschaftsgeschichte* (1963), 50:361–76.

Braun, Rudolf. "The Rise of a Rural Class of Entrepreneurs." *Journal of World History* (1967), 10(3):551–66.

Brepohl, Wilhelm. "Bedeutung der Sozialgeschichte für die Städtegeschichte im 19 Jh." *Beiträge zur Geschichte Dortmunds und der Grafschaft Mark* (1960), 57:101–11.

Croon, Helmuth. "Zur Entwicklung der Städte im 19. und 20. Jahrhundert." *Studium Generale* (1963), 16(9):565–75.

――"Neuere Arbeiten zur Städtegeschichte." *Archiv für Kommunalwissenschaften* (1966), 5:125–34.

Dyos, H. J. "The Growth of Cities in the Nineteenth Century. A Review of Some Recent Writings." *Victorian Studies* (1966), 9:225–37.

Eley, Geoff. "Memories of Under-Development: Social History in Germany." *Social History* (October 1977), no. 6, pp. 785–91.

Fischer, Wolfram. "Rural Industrialization and Population Change." *Comparative Studies in Society and History* (1973), 15:158–70.

――"Stadien und Typen der Industrialisierung in Deutschland. Zum Problem ihrer regionalen Differenzierung." *Wirtschaft und Gesellschaft im Zeitalter der Industrialisierung, Vorträge, Aufsätze, Studien.* Kritische Studien zur Geschichtswissenschaft. Vol. 1. Göttingen: Vandenhoeck and Ruprecht, 1972.

――"Die Stellung der preussischen Bergrechtsreform von 1851 bis 1865 in der Wirtschafts- und Sozialverfassung des 19. Jahrhunderts." *Zeitschrift für die gesamte Staatswissenschaft* (1961), 117:521–34.

Foster, John. "Nineteenth-Century Towns—a Class Dimension." In H. J. Dyos, ed., *The Study of Urban History*, pp. 281–99. London: Edward Arnold, 1968.

Goldstein, Sidney. "City Directories as Sources of Migration Data." *American Journal of Sociology* (1954), 60:169–76.

Gunther, Adolf and René Prévot. "Die Wohlfahrtseinrichtungen in Deutschland und Frankreich." *Schriften des Vereins für Sozialpolitik* (1905), vol. 114.

Gutman, H. G. "Class, Status and Community Power in Nineteenth Century American Industrial Cities: Paterson, New Jersey, a Case Study." In Herbert G. Gutman, *Work Culture and Society in Industrializing America*, pp. 234–59. New York: Vintage Books, 1977.

Heiss, Clemens. "Auslese und Anpassung der Arbeiter in der Berliner Feinmechanik." *Schriften des Vereins für Sozialpolitik* (1910), 134(2):

Hellwig, F. "Unternehmer und Unternehmungsform im Saarlandischen Industriegebiet." *Jahrbücher für Nationalökonomie und Statistik* (1943), vol. 158.

Hobsbawm, E. J. "Custom, Wages and Work-Load in Nineteenth-Century Industry." In Asa Briggs and John Saville, eds., *Essays in Labour*

History: In Memory of G. D. H. Cole, 25 September, 1889–14 January 1959, pp. 113–39. London: Macmillan, 1960.

Hopkins, Richard J. "Occupational and Geographic Mobility in Atlanta, 1870–1890." *Journal of Southern History* (1968), 34:200–213.

Kaelble, Hartmut. "Sozialer Aufstieg in Deutschland, 1850–1914." *Vierteljahrschrift für Sozial- und Wirtschaftsgeschichte* (1973), 60:41–71.

Kerr, Clark and Abraham Siegel. "The Interindustry Propensity to Strike: An International Comparison." In Arthur Kornhauser et al., eds., *Industrial Conflict*, pp. 189–212. New York: McGraw-Hill, 1954.

Kirk, Gordon, W., Jr. and Carolyn Tyririn. "Migration, Mobility and the Transformation of the Occupational Structure in an Immigrant Community: Holland, Michigan, 1850–80." *Journal of Social History* (1974), 8:142–63.

Köllmann, Wolfgang. "Zur Bevölkerungsentwicklung ausgewählter deutscher Grosstädte in der Hochindustrialisierungsperiode." *Jarhbuch für Sozialwissenschaft* (1967), 18:129–44.

——"Industrialisierung, Binnenwanderung und 'Soziale Frage': Zur Entstehungsgeschichte der deutschen Industriegrosstädte im 19. Jahrhundert." *Vierteljahrschrift für Sozial- und Wirtschaftsgeschichte* (1959), vol. 46.

——"Politische und Soziale Entwicklung der Deutschen Arbeiterschaft, 1850–1914." *Vierteljahrschrift für Sozial- und Wirtschaftsgeschichte* (1963), 50:480–504.

——"The Process of Urbanization in Germany at the Height of the Industrialization Period." *Journal of Contemporary History* (1969), 4:59–76.

Lebovics, H. "'Agrarians' versus 'Industrializers': Social Conservative Resistance to Industrialism and Capitalism in Late Nineteenth Century Germany." *International Review of Social History* (1967), vol. 12.

Lorwin, Val. "Working-Class Politics and Economic Development in Western Europe." *American Historical Review* (1958), 63:338–51.

McCormick, B. M. and J. W. Williams. "The Miners and the Eight-Hour Day, 1863–1910." *Economic History Review*, (1959).

O'Boyle, Leonore. "The Middle Class in Western Europe, 1815–1848." *American Historical Review* (1966), 71:826–45.

Rimlinger, Gaston V. "International Differences in the Strike Propensity of Coal Miners: Experience in Four Countries." *Industrial and Labor Relations Review* (1959), 12:389–405.

——"The Legitimation of Protest: A Comparative Study in Labor History." *Comparative Studies in Society and History* (1960), 2:329–43.

R. J. "Erlebnisse eines Metalldrehers." *Archiv für exakte Wirtschaftsforschung. Thünen-Archiv* (1907–8), 2:718-758.

Rosenberg, H. "Political and Social Consequences of the Depression of 1873–1896 in Central Europe." *Economic History Review* (1943), 13:58–73.

Schofer, Lawrence. "Patterns of Labor Protest: Upper Silesia, 1865–1914." *Journal of Social History* (1972), 5:447–63.

Scott, Joan W. "The Glassworkers of Carmaux, 1850–1900." In Stephen Thernstrom and Richard Sennett, eds., *Nineteenth-Century Cities: Essays in the New Urban History*, pp. 3–48. New Haven, Conn.: Yale University Press, 1969.

Seidl, H. "Der Arbeitsplatzwechsel als eine frühe Form des Klassenkampfes der mittel- und ostdeutschen Braunkohlenbergarbeiter in der Zeit von 1870 bis 1900." *Jahrbuch für Wirtschaftsgeschichte*, Teil IV (1965), pp. 102–24.

Shorter, Edward and Charles Tilly. "The Shape of Strikes in France, 1830–1960." *Comparative Studies in Society and History* (1971), vol. 13.

Sorer, Richard. "Auslese und Anpassung in einer Wiener Maschinenfabrik." *Schriften des Vereins für Sozialpolitik* (1911), vol. 135(2).

Stearns, Peter N. "Adaptation to Industrialization: German Workers as a Test Case." *Central European History* (1970), 3:303–31.

Stone, Katherine. "The Origins of Job Structures in the Steel Industry." *Radical America*, 74–6 (1973), 19–64.

Syrup, Friedrich. "Die Soziale Lage der sesshaften Arbeiterschaft eines Oberschlesischen Walzwerkes." *Schriften des Vereins für Sozialpolitik* (1915), n.f. 153:131–218.

——"Studien über den industriellen Arbeiterwechsel." *Archiv für Exakte Wirtschaftsforschung. Thünen Archiv* (1912), pp. 261–303.

Thernstrom, Stephan. "Notes on the Historical Study of Social Mobility." *Comparative Studies in Society and History* (1968), vol. 10.

——"Urbanization, Migration and Social Mobility in Late Nineteenth-Century America." In Barton J. Bernstein, ed., *Towards a New Past: Dissenting Essays in American History*, pp. 158–75. J. Bernstein. New York: Pantheon Books, 1968.

——"Working Class Social Mobility in Industrial America." In Melvin Richter, ed., *Essays in Theory and History: An Approach to the Social Sciences*, pp. 221–38. Cambridge, Mass.: Harvard University Press, 1970.

ernstrom, Stephan and Peter Knights. "Men in Motion: Some Data and Speculations about Urban Population Mobility in Nineteenth-Century America." In Tamara K. Harevin, *Anonymous Americans: Explorations in Nineteenth-Century Social History*, pp. 17–47. Englewood Cliffs, N.J.: Prentice-Hall, 1971.

Tilly, Louise A. "I Fatti di Maggio: The Working Class of Milan and the Rebellion of 1898." In Robert J. Bezucha, ed., *Modern European Social History*, pp. 124–58. Lexington, Mass.: D. C. Heath, 1972.

Tilly, Richard. "Popular Disorders in Nineteenth-Century Germany: A Preliminary Survey." *Journal of Social History* (1970), 4:1–40.

Tipps, Dean C. "Modernization Theory and the Study of National Societies: A Critical Perspective." *Comparative Studies in Society and History* (1973), 15:199–226.

Worthman, Paul B. "Working-Class Mobility in Birmingham, Alabama, 1880–1914." In Tamara K. Harevin, ed., *Anonymous Americans: Explorations in Nineteenth-Century Social History*, pp. 172–213. Englewood Cliffs, N.J.: Prentice-Hall, 1971.

Wrigley, E. A. "The Process of Modernization and the Industrial Revolution in England." *The Journal of Interdisciplinary History* (1972), 3:225–259.

Zorn, Wolfgang. "Typen und Entwicklungskräfte deutschen Unternehmertums im 19. Jahrhundert." *Vierteljahrschrift für Sozial- und Wirtschaftsgeschichte* (1957), 44:55–77.

B. Books

Anderson, Michael. *Family Structure in Nineteenth Century Lancashire.* Cambridge Studies in Sociology. Cambridge, Eng.: At the University Press, 1971.

Ashton, T. S. *Iron and Steel in the Industrial Revolution.* Manchester, Eng.: Manchester University Press, 1963.

Bechtel, Heinrich. *Wirtschaftsgeschichte Deutschlands im 19. und 20. Jahrhundert.* Munich: Georg Callwey, 1956.

Beck, Clemens. *Lohn- und Arbeitsverhältnisse in der deutschen Maschinenindustrie.* Dresden: 1902.

Bell, Lady Florence E. *At the Works. A Study of a Manufacturing Town.* Reprint of 1907 edition. New York: A. M. Kelley, 1969.

Benaerts, Pierre. *Les Origines de la grande industrie allemande.* Paris: F. H. Turot, 1933.

Bendix, Reinhard. *Work and Authority in Industry: Ideologies of Management in the Course of Industrialization.* New York: Wiley, 1956.

Bezucha, Robert, ed. *Modern European Social History.* Lexington, Mass.: D. C. Heath, 1972.

Born, Karl Erich, ed. *Moderne deutsche Wirtschaftsgeschichte.* Cologne and Berlin: Kiepenheuer und Witsch, 1966.

Bottomore, T. B. *Sociology as Social Criticism.* New York: Pantheon Books, 1974.

Braun, Rudolf. *Industrialisierung und Volksleben. Die Veränderung der Lebensformen in einem ländlichen Industriegebiet vor 1800 (Zürcher Oberland).* Ehrlenbach-Zurich and Stuttgart: Eugen Rentsch, 1960.

——*Sozialer und Kultureller Wandel in einem ländlichen Industriegebiet (Zürcher Oberland) unter Einwirkung des Machinen- und Fabrikwesens im 19. und 20. Jahrhundert.* Ehrlenbach-Zurich and Stuttgart: Eugen Rentsch, 1965.

Briggs, Asa. *The History of Birmingham.* Vol. ii. London: Oxford University Press, 1952. *Victorian Cities.* Harmondsworth, Middlesex: Penguin Books, 1968.

Brockhaus, Eckard. *Zusammensetzung und Neustrukturierung der Arbeiterklasse vor dem Ersten Weltkrieg. Zur Krise der professionellen Arbeiterbewegung* (Munich: Trikont Verlag, 1975).

Brody, David. *Steelworkers in America: The Nonunion Era.* Cambridge, Mass.: Harvard University Press, 1960.

Burgess, Keith. *The Origins of British Industrial Relations.* London: Croom Helm, 1975.

Chevalier, Louis. *Laboring Classes and Dangerous Classes in Paris during the First Half of the Nineteenth Century,* translated by Frank Jellinek. New York: Howard Fertig, 1973.

Clapham, J. H. *The Economic Development of France and Germany, 1815–1914.* Cambridge, Eng.: At the University Press, 1963.

Dahrendorf, Ralf. *Class and Class Conflict in Industrial Society.* Stanford, Cal.: Stanford University Press, 1959.

——*Society and Democracy in Germany.* Garden City, N.Y.: Doubleday, 1967. (*Gesellschaft und Demokratie in Deutschland.* Munich: Piper, 1965.)

Dawson, E. H. *Municipal Life and Government in Germany.* London: Longmans, Green, 1914.

Dennis, N., Henriques, F., and Slaughter, C. *Coal Is Our Life: An Analysis of a Yorkshire Mining Community.* London: Eyre & Spottiswoode, 1956.

Dyos, H. J., ed. *The Study of Urban History.* London: Edward Arnold, 1968.

Eckert, Hugo. *Liberal- oder Sozialdemokratie. Frühgeschichte der Nürnberger Arbeiterbewegung.* Industrielle Welt. Schriftenreihe des Arbeitskreises für moderne Sozialgeschichte, Bd. 9, edited by Werner Conze. Stuttgart: Ernst Klett, 1968.

Fischer, Wolfram. *Unternehmerschaft, Selbstverwaltung und Staat. Die Handelskammer in der deutschen Wirtschafts- und Staatsverfassung des 19. Jahrhunderts.* Berlin: Duncker & Humbolt, 1964.

——*Wirtschaft und Gesellschaft im Zeitalter der Industrialisierung. Aufsätze–Studien–Vorträge.* Göttingen: Vandenhoeck & Ruprecht, 1972.

Fischer, Wolfram, ed. *Wirtschafts- und sozialgeschichtliche Probleme der frühen Industrialisierung.* Berlin: Colloquium, 1968.

Fünfundsiebzig Jahre Industriegewerkschaft 1891 bis 1966. Vom Deutschen Metallarbeiter-Verband zur Industriegewerkschaft Metall. Frankfurt am Main: Europäische Verlagsanstalt, 1966.

Geschichte und Gesellschaft. Zeitschrift für historische sozialwissenschaft. I. Jahrgang 1975. Göttingen: Vandenhoeck and Ruprecht. Book 1, *Soziale Schichtung und Mobilität in Deutschland im 19. und 20. Jahrhundert,* Jürgen Kocka, ed.

Göhre, Paul. *Three Months in a Workshop: A Practical Study.* (Translation of *Drei Monate Fabrikarbeiter und Handwerksbursche.*) Reprint of the 1895 ed. New York: Arno Press, 1972.

Die Grosstadt. Vorträge und Aufsätze zur Städteausstellung. Gehe-Stiftung zu Dresden. Dresden: v. Zahn und Jaench, 1903.

Hardach, Gerd H. *Der Soziale Status des Arbeiters in der Frühindustrialisierung. Eine Untersuchung über die Arbeitnehmer in der französischen Eisenschaffenden Industrie zwischen 1800 und 1870.* Schriften zur Wirtschafts- und Sozialgeschichte, vol. 14, Wolfram Fischer, ed. Berlin: Duncker & Humbolt, 1969.

Heberle, Rudolf and Fritz Meyer. *Die Grosstädte im Strome der Binnen wan-derung. Wirtschafts- und bevölkerungswissenschaftliche Untersu-chungen über Wanderung und Mobilität in deutschen Städten.* Leipzig: S. Hirzel, 1937.

Heffter, H. *Die deutsche Selbstverwaltung im 19. Jahrhundert. Geschichte der Ideen und Institutionen.* Stuttgart: Koehler, 1950.

Henneaux-Depooter, Louise. *Misères et luttes sociales dans le Hainaut, 1860–1869.* Institut de Sociologie Solvay. Centre d'Histoire Econo-mique et Sociale. Brussels: Université Libre de Bruxelles, 1959.

Hobsbawm, E. J. *Labouring Men: Studies in the History of Labour.* London: Weidenfeld & Nicolson, 1964.

Hoffman, Josef. *Der Ewige Bergmann. Vier Bücher vom bergmännische Menschen. Das Leben des deutschen Bergmanns im Vergangenheit und Gegenwart. Untersucht und dargestellt im Spiegel der alten und neuen Dichtung. Zugleich ein Beitrag zur bergmännischen Kultur- Sozial- und Literaturgeschichte.* Rheinhausen: Deutsche Wald, 1958.

Hommer, Otto. *Die Entwicklung und Tätigkeit des Deutschen Metallarbei-terverbandes.* Berlin: Heymann, 1912.

Hoselitz, Bert F., and Wilbert E. Moore, eds. *Industrialization and Society.* Unesco. The Hague: Mouton, 1966.

Hue, Otto. *Die Bergarbeiter. Historische Darstellung der Bergarbeiter-Ver-hältnisse von der ältesten bis in die neueste Zeit.* 2 vols. Stuttgart: Dietz, 1910–1913.

Imbusch, H. *Arbeiterverhältnisse und Arbeiterorganization im deutschen Bergbau. Eine geschichtliche Darstellung.* Essen: Gewerkverein chris-tlicher Bergarbeiter, n.d.

——*Ist eine Verschmelzung der Bergarbeiter-Organizationen möglich? Kri-tische Betrachtungen zur Frage der Verschmelzung der beiden grossen Bergarbeiterverbände.* Essen: Fredebeul & Koenen, 1906.

Jaeger, Hans. *Unternehmer in der deutschen Politik, 1890–1914.* Bonn: Röhrscheid, 1967.

Kaelble, Hartmut. *Berliner Unternehmer während der frühen Industrialisi-erung. Herkunft, sozialer Status und politischer Einfluss.* Veröffentli-chungen der Historischen Kommission zu Berlin, vol. 40; Publikationen zur Geschichte der Industrialisierung, vol. 4. Berlin and New York: de Gruyter, 1972.

——*Industrielle Interessenpolitik in der Wilhelminischen Gesellschaft. Central-Verband Deutscher Industrieller, 1895–1914.* Berlin: de Gruy-ter, 1967.

Kerr, Clark and Abraham Siegel. *Industrial Conflict.* New York: McGraw-Hill, 1954.

Kerr, Clark et al. *Industrialism and Industrial Man: The Problems of Labor and Management in Economic Growth.* New York: Oxford University Press, 1969.

Keyser, Erich. *Bibliographie zur Städtegeschichte Deutschlands Acta Colle-gii Historiae Urbanae.* Societatis Historicum Internationalis. Cologne and Vienna: Bohla, 1969.

Knowles, K. G. J. C. Strikes—a Study in Industrial Conflict. New York: Oxford University Press, 1952.

Kornhauser, Arthur et al. Industrial Conflict. New York: McGraw-Hill, 1954.

Kuczynski, Jürgen. Die Geschichte der Lage der Arbeiter in Deutschland von 1871 bis 1900. Berlin: Akademie, 1962.

Kulemann, W. Die Berufsvereine. Vol. 2. Die Arbeiter, Die Arbeiterinnen. Einzelne Organizationen. Jena: Fischer, 1908.

Lambi, Ivo N. Free Trade and Protection in Germany, 1868–1879. Vierteljahrschrift für Sozial- und Wirtschaftsgeschichte. Beihefte Nr. 44. Wiesbaden: Franz Steiner, 1963.

Landes, David. The Unbound Prometheus: Technological Change and Industrial Development in Western Europe from 1750 to the Present. Cambridge, Eng.: At the University Press, 1969.

Laslett, Peter. The World We Have Lost. London: Methuen, 1965.

Lipset, Seymour Martin, and Reinhard Bendix. Social Mobility in Industrial Society. Berkeley and Los Angeles: University of California Press, 1959.

Lorwin, Val. R., and Jacob M. Price, eds. The Dimensions of the Past: Materials, Problems and Opportunities for Quantitative Work in History. New Haven, Conn.: Yale University Press, 1972.

Markow, Alexis. Das Wachstum der Bevölkerung und die Entwicklung der Aus- und Einwanderungen, Ab- und Zuzüge in Preussen und Preussens einzelnen Provinzen, Bezirken und Kreisgruppen von 1824 bis 1885. Tübingen: Laup, 1889.

Mauersberg, Hans. Deutsche Industrien im Zeitgeschehen eines Jahrhunderts. Eine Historische Modelluntersuchung zum Entwicklungsprozess Deutscher Unternehmen von ihren Anfängen bis zum Stand von 1960. Stuttgart: Gustav Fischer, 1966.

Mayntz, Renate. Soziale Schichtung und Sozialer Wandel in einer Industriegemeinde: Eine Soziologische Untersuchung der Stadt Euskirchen. Stuttgart: Ferdinand Enke, 1958.

Mitchell, Harvey, and Peter Stearns. The European Labor Movement, the Working Classes and the Origins of Social Democracy, 1890–1914. Itasca, Ill.: F. E. Peacock, 1971.

Moore, Barrington, Jr. Injustice: The Social Bases of Obedience and Revolt, White Plains, N.Y.: Mitchell Sharpe, 1978.

Mottek, Hans et al. Studien zur Geschichte der Industriellen Revolution in Deutschland. Veröffentlichungen des Instituts für Wirtschaftsgeschichte an der Hochschule für Ökonomie Berlin-Karlshorst. Vol. 1. Berlin: Akademie, 1960.

Park, Robert E., Ernest W. Burgess, and Roderick D. McKenzie. The City. Chicago: University of Chicago Press, 1967.

Pollard, Sidney. The Genesis of Modern Management: A Study of the Industrial Revolution in Great Britain. Cambridge, Mass.: Harvard University Press, 1965.

Prest, John. The Industrial Revolution in Coventry. London: Oxford University Press, 1960.

Preuss, Hugo. *Die Entwicklung des deutschen Städtewesens. Entwicklungs-geschichte der deutschen Städte-Verfassung.* Reprint of the Leipzig 1906 edition. Aalen: Scientia, 1965.

Reports of the Gainsborough Commission of British Workmen: Life and Labour in Germany. London: Simpkin, Marshall, Hamilton, Kent, 1906.

Rosenberg, Hans. *Grosse Depression und Bismarckzeit.* Historische Kommission zu Berlin. Vol. 24. Berlin: de Gruyter, 1967.

Samuel, Raphael, ed., *Miners, Quarrymen, and Saltworkers.* London: Routledge and Kegan Paul, 1977.

Schofer, Lawrence. *The Formation of a Modern Labor Force: Upper Silesia, 1865–1914.* Berkeley and Los Angeles: University of California Press, 1975.

Schott, Sigmund. *Die Grosstädtischen Agglomerationen des Deutschen Reiches, 1871–1910.* Schriften des Verbandes deutscher Städtestatistiker. Ergänzungsheft zum Statistischen Jahrbuch deutscher Städte. Book 1. Breslau: Druck und Verlag von Wilh. Gottl. Korn, 1912.

Schroter, Alfred and Walter Becker. *Die deutsche Maschinenindustrie in der industriellen Revolution.* Veröffentlichungen des Instituts für Wirtschaftsgeschichte an der Hochschule für Ökonomie Berlin-Karlshorst. Vol. 2. Berlin: Akademie, 1962.

Die Schwereisenindustrie. Ihre Entwicklung und ihre Arbeiter. Nach vorgenommenen Erhebungen im Jahre 1910 bearbeitet und herausgegeben vom Vorstand des deutschen Metallarbeiter-Verbandes. Stuttgart: Alexander Schlicke, 1912.

Sennett, Richard, ed. *Classic Essays on the Culture of Cities.* New York: Appleton-Century-Crofts, 1969.

Shorter, Edward. *The Historian and the Computer: A Practical Guide.* Englewood Cliffs, N.J.: Prentice-Hall, 1971.

Shorter, Edward, ed. *Work and Community in the West.* New York: Harper and Row, 1973.

Shorter, Edward and Charles Tilly. *Strikes in France, 1830–1968.* New York: Cambridge University Press, 1974.

Smelser, Neil. *Social Change in the Industrial Revolution: An Application of Theory to the Lancashire Cotton Industry, 1700–1840.* London: Routledge and Kegan Paul, 1967.

Sorokin, Pitirim. *Social Mobility.* New York: Harpers, 1927.

Stearns, Peter. *European Society in Upheaval: Social History Since 1800.* New York: Macmillan, 1967.

Stearns, Peter, ed. *The Impact of the Industrial Revolution. Protest and Alienation.* Englewood Cliffs, N.J.: Spectrum Books, Prentice-Hall, 1972.

Stolper, Gustav. *The German Economy 1870 to the Present.* New York: Harcourt Brace & World, 1967.

Strauss, Rudolph. *Die Lage und die Bewegung der Chemnitzer Arbeiter in der Ersten Hälfte des 19. Jahrhunderts.* Deutsche Akademie der Wissenschaften zu Berlin. Schriften des Instituts für Geschichte. Reihe II. Landesgeschichte, vol. 3. Berlin: Akademie, 1960.

Stürmer, Michael, ed. *Das kaiserliche Deutschland, Politik, und Gesellschaft, 1870–1918.* Düsseldorf: Droste, 1970.

Thernstrom, Stephan. *Poverty and Progress: Social Mobility in a Nineteenth-Century City.* Cambridge, Mass.: Harvard University Press, 1964.

Thernstrom, Stephan and Richard Sennett, eds. *Nineteenth-Century Cities: Essays in the New Urban History.* New Haven, Conn.: Yale University Press, 1969.

Thompson, E. P. *The Making of the English Working Class.* New York: Vintage Books, 1963.

Veblen, Thorstein. *Imperial Germany and the Industrial Revolution.* Ann Arbor: University of Michigan Press, 1968.

Weber, Adna Ferrin. *The Growth of Cities in the Nineteenth Century: A Study in Statistics.* Ithaca, N.Y.: Cornell University Press, 1967.

Weber, Adolf. *Die Grosstadt und ihre sozialen Probleme.* Leipzig: Quelle and Mayer, 1918.

Wehler, Hans-Ulrich, ed. *Moderne deutsche Sozialgeschichte.* Cologne and Berlin: Kiepenheuer and Witsch, 1966.

Index

DEMCO